LEARNING WITH A
VISUAL BRAIN
IN AN AUDITORY WORLD

LEARNING WITH A
VISUAL BRAIN
IN AN AUDITORY WORLD

Visual Language Strategies for Individuals with Autism Spectrum Disorders

Ellyn Lucas Arwood, Ed.D.
Carole Kaulitz, M.Ed.
Mabel M. Brown, M.A.

APRICOT, INC.

P.O. Box 230138
Tigard, OR 97281-0138
www.apricotclinic.com

© 2018 APRICOT, Inc.
PO Box 230138
Tigard, OR 97281-0138

www.apricotclinic.com

Arwood, Ellyn Lucas
    Learning with a visual brain in an auditory world: visual language strategies for individuals with autism spectrum disorders / Ellyn Lucas Arwood, Carole Kaulitz and Mabel M. Brown. – 2nd ed. – Tigard, OR : APRICOT, Inc., 2018.

    ISBN-13: 978-0-9679720-3-9

    Includes bibliographical references and index.

    1. Autistic children – Education. 2. Autism in children. 3. Visual learning. 4. Learning
        disabled children – Education.

First edition (2007) was sold and published by AAPC (Autism Asperger Publishing Company), PO Box 23178, Shawnee Mission, Kansas 66283-0173; www.asperger.net
ISBN-13: 978-1-931282-38-3

Second edition (2018) is sold and published by APRICOT, Inc., PO Box 230138, Tigard, OR 97281-0138; www.apricotclinic.com
ISBN-13: 978-0-9679720-3-9

POD through Lightning Source, Inc.

This book is designed in Warnock Pro and Immi.

Printed in the United States of America.

TABLE OF CONTENTS

Section One: The Learning System:
How Do Individuals with Autism Spectrum Disorders Learn?

Section Two: Language and Learning
How Does Learning Language Affect Social, Behavioral, and Academic Development?

Section Three: Language-Based Learning Strategies: Strategies and Interventions for the Visual Brain

Acknowledgments

We would like to thank our families and friends for their help with this project. Specifically, we would like to thank our colleagues, Kitty Mulkey, CCC-SLP, Lyn Larfield, CCC-SLP, and Neatha Lefevre, OTR/L, for their professional contributions. Without the technical support of Tom Slavin and Tomas Peterson, the figure graphics would have been difficult to produce. Their wisdom of technology made our lives much easier.

We would also like to thank those parents and professionals who live and/or work with persons on the spectrum and who experience what we are talking about in this book every day at school, at home, and in the community for their patience and understanding while we work to develop better ways to help.

Finally, we would like to dedicate the book to Mabel M. Brown, a wonderful friend, sister, and colleague, who took dim copies of children's works, worn pages of drawings, and sketches of ideas, and brought them to life with a fresh, inked drawing. It is Mabel for whom the Mabel Mini-Lectures mentioned later in the book are named. For the figures, mini-lectures, and a whole lot more, we are truly grateful. And, on behalf of all those parents and children with whom Mabel has worked during the last 30 years, we would like to say thank you!

– Ellyn Lucas Arwood
– Carole Kaulitz
– Mabel M. Brown

Preface

Children diagnosed with an autism spectrum disorder (ASD) often present parents and educators with perplexing symptoms. Because of the diversity of symptoms, a spectrum of disorders has been adopted to account for children and adults with both high-end and low-end skills. The underlying assumptions of this spectrum are twofold: (a) diverse symptoms may suggest different disabilities with different etiologies; and (b) different symptoms call for different diagnoses and interventions.

Even though the skills of children with ASD can range from very high to very low, they have similar underlying learning systems. Knowledge about these learning systems helps provide direction for choosing effective assessment and intervention methods for helping individuals with ASD learn to behave, to perform academically, and to become socially competent. This book is unique in that the authors are recommending strategies based on the language of the way individuals with ASD learn. When referring to learning systems, we are not talking about learning styles in the sense of educational preferences that can be taught. Instead, we are referring to the neurobiological systems through which children and adults learn new concepts. Even though many scholars recognize that individuals with ASD use "visual" ways of thinking, most fail to realize that a visual mental language is different from the visual sensory system of seeing something.

Visual language forms have their own unique properties, which can be used for assessment and intervention. And, because visual thinking in a visual language form represents the underlying visual concepts, strategies based on visual language properties can be used to increase a child's cognitive or thinking ability. Therefore, the child's academic, social, or behavioral needs are met through the use of language learning strategies. The result is a very effective way of working with individuals with ASD. Children who have not learned to communicate or socialize learn to communicate and become socially effective. Individuals with ASD who have learning, language, and social challenges learn to be more socially appropriate with more natural language and better learning.

About This Book

The book is divided into three sections. Section One (Chapters 1-5) is about the learning system; how the learning system develops; how learning is different for a person with ASD; and how the learning system develops concepts for language. Section Two (Chapters 6-9) connects the learning of a child with ASD to how the child performs behaviorally, academically, and socially. Finally, Section Three (Chapters 10-15) provides intervention strategies for helping a person (child or adult) with the visual brain characteristic of ASD to fit into an auditory culture. The strategies are language-based and take into consideration the complexity of the underlying biological learning system.

The authors interweave knowledge about how the brain works, how children and adults on the autism spectrum learn, and how language functions to connect cognition with learning. For example, a child diagnosed with autism may not see herself sitting in a classroom with other students. So, we would draw her sitting with the other students so that she can see herself working with the other students. This drawing would also show the child what she thinks about as thought bubbles. In this way, the child's thinking, or cognition, is visible to her, and the way she sees the other students shows her how to learn about what they think as well what she is to think when she is in the classroom. Using this approach, we have developed successful learning strategies for children and adults with a diagnosis on the autism spectrum. By understanding how the "visual brain" of a child or adult with ASD works, we can develop these types of learning language strategies for the many different behaviors that individuals with ASD display, whether they are functioning with high-end skills or low-end skills.

Because individuals with ASD use visual concepts for thinking and learning, the text includes many drawings or figures to visually represent the material. Typically, the communicator would talk and draw at the same time to help the learner see the ideas develop. But since this is a published book, the pictures are already drawn. In many places throughout the text, the reader will be reminded that the pictures should be drawn in "real time," at the same time as the actual communication act takes place.

As you read the book, you are encouraged to use *your* best way of learning, especially since the drawings are static. In other words, not every reader enjoys the same way of processing the printed and drawn material. For example, if the drawings make sense to you, then use them to supplement the meaning of the text. However, if you look at the print and see a picture in your head that doesn't match the picture in the book, make mental pictures that match your knowledge about what the print says. And, if you do not want to use the pictures, make mental notes of your own voice interpreting what you read.

Realize that the drawings in the text show you how you might draw a particular concept, but drawings are never conventional. There are lots of ways to visually interpret a spoken concept. And there are probably as many ways to draw a concept as there are people interpreting the idea. The drawings in the book show many ways to depict all sorts of concepts. In drawing the pictures, the authors used their knowledge about visual language characteristics (Chapter 5) so that the drawings create a level of meaning that will help some people learn. The drawings and the text match so that each provides meaning that can stand alone or overlap. At the same time, the drawings are also part of the text so that the reader can see that all ideas can be drawn.

Drawing for children with ASD is popular because educators have realized that these children do better with visual than with spoken or auditory input. For many individuals with ASD, writing is a form of drawing the shapes or patterns of ideas and is, therefore, easier to understand than the conceptual basis of drawings. However, few people have the brain-based language-learning knowledge to understand the theoretical reason why the drawing works, when the drawing works or does not work, and how drawing is actually just one mode of how to approach a child's neurological learning system. This book will help the reader understand why different types of input make a "learning" difference and how to access a child's learning system by changing the type of input as well as the language level of the input. Knowing how to access a child's learning system provides the educator with language principles for assessing the progress of the child or adult. Numerous examples of how to access the learning, and thus understand how to assess the progress, will be presented.

The authors base their work on what is known about learning and language, not learning styles and modalities. Learning styles are preferences but do not always reflect the way a person learns best. For example, Ellyn has a shower style … she likes to think in the shower. But she does not need to bring the shower to the office or meet people in her shower in order to think. Her shower preference is a style, not the way her learning system acquires new concepts.

Furthermore, the learning system, not our learning styles, creates developmental products like language. Language develops in the way we learn best. When we present material for our sensory systems, we are using a modality approach. This book will *not* emphasize either the preferences or styles or the modalities. For example, just because a picture is drawn so that a person can see (modality) the image does not mean that the child looking at the picture has the appropriate cognitive or language level to interpret what is in the picture. That is, a particular drawing may not have enough language characteristics for a specific child's language level or knowledge level. It is also possible a specific child needs to see the hand move during the drawing, not the drawn object or finished picture. To some, the movement of the hand provides the shape of ideas better than the actual finished drawings.

Learning styles tell us that different people have different preferences. Learning systems tell us how the child learns new concepts best. Modalities are the way that material is brought to the senses.

Many children with autism are taught using learning styles that are different than their learning systems. This book emphasizes the use of the child's best learning system with material presented at the child's language level. Ideally, the child's learning style would match her learning system. When the learning system and the learning style do not match, the child may not make the desired progress. Therefore, this text emphasizes ways to develop the child's learning system with language-based strategies.

We hope you will find the material easy to read, and therefore easy to try. Many of our colleagues tell us that even "dabbling" with some of the suggested practices makes a difference. The authors have more than 60 years of combined professional work from which they will bring examples and case studies representing many different ages and developmental levels. The final drawings are completed by a practitioner, Mabel Brown, who draws every day with her clients. She has more than 20 years of rich experience. Names and identifying information have been changed to protect the children and adults.

At the beginning of each chapter you will find a listing of specific concepts that will be explained within the chapter as well as learner outcomes. Throughout each chapter will be activity checks to help you determine how well you understand the concepts. Finally, at the end of each chapter you will find a summary of the material presented.

SECTION ONE

The Learning System: How Do Individuals with Autism Spectrum Disorders Learn?

SECTION ONE

Preparing Staff to Work with Individuals with Autism Spectrum Disorders: Part 2

Concepts in Chapter 1

What is autism?

Why is there an autism spectrum?

What is the learning process?

How does the learning system process sensory input?

How do children with ASD process sensory input differently than typical learners?

CHAPTER 1

Autism: What Is It?

I see it,

I hear it,

I smell it.

I cannot know it!

Learner Outcomes: As a result of reading this chapter, the reader should be able to draw and explain how the sensory input forms the first stage of meaning of the learning system.

Because this book is designed for parents and educators, the different ways we define autism should be clarified. Since parents often receive the diagnosis of an autism spectrum disorder (ASD) for their child from the medical community, the criteria set forth in the *Diagnostic and Statistical Manual of Mental Disorders,* fourth edition, text revision (DSM-IV-TR; American Psychiatric Association, 2000), we will briefly examine the DSM-IV definition.

Autism is classified as a type of pervasive developmental disorder (PDD) in which children are characterized by severe and pervasive impairment in several areas of development: reciprocal social interaction skills, communication skills, or the presence of stereotyped behavior, interests and activities. (p. 69)

Subcategories of pervasive developmental disorders include autistic disorder, Asperger Syndrome (AS), and pervasive developmental disorder-not otherwise specified (PDD-NOS). Within this definition there are criteria, which include differences in social interaction, communication, and repetitive or stereotyped behavior. Following these criteria, educators recognized the need to have a special definition for individuals with ASD in order to make them eligible for educational services.

The Individuals with Disabilities Education Act (IDEA, 1997) defines autism as a "developmental disability significantly affecting verbal and nonverbal communication and social interaction, generally evident before age three, that adversely affects a child's performance" (34C.F.R. Part 300, Sec.300.7[b][1]). In other words, a child with an ASD experiences developmental differences in three areas: (a) verbal and nonverbal communication; (b) social interaction; and (c) other areas of developmental performance. Two of the developmental areas are specified as communication (nonverbal and verbal) and social development. However, other developmental areas may be affected as well, such as cognition, motor, and/or physical.

Tracking development is similar to watching a child climb a set of stairs. With each step, the child reaches an observable, higher level of development. See Figure 1.1.[1]

Figure 1.1. Developmental Stairs.

The literature suggests five "typical" areas of normal development: Social, language, motor, physical (height and weight, for example), and cognitive (thinking) (e.g., Santrock & Santrock, 2005). Some researchers combine affective or emotional skills within the domain of social development. Children with ASD do not typically show this predictable, stair-step progression. Out of these five areas, three areas – social, language (communication), and motor development – are typically affected in individuals with autism disorders.

Social development is how a child relates to others by initiating and maintaining relationships. See Figure 1.2.[2]

Figure 1.2. Social Development.

---

[1]   Drawings represent a person's mental language but are not conventional. You may have a different mental set of concepts for the figures or drawings in this book.

[2]   You may not feel the need to use the drawings to help understand the meaning of the text. Not all readers will use visual mental images for their comprehension. You may have different pictures or words for understanding the concepts than what you see in the text. Use the meaning that you understand. All important concepts will be presented in several different ways throughout the text.

Language development refers to the way people communicate their thinking or thoughts (cognition) to others in a recognizable or conventional manner and form. See Figure 1.3.

Figure 1.3. Language Development.

"Other areas of developmental performance" include movement skills such as gross-motor (e.g., running or walking) and fine-motor movements (e.g., speech, writing). See Figure 1.4.

Figure 1.4. Motor Development.

The stereotypical or repetitive motions often associated with autism disorders represent a difference in the child's motor system.

Even though the disability of autism affects communication (language and speech), social, and motor areas of development, the degree or severity varies. Therefore, as mentioned, people with autism show an entire spectrum of developmental abilities and disabilities. *Disabilities* define what a child or adult cannot do compared to what others can do. *Abilities* refer to what the child or adult can do that others also can do. Even though it is the disability that is assessed, for individuals with autism, the abilities may

Autism: What Is It?

be stronger than expected. So the diagnosis of autism itself is also part of a spectrum of disabilities and abilities. To be diagnosed with autism, the child has to show disabilities in combination to include communication language differences, socialization issues such as stereotypical or repetitive motions, and onset before the age of 3. These disabilities are on a spectrum of ability or severity of need. Some children with autism have very high skills while others have very low skills. Even though the diagnosis is based on disabilities, this book will focus on the *abilities* of children and adults with autism.

By understanding what individuals with ASD can do, intervention strategies based on their learning promote development in all domains. In other words, all development is a product of learning, and since the developmental products are different for children and adults with ASD, their learning systems must also be different. This book will emphasize the interdependence between learning and development to weave theory and practice together for the best intervention strategies.

Other disorders or diagnostic labels are often related to autism and/or diagnosed along with ASD. These include, but are not limited to, Rett's Syndrome, childhood disintegrative disorder, Asperger Syndrome (AS), and pervasive developmental disorder-not otherwise specified (PDD-NOS) (American Psychiatric Association, 2000). All of these disorders show differences in language/communication, socialization, differences in processing for cognition, and some repetitive or stereotypic movements (motor development). This book will discuss the learning system for all individuals with ASD and will specify the functioning level for specific intervention strategies.

Diagnosis

It is fairly easy to place a diagnosis of autism on a child who displays a specific set of developmental behaviors representative of disabilities or what the child cannot perform; however, it is difficult to come up with effective strategies based on a diagnosis of disability. For example, if a child demonstrates unusual or atypical, even self-injurious or harmful, types of behavior and the educator or parent eliminates the harmful behaviors, what other behaviors does the child use to communicate? ***Knowing what a child can't do does not help develop what a child can do!***

Since development is a product of learning, looking at a child's developmental products such as talking, walking, screaming, throwing a tantrum, and so on, also tells us how a child learns. ***Different developmental products indicate differences in learning.*** By applying the literature about learning to children with autism, it becomes easier to recognize the child's learning system, and knowing how a child learns helps develop ways to support the child's learning. Methods and strategies that match the way a child learns best focus on ability, not disability, and are effective in improving ***what the child can do.***

By using an assessment of a child's learning system as a basis for developing interventions, the child develops performance products that are more recognizable and typical of what teachers and parents expect. For example, if a teacher knows that a child needs to see the written word to understand the movement that the mouth makes for speech, strategies aimed at writing will improve the developmental product of speech. That is, the child will talk more and "better." ***Understanding the neurobiological learning system as a way to understand how a child learns helps us develop effective strategies based on ability. To diagnose a child with the symptoms of the definitions is relatively easy; to establish strategies to help the child is not based on the diagnosis but on the way the child learns best.***

Historically, the diagnosis of autism has been rare; it is called a disability of "low incidence." However, more recent statistics suggest that the number of children with autism is growing at an unprecedented rate. Some local agencies in some parts of the country report as much as a 1,000% increase of autism cases in recent years. Since autism affects communication, social, and other areas of development, the relationship between learning and development is important to understand.

Figure 1.5 is a drawing summarizing the concepts in this section. The next section explains the way a person learns and how learning and development are related.

| Occurs before age 3. | Communication problems. | Social problems. |

Figure 1.5. Summary of Definition of Autism.

Autism: A Sensory Problem in Learning

The *neurobiological learning system* refers to the way that information is taken into the body, processed, and then understood and acted upon. One of the first steps in the process of developing a mature learning system rests with the learner or child being able to receive sensory input.

How Does the Learning System Process Sensory Input?

Most neuroscientists (e.g., Bookheimer, 2004; Bragdon & Gamon, 2000; Caine & Caine, 1994; Calvin, 1996; DaMasio, 2000, 2003; Goldberg, 2001; Goldblum, 2001; Hart, 1983; Lucas, 1977; Naugle et al., 1998; Obler, 2000; Restak, 1984; Sousa, 1995; Sprenger, 1999; Sylwester, 2003; Webster, 1999; Wesson, 2004) agree that the neurobiological learning system begins with an intact set of sensory receptors: the mouth, the skin, the eyes, the ears, and the nose. These receptors connect the outside world to the inside space of a learner, who acquires information about the world through these sensory receptors. Each receptor brings different kinds of information.

The first level of learning is a form of sensory input that the receptor recognizes (Arwood, 1991). At first, the child assigns no meaning to this input, but does show a motor response. The adults in the child's environment assign meaning to the child's motor responses. The following section explains what each of the receptors provides a learner, and how children with autism may respond to the different sensory inputs. In other words, some children with ASD respond differently to ordinary tastes than typical learners. And, because the learning system consists of input from the different sensory systems (taste, touch, smell, proprioception, sight, and sound), understanding what type of information these systems provide helps the parent and educator understand the child's responses.

Taste. The taste, or the gustatory, system provides information about sweet, sour, bitter, and salty inputs. The newborn has no words for these taste differences, only the receptor cells receive the differences and code the information for processing later as concepts. For example, a mother gives a young baby a taste of applesauce. The baby makes a "pucker-like" face because the taste is different – not because it is sweet, sour, bitter, or salty. Without the conceptual understanding of the differences received by the sensory system, the baby spits out the new tastes. Some parents and caregivers interpret this behavior as meaning that the child doesn't like applesauce. Others help scoop up the applesauce on the chin and give it back to the child, knowing that the child needs more of the same input to create more meaning.

Children with autism often show these negative types of responses to certain tastes. For example, a study by Myles, Cook, Miller, Renner, and Robbins (2001) revealed "more than one third of the individuals with Asperger Syndrome (AS is a high functioning form of autism) (a) avoided certain tastes that are typical of children's diets, (b) would only eat foods with certain tastes, and (c) were picky eaters" (pp. 37-38). See Figure 1.6.

Figure 1.6. Child Spits out an Unfamiliar Taste.

The sensory input of the different tastes is sent through the nerves to the cerebrum of the brain where the cells decide whether these inputs have meaning. See Figure 1.7.

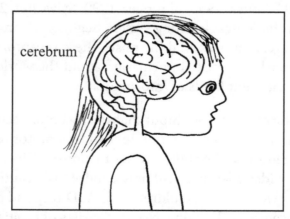

cerebrum

Figure 1.7. The Cerebrum Is the Center for Recognizing Sensory Input.

Interesting, the tastes may be found in an area of the cerebrum (parietal lobe) that is close to the tactile system. Children with autism also negatively respond to certain consistencies of food, a tactile, not just a gustatory, phenomenon.

Touch. The tactile or touch system recognizes pressure by the skin, a receptor organ. Our whole body is covered with skin, an organ that is sensitive to pressure or touch. The brain records the intensity of pressure from outside touch as well as the temperature of the difference between the outside air and the inside body temperature. Newborns, for example, require some interaction with this temperature differential between inside and outside of the body to develop the ability to adjust to temperature changes.

The skin cells respond to the differences in pressure and temperature, sending a biochemical record of these differences in pressure and temperature to the brain. Later, sometimes months to years, the brain assigns meaning to these differences as concepts. Language in the form of conventional words represents the meaning of the concepts with words such as "hot," "hurt," "hard," and "cold." Figure 1.8 shows three learning steps: The child touches, tastes, smells, and bounces the sensory input from the ball. Next, the child recognizes these inputs, and finally she begins to understand what the ball can do.

| Sensory Input: | Perceptual Recognition: | Conceptual Understanding: |
| Child touches, tastes, smells, and bounces ball. | Child feels the ball. | Child is careful about throwing the "hard" ball. |

Figure 1.8. Sensory Stages of Learning.

More on these different stages of acquiring meaning from different types of input will be presented in later chapters.

As a child moves through space, his body receives touch, which helps develop his tactile system. The brain is recording the points of touch as concepts of space. Thus, each movement creates more points of touch or conceptual space. Brain research studies (e.g., Sadato, 1996) show that the movement of the hand, for learning Braille, records the meaning of the movement of the hand in the visual cortex. These movements create the space of concepts. Movement is the recoding of space or visual concepts. These visual concepts or meanings contribute to the development of spatial orientation and visual perception (Pierce, 1992). Spatial orientation refers to where a person is in relationship to a physical object or ground, and visual perception refers to the way a learner organizes the sensory input from the eyes. So, movements integrate both meaning about spatial orientation and meaning about integrated visual patterns. ***Movement connects both space and patterns of sight into visual concepts.***

Children with autism often display different types of movements such as rocking their bodies back and forth, flapping their hands as they run, bonking or using their fist to hit their head, or clicking their fingers in front of their eyes. Any other movement pattern with which a child with ASD experiences difficulty may be repeated and become stereotypical. These movements suggest that the child is not processing the meaning of the patterns into visual concepts. Further evidence of such lack of meaning comes from other researchers (e.g., Ayers, 1979), who suggest that children with autism show hypersensitivity or hyposensitivity to touch, resulting in difficulty using their space. Similar to taste, where children with autism have difficulty assigning meaning to tastes, some children receive the messages of touch but do not have sufficient meaning of these messages to attach concepts for language. Figure 1.9 illustrates how the child pulls away in reaction to Mom's touch.

Mom tries to pick up the child, who pulls away
to her touch.

Figure 1.9. Tactile Sensory Response.

The tactile system works in tandem with the proprioceptive system. The proprioceptive system provides input from internal movements of muscles, tendons, and so on. The skin or tactile system is the receptor for sensory touch and movement from outside the body, and the proprioceptive system is the internal feedback to the tactile sensory system. For example, whereas touch connects the child's skin on the outside of the child's body to world-based physical experiences, the proprioceptive system connects the child's muscles, tendons, and joints from inside the child's body to movements of the body.

As a child sits or stands, the proprioceptive system responds to the positions of the muscles, tendons, and joints. For some individuals with autism these types of positions are not automatic. Thus, even though the child is able to receive the sensory information from outside the body, integration with the internal movements or positions may be weak or different. The child may have difficulty feeling where her body is in relation to what she does. In other words, the child may be able to move and receive touch but may not know the meaning of such movements or touches.

Figure 1.10 shows a child trying to balance his internal proprioception by touching the door as he moves from one space to another space. The child touches the sides of the door with his feet and hands to create a stable relationship between internal recognition of input and outside input.

Child touches door with feet and hands to create a
stable relationship between
internal recognition of outside input.

Figure 1.10. Proprioceptive Equilibrium.

When our body changes positions, input from outside the body through touch connects to the body's internal muscle responses. Simultaneously, the vestibular system records the shift in movement in relationship to the pull of gravity. The vestibular system, located in the inner ear, controls the sense of movement and balance to gravity. So when an individual moves, external input to touch connects with the internal response or movement of muscles, joints, and tendons, recording such movements in physical connection to the force of gravity on the movement of the body. For example, when an infant is lying in his mother's arms, his skin records the pressure of the touch. This sensory input activates the body to physically respond, which in turn moves the muscles, joints, and tendons. As the child moves, the vestibular system of the inner ear along with the eyes records the child's body position in space. These systems (touch, proprioception, and vision) are integrating the information to create patterns of spatial positioning and movement.

A child with autism does not typically have difficulty with the receptors; so input from any of these sensory systems is okay. But for these systems to work beyond receptor input, they must be able to integrate the patterns of the sensory information from the interconnectedness of the different systems into meaningful concepts. *For individuals with autism, the receiving ability is fine, but the integration of the systems to assign meaning is difficult.* Chapters 2 and 3 explain the relationship between the sensory sets of patterns and how concepts form from these patterns.

Smell. One of the oldest biological sensory systems is that of smell. Like the other sensory systems, the olfactory system is ready to record information at birth. However, unlike the other systems, it does not need integration with other sensory inputs to record an olfactory tracing. (A tracing is a cell's way of remembering information from past situations.) Olfactory input continues to come into the receptor waiting for the input to be assigned meaning. If the learner's system cannot assign meaning, the input begins to build up, and the child appears to be very sensitive to smell.

Children with ASD often appear to be sensitive to smells, especially when they are young and do not have the language to interpret the smells. Myles and her colleagues (2001) found that over 75% of children with Asperger Syndrome experience olfactory sensitivity. This suggests that the sensory receptors work fine for smell, but the processing of the sensory information to assign meaning for conceptualization of smell may be difficult.

Olfactory input works to protect us from dangerous situations (fire, chemicals, etc.), and plays an important role in sexual development such as in puberty when pheromones are released and sensed through the olfactory system. Smell also plays a role in memory related to concepts and language. The use of language to represent concepts that form from the integration of sensory input requires more than just reception of the input. More about integration of input will be discussed in later chapters.

Sight and sound. We have two distance sensory receptors: the eyes and the ears. The eyes are able to record the input of light and movement close to 180 degrees whereas the ears record the physical dimensions of a sound wave (pitch or frequency, loudness or amplitude, and duration or on-off set) in a 360 sphere. The eyes provide sight and the ears provide sound. Figure 1.11 shows how the eyes and ears work to provide distance input.

Sight: Mom sees child playing.

Sound: Child hears sound of mom's voice.

Figure 1.11. Eyes and Ears Provide Distance Input.

Much more about the visual and acoustic sensory senses will be presented later since these systems are the primary ways for reception of meaning used for communication and language.

How Does the Learning System Create Meaning?

The sensory receptors bring the input into the child, and then the child's biological system begins to organize the input. Figure 1.12. shows a child's learning input when all sensory systems connect together.

Figure 1.12. Sensory System Interconnect.

When the sensory input comes in through the eyes, ears, skin, touch, and taste, the cells integrate the information. Most of the information is relayed through the brain stem and is integrated through cellular nuclei to create patterns. These patterns of cells form networks of interconnected cell function, also called cellular systems. The cellular systems are the biological parallels to the developed concepts. As the networks of cells transport information to higher parts of the brain, systems of *sensory integration* form as concepts. Language represents these concepts as sets of symbols (symbolization). *Language, the highest function of cellular systems, represents the underlying concepts (Arwood, 1983).*

To create meaning requires increased development of the learning system through sensory input, integration, and inhibition. Input from sensory systems integrates throughout the brain stem on up to the cerebrum. If the cellular structures of the learning system recognize the integration, then the cells biochemically respond that the sensory integration is present. This recognition of input is called inhibition. Inhibition tells the body that sensory input is recognized. For the typical learner, this process occurs without notice (e.g., Hannaford, 1995, 1997; Trott; 1993; Wallace et al., 2004) as does the typical learner's development of cognition, language, and socialization. So, for the typical learning system, meaning occurs by sensory input forming the development of cellular patterns that *inhibits recognizable* patterns for the development of concepts. Figure 1.13 shows how the integration of sensory input allows for learning.

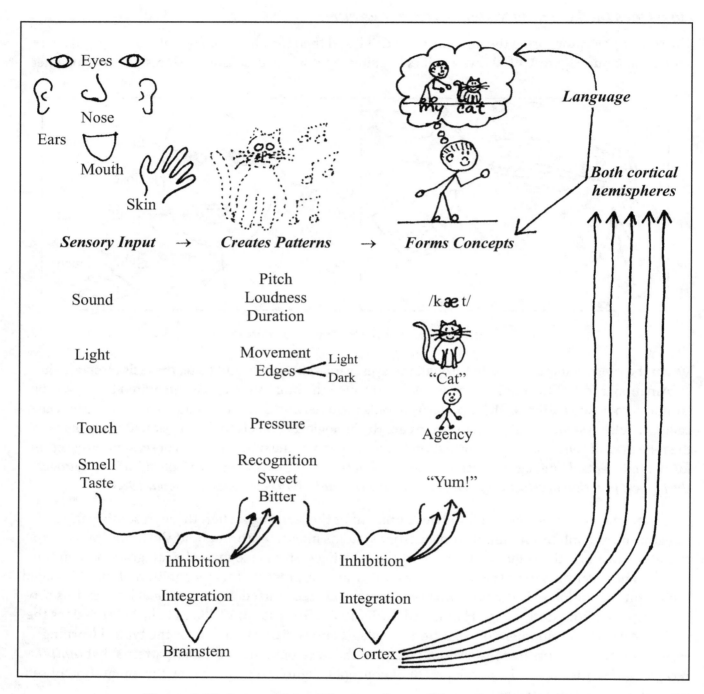

Figure 1.13. Integration of Sensory Input Allows for Learning.

The typical child can hear, see, taste, touch, and smell others' speech, music, print, objects, and so on. *The sensory input creates patterns. These patterns become concepts, and language forms to represent the concepts.* To learn concepts, there must be inhibition and integration of sensory input patterns. This neurological integration and inhibition of the patterns for development of concepts allows the child to acquire higher forms of socialization, communication, and language. Language symbols represent the concepts that form from the systems of sensory integration. Therefore, from a neurobiological view, *the use of language is the most complex function.* Likewise, the most complex level of meaning is the use of language.

Activity: Explain how sensory input results in patterns that form concepts for language use.

What Is the Learning System Like for the Child with Autism?

The child with ASD can hear. The child with ASD can see, and so on. The child with ASD is able to receive all of the sensory raw data, but does not easily move the patterns of these sensory inputs into concepts for language symbols. Instead, the child often continues to develop patterns without concepts (see Chapter 2). Since patterns are not easily recognizable, the child's learning system does not inhibit them. Without inhibition the child does not form the concepts or the language to represent the concepts. Therefore, intervention is needed to help the child with ASD to form concepts related to socialization, communication, and language. Figure 1.14 shows the learning system for a child with autism. Note how the language and conceptual pieces of learning do not connect with the sensory pattern development.

Activity: Compare Figure 1.13 to Figure 1.14. What are the similarities and what are the differences?

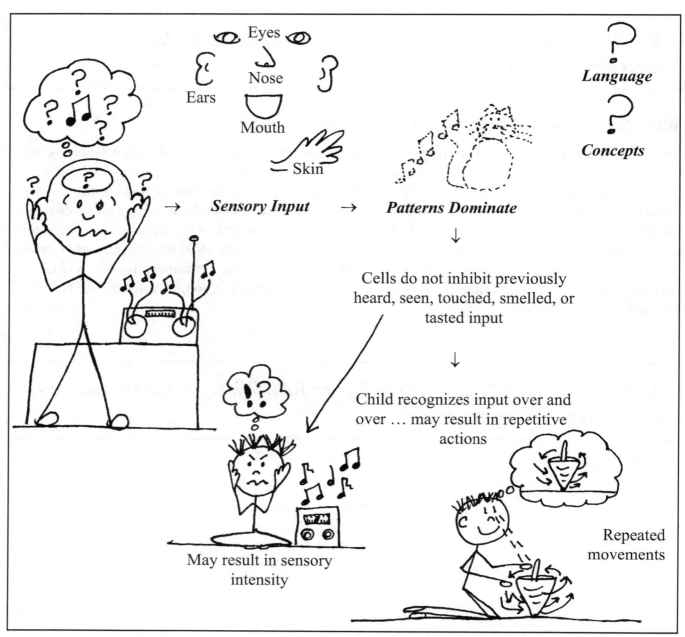

Figure 1.14. Learning System of a Child with Autism.

Summary

This chapter described how the definition of autism relates to the development of social, cognitive, and language abilities that are acquired through the neurobiological learning system. This learning system begins with the input of sensory information, which then forms systems of patterns through inhibition and integration. Chapter 2 explains how the sensory input organizes perceptual patterns through inhibition and integration to form concepts, the next level of learning.

Concepts for Chapter 2

What does the brain seek to process?

What does sensory integration form?

When significant integration of perceptual patterns occurs, what forms?

Why does autism cause challenges with perceptual patterns?

CHAPTER 2

Autism: Why Is It Developmental?

I see it, but I don't recognize it.
I hear it, but it doesn't make sense.
I smell it, but I don't know its name.
I perceive it, but I don't know how!

Learner Outcomes: As a result of reading this chapter, the reader should be able to explain and give examples of learning patterns and how patterns form concepts. The reader should also be able to recognize the difference between typical learning of patterns for concept development and the lack of pattern recognition that results in a lack of concepts.

The child with autism can hear, see, smell, taste, and touch. The raw data of these sensory inputs form patterns – recognizable forms of input. For example, as you walk into a room, you see squiggles on the carpet. As you look around, the squiggles become more discernible. Finally, you recognize the paisley design on the carpet. Your brain's function is responsible for the ability to make sense out of seeing the squiggles on the carpet. This chapter discusses how the brain creates these patterns of sensory input, also known as perceptual patterns.

The Brain and Learning

The brain is like a lighthouse. It is always scanning for new information. If the brain sees, hears, tastes, touches, or smells a new input, it is doing what it is designed to do – recognize new input. Sensory input is the only way that information comes into the learner. But the sensory input must be sorted as it comes into the body through the receptors to allow the learner to begin to see, hear, taste, touch, or smell familiar input. Familiar sensory input forms a recognized set of patterns.

Figure 2.1 shows how new input through the sensory systems forms a recognized set of patterns. The simple activity of playing ball with Mom consists of numerous types of input that overlap into a recognizable event.

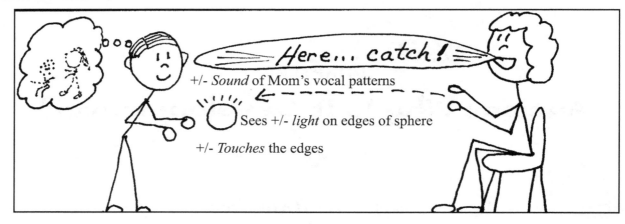

Mom throws the ball.

Figure 2.1. Sensory Input Forms Patterns.

Patterns of sensory input increase as long as there are sounds, sights, tastes, touches, and smells. For example, every time he sees the "ball," the child sees the sensory pieces of the ball as parts of the whole ball. When the ball is thrown, the ball moves through many different positions, each is another frame of sensory input. When the child is at a developmental level of using the sensory input, he literally sees dozens of shapes for the one ball thrown through space. Because the brain continues to build sets of patterns from these types of experiences, the child eventually is able to see the object, catch the object, and so on.

> **Remember: Children are not born able to see objects or hear words. These abilities are learned through the constant neural or "brain" recognition of past sensory input. The newborn sees differences in light that continue to expand, either by moving the object or by the child moving through the various spatial planes, until the child begins to see the consistent shape of points of light on a plane in the shape of the object.**

Figure 2.2 shows how the light shapes the edges of objects through pattern recognition. First the child sees the "flat" points of light reflect from the side of an object that, in reality, is round. The brain then recognizes those points of light so a new plane or dimension of input is formed. This enables the child to see the round object as a flat sphere or as two-dimensional. The original dimension was horizontal to the child; the second dimension created some depth or vertical dimension. Eventually, the third, or diagonal, set of light points on the planes' edges creates a spherical dimension of roundness. Now, the child actually sees the shape of a ball.

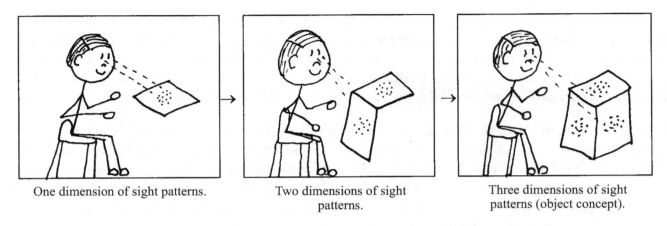

| One dimension of sight patterns. | Two dimensions of sight patterns. | Three dimensions of sight patterns (object concept). |

Figure 2.2. Light Patterns Form Shapes of Light Points on a Plane.

These overlapping patterns of visual input for each dimension create the shapes of objects. Such systems of patterns are concepts. Once the child's brain recognizes the input in these dimensional shapes of patterns, she has the conceptual meaning of the object. As shown in Figure 2.2, the child has two *overlapping* sets of patterns that the brain sees *before* the third set of *overlapping patterns* forms the concept of the object.

A child with a typical learning system is able to naturally organize the sensory input into patterns that form concepts. Sounds, tastes, touches, smells, and sights all *integrate* as sets of perceptual patterns. These perceptual patterns *overlap* into concepts. There are two key elements to conceptual development: (a) the child's neurobiological system is able to "recognize" new perceptual patterns from old perceptual patterns; and (b) there is sufficient integration of different forms of input to inhibit the old patterns for recognition.

These principles are critical in the development of the learning system for language, cognition, and socialization. If a child has a learning system that does not recognize new input separate from old input, she may have difficulty inhibiting past input, acting as if sensory input is always new. For example, children around 12 to 18 months of age often play with sensory input such as trying to catch water that comes out of the bathtub spout. The young child is trying to recognize the patterns of water as something that can be caught in the hands; yet, with each attempt to catch the water, the water runs out between the fingers.

For a typical learner, a few attempts to catch the water in the fingers result in enough overlap of patterns so that the child begins to use a toy or cup to catch the water drips from the bathtub spout. That is, the child's learning system integrates the overlap of patterns and the child begins to develop a concept about water, and eventually quits the pattern repetition of running water through the fingers.

Children with autism, on the other hand, often repeat the sensory play of a set of patterns over and over. For example, one 9-year-old nonverbal child had spent so many hours sitting in a watering trough playing with the water that his legs were deformed into the shape of the rectangle trough. This child had lots of experience with the patterns of water but could not form them into concepts.

To learn concepts, the child's neurological system of cellular structures must be able to recognize the sensory patterns of input. Once the brain recognizes past input, the child can begin to attend to other input. This ability to shift from recognition of past input to attending to more complex new input is a form of integration and inhibition. To develop the concepts from the perceptual patterns, *a child's learning system must be able to inhibit the old patterns while integrating new perceptual patterns.*

Once sensory input forms patterns of recognition, the brain looks for new input. This new input overlaps to form concepts. For example, in the case of a spherical object like a ball, the recognition of the concept "ball" comes from the many visual inputs of the ball as it moves through space. The overlap of these visual inputs across spatial planes allows for conceptualization of the actual depth of the object. *Not all types of overlapping sensory input will form concepts.* More information about which patterns create concepts will be presented in Chapter 3.

Figure 2.3 shows another example of how perceptual overlap of visual input forms a basic concept. With each input, more and more pieces of visual input overlap to form an object (cat). Even if the cat changes positions or looks, the child will still be able to recognize the form of the patterns as the concept "cat."

Figure 2.3. Visual Perceptual Patterns Overlap to Form Concept Knowledge.

Autism: A Perceptual Difficulty in Learning

As we have seen, autism is not a problem with sensory input. Instead, individuals with autism disorders have difficulty integrating and inhibiting the perceptual patterns of sensory input they receive to form concepts. More specifically, they have difficulty recognizing the input as previously tasted, touched, smelled, heard, or seen. As a result, the child with autism is supersensitive to all sensory input that does not become organized as perceptual patterns from adequate integration and inhibition to form concepts. The child who finds the tastes of foods unfamiliar, the fluorescence of a light too bright, or the sound of a fire drill alarm too loud is experiencing difficulty in turning the sensory patterns into concepts.

This inability to process the sensory input into recognizable patterns to form concepts is sometimes referred to as *hypersensitivity*. The child appears to be too sensitive to the input; however, the problem really is that the input is not meaningful enough. The child does not lack sensitivity because the child is responding to the sensory input. But because the child "over-responds," she attends to sensation rather than blocking out the sensation by forming concepts. Some children appear to lack sensitivity, such as when they chew off the ends of their fingers. When this happens, it means that the child is not gaining cortical meaning from the intense pressure ... the pressure on the finger is recognized as sensory input, not as pain, a language function.

The ability to form concepts from patterns of integrated and inhibited sensory input usually occurs as an automatic neurological organization of systems within the brain. The following section explains how perceptual patterns occur in our world with or without conceptual meanings.

Perceptual Features of Learning

Perceptual patterns develop from the neurobiological learning system seeking new sensory input. As the sensory receptors bring new sensory input into the learning system, structures within the brain stem inhibit old sensory patterns while the brain seeks new patterns. For typical learners, these patterns overlap and begin to form concepts. However, for children with ASD patterns do not always form concepts. Some children lack the ability to integrate certain types of sensory patterns, so their learning systems are constantly seeking meaning from perceptual features. For example, some children with ASD spin objects over and over. As the child looks at the spinning object, the sensory input brings in the visual features of patterns of the spin over and over and over. However, the learning system does not recognize the patterns and, therefore, is not able to overlap patterns to form concepts.

But not all learning is conceptual. Many typical activities in education use perceptual patterns. For example, a child who can say the names of the patterns on a page, or word call, is recognizing the sound patterns that go with the sight patterns without necessarily understanding the meaning of the ideas or concepts. This is what we typically call "reading aloud." Or, a child can tell you back exactly what patterns he heard without being able to attach conceptual meaning. Children with autism can often repeat acoustic patterns such as entire TV commercials verbatim, but do not have the conceptual meaning of what they are repeating. In school, when typical learners are asked what a rule is for behavior, they often repeat back the rule, "You don't push," but do not understand the meaning well enough to "not push."

The ability to match patterns, repeat patterns, reiterate patterns, or copy patterns is the result of being able to integrate enough sensory input to respond. These types of perceptual patterns do not require conceptualization. Figure 2.4 shows how copying in school is a perceptual task of pattern recognition.

Figure 2.4. Perceptual Pattern Recognition.

Pattern repetition includes the following tasks: doing math problems as patterns without understanding the concepts of the numbers; copying letters; matching letter patterns for writing; matching the patterns of an end-of-chapter set of questions to patterns in the chapter without understanding the questions; word calling for reading fluency; imitating patterns of sound in speech therapy; matching shapes and colors; imitating spoken sounds to pictures (show the picture, and child says "dog"); matching patterns for filling in worksheets. The list goes on and on. A great number of tasks in the pre-primary and primary grades expect nothing more than pattern imitation, repetition, matching, and copying. Most educators see this pattern learning as "normal." However, when a child with ASD does this type of pattern learning in the quest for more meaning, such as spinning an object or rocking back and forth, educators see it as atypical.

What is the difference between typical learning of patterns and a child with ASD who uses perceptual pattern learning? The difference is that the child with autism cannot always make conceptual meaning from the patterns that she is repeating. On the other hand, the typical learner repeats patterns for parents or educators because they are asked to do these types of tasks, especially in literacy activities.

The typical learner converts naturally occurring sights, smells, sounds, tastes, touches as patterns into concepts. The child with ASD cannot always make concepts out of some of these patterns, and therefore does not form concepts. Instead, the child appears to "get stuck" with the patterns, continuing to seek meaning from these naturally occurring patterns.

In a typical learner, the brain is constantly finding new information from naturally occurring patterns, so the child gravitates to those things that are conceptually meaningful. In school, the educator may ask a typical learner to repeat patterns that are not conceptually meaningful, so the typical learner will begin to seek new meaning. For example, staff at a Title I elementary school, with many at-risk students with low language development, decided to have the primary-age children change classrooms with each change of content. The children were also to change classes by ability level. So for 20 minutes a group of children would work on patterns of sound for phonics. Then the period would be over and the children would change teachers, sometimes rooms, and even groups. It was amazing to see many children – with typical learning systems – pounding their heads (bonking), spinning objects or their bodies in circles, or engaging in repetitive patterns such as pencil sharpening or rhythmic drumming during these transitions and into the next period. The children simply did not have enough conceptual understanding of what was happening to recognize the patterns of where they were to go, with whom, and for what. Thus, their unusual behaviors represented the learning system looking for more meaning.

When a child with autism is engaging in atypical behaviors such as spinning, the child's learning system is looking for how to make conceptual meaning from the patterns of sensory input. Each spin of an object is like a new frame of perception. Figure 2.5 shows how a child with ASD continues to seek meaning of the patterns of an object but without the ability to form concepts from the patterns. The child moves the car, and each movement of the car creates a new shape of the car. Since a child with ASD learns concepts through the motor movements to create shapes, this means the child continues to receive meaning from each movement of the car. However, this meaning remains perceptual like the frames of a film with no story line – *there are no concepts with these movements until the motor patterns can be integrated or overlapped to form conceptual meaning.*

Each spin creates a new pattern. The object is seen in a new position, shape, etc.

Figure 2.5. Movements Form Patterns Without Concepts.

Figure 2.6 shows a child with autism creating the same patterns with body movements.

| Child sees object. | Child moves, and object is different in patterns. | Child turns all the way around, and object disappears. | Child moves, and object is different in position. | Child moves and sees the whole object again. |

Figure 2.6. Creating Patterns with Body Movements.

Sights, sounds, tastes, touches, and smells create patterns to form concepts. Some children can make concept meanings from the usual environmental sensory inputs. Other children, such as children with ASD, cannot always make enough conceptual meaning from the perceptual patterns. Educators tend to try to teach patterns at an early age; but typical learning systems naturally use patterns for developing concepts without intervention. Children diagnosed with ASD have difficulty separating nonmeaningful pattern recognition from patterns that will create concepts for them. Therefore, they need intervention.

It is important to realize that a child with ASD does not need more patterns but more meaning, and therefore more concepts. Later chapters will discuss intervention methods for increasing conceptual development. For children with ASD, the sensory input consists of the individual "features" of the sensory input; that is, the movements of the child, the planes of shapes of objects, the differences in voices, the differences in tastes, or the differences in touch. *For these features to take on conceptual meaning, the patterns of the learning system must overlap so the child can create concepts.*

Assigning Meaning to Patterns

As we have seen, typical learners and children with ASD are able to receive sensory input and form patterns from the sensory input. As all children's learning systems seek out new input for pattern development and meaning, the adults in the environment assign meaning to the children's motor acts. For example, at birth a child produces a reflexive cry by having air rush past the laryngeal folds of the throat. Figure 2.7 shows this pattern of reflexive cry. The child does not intentionally cry to receive something from someone. The child's body produces sound. But this act creates the pattern of the next act, to take another breath, and so on. With each change of input, the child's body responds, creating behavior that the adult assigns meaning to.

| In the womb, the lungs do not inflate. | Child is born. Air rushes in, inflating lungs. | Child's airways open, and air flows past folds that vibrate. |

Figure 2.7. A Reflexive Response to Changes in the Atmospheric Pressure.

By the third day after birth, the child's cry is beginning to take on new patterns (Mehler et al., 1988). The child's neurological system responds to different sensory inputs with different patterns of recognition. In this way, the crying patterns have different meanings – one cry is for hunger, another is for thirst, another is for sleep, and yet another is for pain. Most moms can tell the differences in these cries, even in babies of other cultures. The different cries are seen as the child and parent adding meaning to specific patterns of behavior (see Eimas et al., 1971).

Learning with a Visual Brain in an Auditory World

34

Figure 2.8 shows how a mom responds to one cry with one type of meaning.

Figure 2.8. One Assignment of Meaning.

As the parent assigns meaning to the child's behavior, the child's behavior receives new input. The parent picks up the baby and gives the baby a bottle. Mom's acts provide new touches, smells, sounds, sights, and tastes for new sets of patterns. Mom does something and the child does something. The child does something and Mom does something. This back-and-forth or dyadic relationship creates meaning for the child. Dyadic interactions between Mom and child (Lucas, 1980) help develop sets of patterns with specific meanings for later conceptual development (Arwood, 1991).

This overlap of perceptual patterns on the way to concept development is also the first step toward language learning. Language represents the learned concepts. So, as a child forms concepts, she is also beginning to learn language. If a child can take natural sounds, tastes, touches, sights, and smells and turn them into patterns, she is beginning to recognize the meaning of the concepts of these patterns. As parents assign meaning to these acts, they use language. For example, when a parent interprets a child's cry as hunger, the parent might ask, "Are you hungry?" The parent doesn't expect the baby to respond to these words, but to respond to the taste of milk, the sight of the bottle, the sound of Mom's voice, the smell of Mom's perfume, the touch of Mom's arms, and so on. The familiarity of these patterns indicates that the child is beginning to form concepts from the patterns.

The use of language by the parent is also new sensory input to the child. Mom's spoken utterance has acoustic features that are sensed by the neurobiological system – first as sensory input and then as patterns. In essence, children acquire language through their learning systems from the people around them using language.

Implications of Pattern Learning

Children with ASD learn patterns exceptionally well, making it relatively easy for educators, as well as parents, to "train" them to recognize patterns. For example, a teacher can use a hand movement, a vocal command such as "sit," and/or a picture of a child along with a "payoff" such as food or stickers, to "teach" a child a particular pattern. However, recognizing the features of sensory input to produce patterns of behavior is not the same as learning to choose to sit because it is time to work. To think about "sitting" without pattern recognition requires more learning at a higher level.

Recognizing sensory input as patterns is a lower than conceptual level of learning, as seen in Figure 2.9. Patterns form from the sensory input. Then the child's neurological system must recognize the patterns to form concepts. Children with ASD tend to show a breakdown between forming patterns, which they do well, and being able to neurologically recognize the patterns to form concepts.

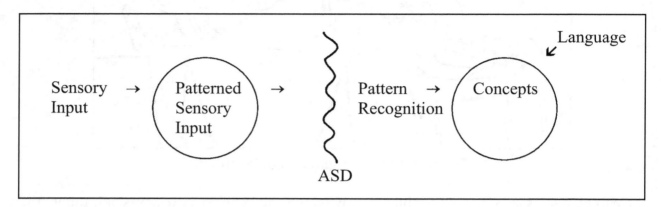

Figure 2.9. Breakdown for Individuals with ASD Happens Between Patterns and Pattern Recognition.

As a result, they create patterns and more patterns. The repetition of patterns within the child's environment creates a soothing routine for many children with ASD. As long as environmental input is routinely a set of patterns, many children with ASD function extremely well. In fact, children who can match the sound patterns to the patterns they hear can echo what others say. Similarly, children who can match sound patterns to print patterns word call or read aloud very well, even though they often do not comprehend what they read. Many children with ASD can match one set of patterns to another set of patterns. Figure 2.10 shows a child repeating the alphabet rhymes over and over.

Figure 2.10. Repetition of Patterns.

Pattern learning shows changes in products and often results in parents and educators encouraging greater development of even more patterns. Math, oral reading, speaking, and behavior compliance can all remain at a product level of pattern development. However, the more patterns that develop without conceptualization, the more inflexible the child or adult becomes. Thus, learning patterns without conceptualization limits a person's functional ability to working from routine-like sets of patterns. A person with a set of patterns for the routine of "getting ready for school," for example, may do the same actions in the same order day after day: Get up, use the toilet, get dressed, get breakfast, brush teeth, get backpack, and go out the door. Anything that interrupts the patterns of the routine also interrupts the child's ability to function. For example, if the child doesn't have time for breakfast at home, the child's parent may try to get the child to eat in the car. Without an understanding of how these activities, in whatever order, constitute the concept of "getting ready," the child will reject the change in routine and the parent may have difficulty getting the child to leave the house. In fact, the child may start repeating patterns such as taking off clothes and putting on other clothes over and over to try to find the patterns of the routine. Meanwhile, parents become upset because they are going to be late.

An adult with Asperger Syndrome graduated from high school and obtained a job. The job began at 8:00 but when this young adult got up the first morning, he realized that the cats needed to be fed (part of his routine). There wasn't any cat food, so he went to the store and got some. Then a friend called, and he answered the phone and talked to the friend. He showed up for his first day of work around 10:00 and was fired. He did not understand! He kept saying over and over, "But the cats were hungry!"

Pattern learning works for a limited level of functioning. To understand why and how something happens requires the development of concepts and the ability to use language to explain the relationship among concepts. The higher the level of language, the better a person is able to function flexibly in the "real world." Chapter 3 will discuss the way concepts develop from patterns for individuals with ASD.

Activity: Explain how children with ASD can acquire so many patterns yet not be able to form concepts.

Summary

The learning system consists of layers of development: (a) the senses receive input; (b) the sensory input creates patterns of input; (c) the neurological system recognizes these patterns; (d) the patterns form systems of pattern integration and inhibition; and (e) the systems of patterns create concepts. Language patterns represent the underlying concepts.

Concepts for Chapter 3

Which patterns form concepts?

What is the difference between acoustic and auditory patterns?

How do movement patterns form visual concepts?

What type of patterns do individuals with ASD use best to develop concepts?

Autism: How Does the Child Learn Concepts?

I see an object, but I don't know the name.

I spin the object, but why does it change the way it looks?

I touch the object, but it isn't a familiar touch.

I know what others don't know, but I don't know what I need to know.

Learner Outcomes: As a result of reading this chapter, the reader should be able to explain which patterns become which concepts and why many children with ASD struggle to develop concepts.

As you may recall from reading the first two chapters, the first stage of learning consists of sensory input. As the child's neurobiological learning system recognizes the sensory input, new sensory input combines or overlaps with the old input to form sensory patterns. These patterns may or may not create conceptual meaning. The purpose of this chapter is to show how a child with autism *uses* the patterns that typically develop concepts for socialization, language, and communication.

Concept Development from Patterns

Children naturally acquire the meaning of differing sensory inputs. Sensory organs consist of specific receptor cells (Chapter 1). Each type of receptor organizes specific features of the sensory input. The ears receive the features of sound as different pitches (how high or low in tone), different loudness levels, and/or different lengths of time to produce the sound (how long a sound occurs before the next sound). For example, the acoustic spoken pattern "cat" may be heard as "cat?" or "cat!" or softly spoken as "my sweet cat" or in exasperation such as "Get out of here, CAT!" Thus, each time a learner hears the pattern of "cat," there are slight differences in the features of sound patterns according to changes in pitch, loudness, and timing or duration.

If the child is able to hear the actual pattern of "cat," he also recognizes the sound pattern of "cat" separate from the features of the sounds of the overhead lights, the sounds of the computer in the background, the sounds of a chair moving, the sounds of a person walking outside, the sounds of the traffic on the street, and so on. All of these different patterns of sounds have competing and overlapping acoustic features. For a child to be able to sort the acoustic features to create conceptual meaning, his learning system must sort background features of sound from the important, foreground features of pitch, loudness, and duration. Sorted features create perceptual or recognizable patterns. Figure 3.1 shows how difficult it is to distinguish among similar acoustic features emitted from differing sources.

Figure 3.1. These Sounds Produce Acoustic Features.

Visual input works in a similar fashion as the acoustic input. As you recall from the previous chapters, the visual input comes in as features of light or movement. So, for the child to recognize an object, her learning system must be able to see all the points of light on the surface of the object. Since objects come in different shapes, the eyes or body must move to follow the shape of the edges of points of light. Without movement, the learner sees a single set of points that will not overlap and will not form the shape of what the person is looking at. Figure 3.2 shows how the movement of the eyes, hand, or mouth creates the shape of an idea. In this way, the eyes create the mental images of shapes and objects. To see a moving object such as a human face, the learner must be able to sort moving patterns of shapes, a task that children with ASD have difficulty doing.

Figure 3.2. Movement Creates the Shape of an Idea.

When a child's learning system sorts the acoustic or visual features, the brain stem and other cerebral structures begin to *integrate* the sorted groups of features into recognizable patterns. One pattern of sound, for example, integrates with another pattern of sound. These patterns are sorted from other acoustic patterns. After sorted patterns begin to integrate, the child's learning system is able to *inhibit* recognizable patterns. The recognition of patterns allows the child's learning system to be more efficient. As old patterns are inhibited, new information can be brought into the system. Figure 3.3 shows how this integration and inhibition allows information to become increasingly more complex in nature.

Figure 3.3. Integration and Inhibition of Patterns.

When the learner can inhibit previously heard or seen features while integrating new sets of features, she is able to distinguish among patterns of sounds or sights from different sources. For example, to hear a spoken pattern such as "cat," the learning system must be able to inhibit and integrate sensory features. The background sounds of lights, computers, or others moving around the room must create sorted groups of patterns that are recognized as neurologically different from the pattern of the spoken idea, "cat."

If patterns of input cannot be sorted into recognized patterns of greater complexity, concept development lags behind. Children diagnosed with ASD experience varying levels of pattern organization and recognition. Consequently, the basic concepts for socialization, language, and communication also occur at varying levels. Chapters 4 through 7 will discuss concept development for socialization, language, and communication. The next section describes which patterns form which types of concepts.

Activity: Being able to create patterns is not the same as being able to integrate patterns to create concepts. Explain the difference between creating patterns and integrating patterns.

Patterns Form Specific Types of Concepts

Since the different sensory systems process different forms of input, the resulting different patterns create different types of concepts. For example, the ears process acoustic features of pitch, loudness, and duration, and therefore produce acoustic patterns. The eyes process visual features from light and movement. Some of these patterns integrate and some don't. If the patterns integrate to inhibit old patterns for new input, the complexity of the patterns increases to form concepts.

Activity: Explain the importance of inhibition and integration of patterns.

One interesting aspect of the human brain is that as long as the brain is alive, it will seek new information from the five senses. Some of these sensory inputs form patterns that reorganize to form concepts, whereas others do not. In other words, not all patterns integrate to form concepts. And, not all people are able to use the same types of patterns for acquiring or developing concepts.

Figure 3.4 shows that the human brain processes typical sensory input as perceptual pattern development.

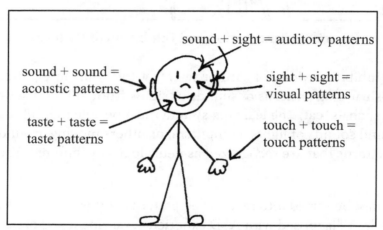

Figure 3.4. The Human Brain Processes Different Input.

The following section shows the educational significance of understanding the difference between pattern and concept learning and explains which sets of patterns form which types of concepts.

Activity: The brain seeks out patterns, so patterns are easy to acquire. But what happens if the patterns do not integrate?

Acoustic patterns. In education, acoustic patterns may be copied, echoed, and/or imitated, but acoustic patterns alone do not form conceptual meanings. For example, a child with autism might learn to "word call" but not comprehend. More specifically, a child with ASD may word call at between the fifth- and eighth-grade level, but his comprehension is often arrested at the third- to fourth-grade level, the level where language must be used to make meaning out of the print. In other words, more than just acoustic patterns have to be used to understand the meaning of the print for reading comprehension.

Acoustic patterns are the specific sounds that the child copies, echoes, or imitates much like a phonograph. But acoustic echoing, copying, or imitating does not improve language or the meaning of concepts. Figure 3.5 shows a child with ASD who is imitating the sound patterns of another person.

Figure 3.5. Imitation of Acoustic Patterns.

The imitation usually lacks the quality of typical speech, sounding robotic or mechanical, as if great effort were expended on producing it. The child's speech might even appear to get stuck as if she is stuttering. Or the child might imitate borrowed phrases that are repeated such as "You betcha." Again, this type of imitation of acoustic patterns lacks the underlying conceptual comprehension of language.

The amount of imitation and level of imitation varies among children with ASD. As illustrated in the following, many children with ASD can often repeat *all* acoustic patterns while others cannot pick up enough patterns to make sound patterns that are similar to speech or even the prosody of a natural cry or laugh. Yet others are able to pick up a lot of acoustic patterns, often sounding like they have formal adult language but are unable to socially communicate about their spoken ideas. Figure 3.6 shows a representation of a child with a moderate level of acoustic pattern matching. The child sees the print and says the print, but his word call of the sounds of the print doesn't mean anything to him.

Figures 3.6. Moderate Level of Pattern Matching.

Figure 3.7 shows a child who repeats patterns but does not match the patterns well. While he is acquiring a lot of patterns, he is not forming many concepts, so he repeats the patterns.

Figure 3.7. Pattern Acquisition and Repetition with Limited Matching.

Figure 3.8. shows a child who acquires the patterns but with almost no matching of patterns. Therefore, the sensory input around him remains irritating and meaningless.

Figures 3.8. Pattern Acquisition But Very Limited Matching.

Figure 3.9 shows a child who acquires a lot of patterns and can match a lot of patterns to form concepts. These concepts are based on how well the patterns match what the child can do within the context. In this case, the child knows that the patterns of letters mean the concept "alphabet." This child may not be able to alphabetize files or sound out words for spelling, but would be able to match the patterns of a word to exactly what the child mentally remembers the word looking like.

Figure 3.9. Lots of Matched Patterns for Concept Development.

Acoustic patterns by themselves do not form concepts and therefore have no language basis. With this knowledge about the learning system, it would make little sense to have a child practice sounds without previously developing a full language system, or to ask a child to work on phonics if he cannot already tell a full language story. Yet, many educators and therapists try to input more acoustic patterns in the hope that the child will learn to speak from these sounds or learn to read from the sound patterns of phonics. *Acoustic patterns can increase in number but will not form concepts or create language. Straight acoustic patterns are speech forms without underlying conceptual meanings.* Strategies that are consistent with how a child with ASD learns concepts will be offered later in the book.

Whereas the learning system of children with ASD does not automatically connect acoustic patterns with other sensory input, other types of learners may be able to integrate acoustic patterns with visual patterns. In about 15% (Arwood, 1991; Arwood, Kaakinen, & Wynne, 2002) of typical learners, acoustic patterns moving from the ear to the brain integrate with visual patterns in the "auditory," not acoustic, pathways of the brain stem. These types of auditory patterns form language-based concepts. Individuals whose learning systems can simultaneously integrate visual and acoustic patterns form auditory types of concepts. Most children with ASD are unable to do so, and therefore do not develop auditory types of concepts. A later section in this chapter will explain auditory concepts.

Activity: Explain why working on acoustic patterns will not benefit concept development. Also, explain how matching patterns may not produce concepts.

Educators attempt to teach many skills that require the ability to neurologically integrate acoustic and visual patterns. For example, spelling is a task that is auditory in nature. The speller is expected to say the names of the letter sounds of a pattern or word, remember these acoustic and visual patterns, and be able to write the correct integrated sound and sight pattern on a spelling test and then in an essay. People whose learning systems naturally integrate visual and acoustic patterns find spelling easy as long as they have learned the letters and sounds (phonics). Remember that about 15% of U.S. population is able to integrate these types of patterns.

Activity: Acoustic patterns are different from auditory patterns. Acoustic patterns consist of sound only. What do auditory patterns consist of? Give at least one example of an auditory set of educational patterns.

Children and adults with ASD do not integrate acoustic and visual patterns for these types of auditory concepts. Arwood (e.g., 1991) has been conducting workshops on this topic for years. During many of these workshops she will choose a participant to "Sh-boo-ee the door." In response, the participant will typically try to do something to the door. Then the participant is asked to use "sh-boo-ee" in a sentence. The participant always is able to create a sentence using "sh-boo-ee." Many times the participant says, "I sh-boo-id the door." The participant is able to say the nonsense pattern, to act on the pattern, and even to modulate or change the pattern to form a past tense version of "sh-boo-ee," such as "shabooied." Then all participants are reminded that as educators they are well versed in phonics and spelling (e.g., Heilman, 2002). They are then asked to write out "sh-boo-ee." Many different patterns are offered, such as "chabui," "shebui," "shabuey," "shibui," "shabooey," "schabouey," or "shebouy." There is no correct pattern, as "sh-boo-ee" does not represent a conventional meaning or agreed-upon language term for a concept. Furthermore, the reason why the educators cannot spell the pattern in a conventional way is that they have not *seen* the pattern, only heard it (e.g., Holmes & Davis, 2002).

Remember: Acoustic patterns do not form concepts. Spelling in English is typically taught as a visual and acoustic or auditory concept.

Activity: Why can't most people with phonics background correctly spell a word they have only heard? Why is spelling an auditory task for most people?

As we have seen, the acoustic and visual patterns do not integrate in children with ASD. These children can hear and they can see, and they can combine acoustic patterns to imitate or copy what they hear. But these acoustic patterns do not create concepts. For a child or adult with ASD, the educational "rule of thumb" might be stated as follows: Individuals with ASD do not create auditory patterns, but they do form acoustic patterns. The more acoustic patterns a child or adult with ASD exhibits, the fewer the concepts, and subsequent language, the individual possesses to represent the concepts.

In the next session we will look at visual patterns. Children with ASD can see and they create visual patterns. Do visual patterns become concepts?

Visual patterns. Visual patterns from the visual sensory input overlap to create visual concepts. Figure 3.10 shows how the visual input from external sensory information may form a visual mental image.

Figure 3.10. Visual Input May Form a Visual Mental Image.

Overlapping visual input creates mental visual images that are conceptual in nature. Therefore, a child with ASD can look at a visual pattern and create a visual pattern mentally. Figure 3.11 shows a child with ASD creating a visual mental image from a written pattern.

Figure 3.11. Mental Visual Concepts Develop from Visual Print Patterns.

Just like children with ASD can imitate acoustic patterns, they can also imitate or match visual patterns. However, ***the significant educational point is that the acoustic patterns will not form concepts for language whereas the visual patterns will.*** Figures 3.12a and 3.12b show the conceptual difference between acoustic and visual patterns for children with ASD.

Mom asks Sally if she wants some juice, and Sally imitates.

Figure 3.12a. Acoustic Patterns.

Mom asks Sally if she wants juice. Sally sees the pattern "juice" and mentally sees herself drinking juice.

Figure 3.12b. Visual Patterns.

The problem with using visual patterns for conceptualization is that our society functions in an auditory way. This means that we expect people to learn to listen and form concepts based on sound. However, only about 10-15% (Arwood, 1991; Arwood et al., 2002) of society actually use an auditory way of thinking; that is, the sound of words seen and heard (visual and acoustic patterns integrated into concepts). However, many children without ASD, about 55% (Arwood, 1991) of pre-K to 12th grade, are able to use the visual patterns to form concepts that can be added to the sound of what people say. Therefore, even though these learners do not integrate auditory and visual patterns into auditory concepts, they are able to attach their sound patterns to their visual way of thinking. Figure 3.13 shows how a typical learner uses the visual patterns of speech (spoken as acoustic patterns) to create mental visual concepts for understanding and developing language.

Figure 3.13. Visual Input Forms Visual Concepts.

This group of visual metacognitive learners acquires concepts from matching visual patterns such as reading Mom's visual movements matched to Mom's actions of putting away blocks. They are able to attach the acoustic patterns of speech to what they see as mental visual concepts. In this way, these learners speak English and think in pictures or shapes of ideas. Likewise, they become skilled at hearing sound and matching their pictures to the sounds even though they don't use sound to develop language or understand meanings. For example, they might be able to read aloud with emphasis but not know what they read until they quietly look at the print on the page.

Individuals with ASD have varying abilities of attaching sound to their visual concepts or shapes of thoughts. Some cannot attach sound to any of their thoughts. Others are very good at picking up sound but cannot use sound or acoustic patterns for learning concepts. Instead, they imitate lots of acoustic patterns and create lots of visual patterns but do not integrate these patterns into concepts.

There is one more way to create concepts from patterns. Up to 30% of the school-age population can create visual types of concepts or thoughts from the shape of movements. In other words, when the mouth or eyes or hands move around the edges of something seen or touched, the brain stores this information as shapes in the visual cortex (Sadato, 1996). Figure 3.14 shows how the learner is able to create a concept from the shape of motor patterns. Since print patterns are static, that is, they don't change the shape of features, these children use print better than any other input for learning concepts for language development. Children with ASD are exceptionally good at using the patterns of movement to create visual mental shapes for visual language.

Figure 3.14. Visual Concepts Develop from the Shape of Motor Patterns.

Activity: Can visual patterns form visual concepts?

Movement patterns. The sensory input for patterns of movement comes from the motor system. The motor system is the response form of sensory input. That is, the receptors accept the sensory input, and the body responds. For example, the eye receives light, and part of the eye moves to see all the points of light. Or, the head moves to see what else is in the space of light. The child sees an object that consists of past recognizable patterns and uses a motor act such as reaching with the hand to grasp the object or extending the leg to kick the object. ***Patterns of movement create mental shapes of ideas.*** The mental shapes of ideas follow the movements of the hand for writing, the movements of the eye for scanning, and/or the movements of others' hands, mouths, and so on.

Figure 3.15 shows how the learner might follow the shapes the mouth makes to mentally form a concept of shape.

Figure 3.15. Learner Watches the Mouth Change Shapes to Form Concepts.

Educators typically do not use movement as a way to access learning. Therefore, children who use movement for learning, such as those with ASD, often lag behind in concept development for language. The knowledge that children with ASD use movement to develop shaped ideas can be instrumental in developing effective academic, social, and behavioral programs. Later chapters will describe how to capitalize on movement for developing concepts and subsequent language in children with ASD.

Activity: Visual patterns can form visual concepts. Explain how motor movements also can form visual concepts.

How Does Pattern Acquisition Affect Children with Autism Spectrum Disorders?

Children with ASD can see, hear, smell, touch, taste and respond to all of these sensory inputs with movement or motor skills. At first the learning system of a baby with ASD appears normal. The baby's physical body responds to the sensory input in typical ways because all of the input is new. The baby's brain seeks this new input and the baby's body responds. In a child with ASD, the sensory input stacks to form basic perceptual patterns for early conceptual development (6 months to 18 months). The stacking of the patterns allows for normal types of development. For social development, the child is able to match patterns with others, so the child does something and the caregivers respond. Then, the child does something else and the caregiver responds. This give-and-take appears to be social in nature. For communication or language, the child may even begin to pick up and use acoustic patterns of simple words and phrases. The child with ASD learns to walk and even begins to play.

U.S. culture primarily inputs acoustic, auditory patterns or visual patterns to children by talking to or around the child, reading books, watching TV, and so on. Since children with ASD do not use these types of patterns for concept development or language, the acoustic and visual patterns stack in quantity but do not overlap to form concepts. (Remember that children with ASD do not integrate visual and acoustic patterns and, therefore, do not use auditory patterns.) As these patterns stack, the child shows atypical behavior such as echolalia or repetition of acoustic patterns without the conceptual meaning of the spoken words. Or the child might be seen flicking her fingers to create new visual patterns (more about this in a later chapter).

Why the patterns stack and don't overlap through integration is unknown. The stacking may stem from specific gene function and/or body chemistry differences and/or the absence of certain brain stem structures. With the additional stacking of sensory patterns, the child's brain grows but the brain systems do not function together to create concepts from the patterns. The stacking of patterns results in the brain having constant repetition. Recent brain research (e.g., Bookheimer, 2004) shows that under repetition of patterns, the brain begins to shut down. In response to constant repetition of patterns, the child's behavior must change to create unusual or new input so that the brain receives new patterns. For example, rocking back and forth changes what the child sees or feels from the motor movement, thus creating new input of patterns over and over. Every time the body moves, the child sees and feels new input. Children with ASD use the motor access to visual pattern development so the rocking helps bring in new input. *The brain must have new input.*

> ### *Activity: Why does a child with ASD often appear to develop early sensori-motor development in a typical way?*

Children with ASD have differing levels of integration and inhibition of the visual-motor sensory patterns for concept development. The extent to which they are able to create concepts from patterns, and the extent to which their environment modifies the auditory input so that it is more like a visual way of thinking for language, determines the severity of disability from the ASD.

The more severe the disability, the fewer ways the child with ASD has to integrate and inhibit patterns. This means that the more severe the disability is, the more difficult it is to learn concepts. It also means that the more severe the disability is, the more conscientious educators must be to ensure that the correct input is given to create the best learning. In later chapters, case studies will show how to use various input for best pattern development of concept learning.

The logical approach to a child who has ASD and is developing lots of patterns but not concepts would be to work on the missing pieces. For example, if a child isn't developing speech, it would seem important to work on speech. Speech is a set of matched acoustic patterns with motor pattern production. This is a deficit approach to the problem. In other words, if a child cannot make sufficient acoustic-motor or speech patterns, then the logical approach would be to teach speech patterns. But speech patterns are acoustic, and acoustic patterns don't form concepts. So, teaching acoustic or speech problems won't solve the underlying problem of not being able to integrate patterns to form more concepts for the language of socialization, behavior, and academics. Furthermore, children with ASD develop lots of patterns. So teaching more patterns that naturally occur in the environment such as acoustic, auditory, or visual patterns will not help the child develop concepts or language for socialization, language, or behavior.

Activity: Describe the problem that individuals with ASD have with pattern integration.

Without the specific motor patterns for visual integration that children with ASD need to learn concepts, they begin to developmentally lag behind normal expectations. Giving children with ASD more drills consisting of acoustic, visual, or auditory patterns stymies the learning of concepts. The child's brain works at trying to make the intensity of the stacked input more meaningful. Maybe the child digs at his skin with his fingers, bangs his head, chews his fingers into constant infections that deteriorate the bone tissue, or even lights the skin on fire and watches it burn. The more the child's brain shuts down by constant pattern repetition, the more persistent the brain tries to make meaning out of the sensory input of patterns. The child increases the intensity of input by, for example, screaming in high-pitched sounds, rocking the body until she flings herself out of her seat and across an open space, or throwing an object such as a table or toy to create varying inputs out of the same sensory input. The normal input is nonmeaningful. Nonmeaningful input is sensory patterns that have been seen, heard, tasted, touched, or smelled, but the brain does not recognize the organization of the patterns to form concepts. So the brain with ASD asks for more input. However, since the input is already stored, it just stacks, and stacks, and stacks!

The older the child with ASD becomes without being able to manipulate the input in a way that allows him to create patterns of concepts for language, the more intense his atypical way of functioning becomes. Meanwhile, the child is becoming bigger and more difficult to "handle," which brings additional challenges. The physical ways of keeping the child under behavioral control when he was younger don't work as well when the child is 6 feet tall and weighs 200 pounds. And, this bigger child has more body to move and more years of trying to intensify input to make meaning to keep the brain active, and therefore often more severe ways of inflicting injury.

How Do Patterns Intensify Without Overlapping to Create Concepts?

Children with ASD will see patterns such as the visual patterns of an object spinning and then repeat the act. On one hand, the child's brain wants new patterns. The visual patterns are all new and at the same time old. The old components are the visual features of light and movement. The new components are the millions of different spaces created as light reflects off the edges of the object as the object spins. In a typical learning system, these different spaces of occupied light points would create a plan or shape of light points. These shapes of light points form a visual concept. The individual points of light would no longer be wanted by the brain because it can now see the concept. Since the features of sensory light are no longer needed, they are inhibited from the larger shape of knowledge. With inhibition of the features, the brain (cortex of the cerebrum) can attend to the concept – the spinning object. Therefore, the typical child's brain would not need to see the object spin any more unless additional conceptual meaning were added, such as when we spin a spinner in a game to determine how far to move a game piece. In other words, *once the brain recognizes the whole concept as greater than the parts, the parts need not be attended to.*

> **Activity:** *The term "pragmaticism" means that the whole is greater than the parts. Children with ASD tend to focus on the parts instead of the whole. What are the parts?*

Since the child with ASD cannot integrate much of the sensory input, he also cannot inhibit the pattern pieces. Therefore, the child's brain pushes forward to make these inputs into something conceptual – something more meaningful. What appears to be repetition to us actually creates changing input for the child with ASD. The child continues to try to use the sensory input, spinning, flicking, repeating acoustic patterns, spitting out the food, and so on. The typical response by those of us watching these behaviors is that the child is bothered by the fluorescent lights, enjoys the spinning top, or covers the ears to shut out sound. We have the language to make these interpretations. However, *the child with ASD is just trying to make meaning from a sensory world that is not conceptual.*

> **Activity:** *Why does a child with ASD repeat patterns?*

As the child's brain continues not to recognize larger units of input from the smaller sensory pieces, the child shows more and more need, almost like an obsession, to stack the sensory input into millions of features or components that lack conceptual meaning. The more severe the lack of integration of sensory input into perceptual patterns of concepts, the more severe the disability and the more intensified the brain's pursuit to make meaning from sensory input.

Higher-functioning children with ASD, including those with Asperger Syndrome (AS), are often able to make more concepts out of patterns, especially the movement or motor patterns, to form visual concepts for more language. As a result, the child with AS might use a lot of oral language as a way to move her mouth for more motor patterns for conceptualization. Sometimes these motor speech patterns are not recognized by the speaker as having sound. In other words, when the child's mouth moves, she accesses her thoughts, which are visual concepts. More about the motor access to language for all individuals on the autism spectrum will be provided in later chapters. Chapters 4 and 5 provide the structure of visual thinking or language as well as how the visual thinker uses the visual brain in an auditory world.

Activity: How does pattern integration and inhibition affect the level of severity of a child with ASD?

Summary

Acoustic patterns do not form concepts or language. When visual and acoustic patterns are integrated neurologically, auditory patterns form auditory concepts for auditory language. Similarly, visual patterns form visual concepts of shape, and the shape of ideas or concepts may also be developed from motor patterns. Individuals with ASD use motor patterns for acquisition of visual concepts for language. Chapters 6-9 describe how to use these motor patterns for intervention to help develop the concepts of socialization, behavior, and literacy. Programs that emphasize motor access to behavior, academics, and socialization provide the most meaning and, therefore, the most learning for individuals with ASD.

Concepts for Chapter 4

What is language?

How does a child acquire language?

What does language represent?

What is the difference between language structure and language function?

CHAPTER 4

Autism: Language Structure or Function?

I can say a word.

Do you know what I mean?

I can ask your question.

Can you ask mine?

Learner Outcomes: As a result of reading this chapter, the learner should be able to describe how visual patterns create visual concepts for language and how visual with simultaneous acoustic patterns create auditory concepts for language.

Chapters 1 through 3 provided the reader with an explanation of how learning develops within the neurobiological system. Sensory receptors receive input, which is then organized into perceptual patterns. Some of these patterns become concepts, depending on the type of sensory input and the person's learning system. Finally, as the concepts develop, the child learns to represent the concepts.

The most typical way of representing concepts is to use language. Language is a set of conventional and arbitrary symbols that represent a person's underlying thoughts or concepts (e.g., Arwood, 1983; Carruthers, 1996; Chiat, 2001; Cooper, 2003; Halliday, 1994; Jonisee & Seidenberg; 1998; Lucas, 1980; Piaget, 1971). This chapter will define what language is and is not. In the previous chapter, it was noted that some children with ASD have patterns that stack and do not become concepts. This will affect language development. This chapter will expand on why some children with ASD have difficulty acquiring language and why others show superior skills in acquiring some aspects of language structure while experiencing difficulty with certain functions of language.

Language Acquisition

Languages consist of symbols. Symbols represent the meaning of a person's thoughts. As thoughts or concepts are developed from the perceived patterns of input, they help guide the learner into communication between two or more people. For example, the child senses hunger and cries. Mom picks up the child and says, "Oh, you are hungry." To the baby, Mom's words are sounds and at best patterns. But these patterns are forming concepts as well. The idea that this other person will do something for the child is the beginning of concept development. Perhaps Mom will feed the baby, give the baby something to drink, change the baby's diaper, and so on. In other words, the concept of Mom – the person who does something – is developing. As the baby recognizes the patterns of Mom doing something, the baby changes his cry in response to Mom's act. The baby hesitates, waiting for the mother to do something else. Mom begins to feed the baby. Mom's voice, as well as her actions, also consists of patterns, and it isn't long before the baby hears the pattern "hungry?" and begins to anticipate being fed. The pattern "hungry" stands for the act of eating when someone gives the baby something to eat. The connection between the sensory patterns and their contextual meanings typically forms concepts that language will represent.

This constant give-and-take between Mom and the baby forms cycles of patterns that typically develop into concepts. The concepts are about people or agents (Mom), their actions (picking, reaching, speaking), the objects (bottle, diaper, blanket), and the places (bed, arms, sofa). These concepts can be named or given an arbitrary pattern such as "bottle" by those in the context.

From an adult perspective, the word "hungry" is the language that a person uses to refer to a state of wanting to eat. From the child's perspective, someone, an agent, is there. The agent is doing something. The child may be acquiring the meaning of the person, object, or the action. *As the interaction between patterns and concepts increases, the child is beginning to acquire language – words like "hungry" that as acoustic patterns represent the child's underlying ideas or concepts.* Figure 4.1 shows this process of language acquisition. Mom talks to the baby, and the baby's learning system associates the meaning of Mom's actions with the acoustic patterns of Mom's words.

Figure 4.1. Language Acquisition.

Language represents the child's underlying concepts. The underlying ideas or concepts are meaningful or semantic in nature; they are formed from the child's cognitive learning processes interacting with the physical experience of others around. Mom is providing the child with numerous sensory input patterns within a meaningful context. For example, she is using *acoustic patterns* when she speaks. She is using many different *visual patterns* from what the baby sees of her face, her hands, and so on. She is also providing *motor patterns* when she reaches or lifts up the baby.

The child's neurobiological learning system filters background "noise" or non-recognizable sensory inputs from recognizable patterns. If the child begins to say or imitate these patterns, it means that her learning system is capable of recognizing those acoustic patterns. If the child reaches for the bottle, it means she is beginning to develop those recognizable visual patterns as meaningful. The child might even smile when Mom smiles, which means she is matching these types of visual-motor patterns. Without this type of recognizing, sorting, integrating patterns, the child cannot develop the concepts for language to represent. ***Language development is as mature as the child's conceptual development.***

Vygotsky (1962) provided an excellent explanation of how cognition or concept development affects language production and how language production, in turn, affects cognition. Arwood (1983) explained the relationship of this synergistic process of acquiring language as part of the learning system of the brain. She showed how language development is a product of the socio-cognitive learning process of the neurobiological learning system, also known as Arwood's Language Learning Theory. According to this theory, language acquisition is the result of the neurobiological learning system that represents concepts produced from pattern integration and inhibition.

Activity: How is language part of the learning system?

Oral Language

Most people think of language, a set of arbitrary symbols, as spoken or oral. Symbol usage can present itself in many forms, such as the symbols of print on a page, the symbols of the hands for American Sign Language (ASL), the symbols of art, and so on. For patterns to truly be symbolic, they must represent shared or agreed-upon concepts. That is, whether the symbol is spoken, printed, or drawn, the recipient must be able to recognize the shared meaning and continue to assign meaning. In other words, language is a two-way street of symbolic exchange.

The child's ability to produce spoken patterns such as "hungry" does not mean the child can sort and inhibit the recognizable acoustic patterns to form language. In fact, just because the child produces these patterns in context does not mean that the child "knows" or conceptualizes the pattern as a meaningful adult-like word. Remember from the previous chapter that acoustic patterns, those patterns that are only made up of sound, do not form concepts for language. For example, the child hears a music box several times and begins to sing the words of the song produced. The child sounds as if he is learning the song, but he may only be learning the patterns, not the song. The child signs the song, but he may not have language.

For a typical learner, as sensory patterns increase in number, the concepts also increase. While the concepts increase in number, the world makes more sense; is more meaningful. The concepts of the world have meaning or semanticity (Arwood, 1991) as interpreted by other speakers. These interpretations allow for a scaffolding of meaning between the child's learning system and those who assign meaning to the child's acts and words. The adults are assigning meaning in the pattern forms of their language, English, French, Farsi, Hopi, and so forth.

The development of language is the result of this interaction between the child and his learning system within a context of others assigning meaning. Typical sensory input integrates or combines to form patterns of concepts, which are then matched against what others assign meaning to. These meanings are matched to patterns of language seen and/or heard in the child's environment. Figure 4.2 shows the typical language learning system.

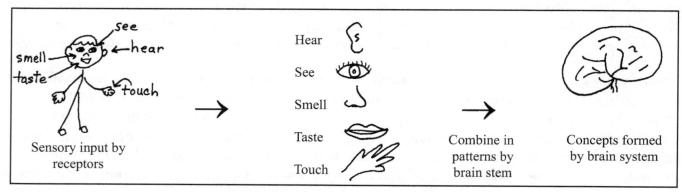

Figure 4.2. The Language Learning System.

The learning system of a child with ASD is not always able to filter out the meaningful patterns from the nonmeaningful patterns. As described in the previous chapters, the child may hear environmental sounds such as the hum of a fan equally as loud as her mother's voice. As a result, the child may not be able to pick out the mother's meaningful acoustic patterns for speech development. Without speech developing, the child's ability to recognize meaningful patterns to form concepts for conceptualization is limited. Because caregivers and educators typically wait for oral language, the child's language may not develop as quickly as expected.

Children with ASD display great variety of ability to sort patterns into concepts for language. There are those who are able to pick up the acoustic patterns and produce them without underlying meaning or conceptualization. Further on the spectrum of disorders, there are those who pick up speech and a lot of concepts for language. It is also possible that the child with ASD does not hear himself talk even with a lot of language development but is able to use a lot of oral as well as written language. Figure 4.3 shows the continuum of speech to language development for children with ASD. More information about the relationship between speech and language will be provided later in this chapter as well as in Chapters 5 and 9.

| Child hears but can't pick up speech patterns for concept development and language. | Child hears and can pick up speech patterns but doesn't understand the speech for language development. | Child hears and can pick up speech patterns. Language develops, but the child may not know if his concepts match his oral language. |

Figure 4.3. Continuum of Processing Oral Language.

Activity: What are some of the various levels of oral language processing for children and adults with ASD?

Concepts for Language

When a child's learning system recognizes patterns as meaningful, the assumption is that the underlying concepts are increasing. It is also assumed that if the child's concepts grow, the child's ability to represent these concepts with language grows. But for a child with ASD, the patterns do not always form concepts, so the concepts do not automatically grow. Typically, feedback from the child's own voice or from others' voices provides an interaction between internal and external patterns. But a child with ASD may not recognize these patterns and, therefore, cannot inhibit the constant input from background sounds as well as spoken sound patterns. The child's learning system lacks the necessary integration and inhibition of recognizable patterns to form the concepts for language. *Therefore, language does not always develop without intervention.*

The tool that is used to assess the child's language integrity is language sampling. Sampling is performed by asking the very young child to tell a story to a picture of an event, such as parents having a picnic with their children, and then recording by audiotape the child's spoken ideas. These taped ideas are then played back and the educator writes down the child's utterances exactly the way the child spoke them. This way, the educator can look at the child's utterances and see how the child is using language. For older children, sampling can be performed by asking the child, adolescent, or adult the question, "What do you do on a typical day?" This specific question has been normed (Arwood & Beggs, 1992). Again the utterances are audio recorded and then transcribed just as they were spoken. When the language is written exactly the way it is spoken, not the way we often interpret it or think we hear it, we can see how well the language functions. By sampling the language of a child with ASD, therefore, the educator can determine how well the learning system is developing, how well the concepts are growing, and what types of patterns the child needs to learn concepts for language development. If a child with ASD does not show development of oral language, a sampling of how the child uses behavior for communicating may be used to determine how the child is learning, what types of patterns are needed for learning concepts, and the child's rate of learning.

Case Study One: Jackie is a 12-year-old female diagnosed with autism, with no language but lots of communicative behavior. She hits, kicks, bites, and throws objects very well. Her behavior will tell us how she learns best, what she needs to learn language, and her rate of learning.

Prior to intervention, Jackie was removed from contact with all students because of her hitting. The support specialists were given six weeks to make the necessary changes to her behavior to keep Jackie at school. Otherwise, Jackie would be sent to a residential psychiatric placement. A typical functional behavior assessment was completed.

Jackie had participated in many different behavior programs aimed at identifying the wanted behaviors, the unwanted behaviors, and working on reinforcing those wanted behaviors while suppressing or punishing the unwanted behaviors (more on behavior will be provided in Chapters 7, 11, 12). Using Arwood's Language Learning Theory (Arwood, 1991; Lucas, 1980) as a basis for interpreting Jackie's behavior, Jackie was learning to hit, slap, bite, kick, take off her shoes, and so on. But she did not show the development of language concepts from all of the talking, physical redirecting, isolated use of manual signs or single pictures. In other words, these types of input were not forming concepts and, therefore, not forming language. Furthermore, all of Jackie's motor movements suggested she could learn the motor patterns. She watched others' hands, feet, and bodies, which suggested that she could sort incoming visual patterns, but educators used few visual structures for her conceptual or language development. So, all sorts of visual language interventions were used so as to match language with the way she learns concepts. Figures 4.4-4.5 show some of the drawings that were used with Jackie. Chapter 5 explains why these drawings changed her behavior within the six weeks.

Figure 4.4. Jackie's Schedule of Pictures.

Figure 4.5. Jackie's Choices for Language Development.

Using a visual-motor way of inputting the meaning of concepts gave Jackie the type of patterns her learning system could process so she could learn. Even though, in addition to autism she is also diagnosed with mental retardation, Jackie's rate of learning is fine. Given the sensory patterns in a conceptual way that has meaning for Jackie, she can learn. In fact, instead of waiting for oral language, Jackie can access reading and writing for increasing oral language if her educators give her those patterns.

Language acquisition is as good as the development of concepts from patterns. If a child needs specific types of patterns to form concepts, then those types of patterns are necessary for the development of language. Jackie could not use the acoustic oral-motor patterns of speech to access the oral language patterns for conceptualization and, therefore, did not develop language. Consequently, her conceptual development also lagged behind.

Case Study Two: Timothy is a 7-year-old male diagnosed with autism. In contrast to Jackie, Timothy has lots of oral patterns. He talks constantly! But much of his oral language is difficult for outsiders to understand. His speech sounds cluttered, and adults say he "just has so much to say." When using an audiotape recorder to record exactly what he says and then transcribing the tape, it becomes apparent that Timothy is not acquiring all of the language structures. He is learning the patterns that he sees others produce over and over.

In order to assess Timothy's language while also setting the basis for where to being with intervention, Timothy is given a picture to look at. The picture is of an event that shows the visual concepts of what the people are doing together. In this way, the picture provides Timothy with visual concepts. Now, the adult gives the oral language that goes with the visual concepts that Timothy can see in the picture. While looking at a picture, the adult says, "Timothy, I am going to tell a story about this picture and then you can choose a picture to tell a story about." The adult told a story with a beginning, several actions in the middle, and an end. She then asked Timothy to pick a picture and tell a story. He picks a picture and then holds the picture very close to his eyes and asks "Is it easy?" The adult says yes and pauses. She tells him to put the picture down and she will tell another story (second model) about another picture. He says, "I don't know how to read." The adult gives a third example about another picture. He says, "Now I can see it. Two boys 'en one grandpa, uh, grabbed the corn (they were shucking the corn). He's holdin' a bak-set for him to put all the stuff in." The adult asks him if he has anything more to say about his story. He says, "Well, I think, there is one dinosaur and one ..." The adult interrupts and says, "Anything else you want to say about this story." Timothy says, "Yes, once upon a time, a grandpa and a boy and a boy and a corn."

Even though this boy talks and talks and talks, the fact that his language structures are not at age level and the fact that he borrows utterances or patterns suggest that his language is not as good as his learning rate. The following is an analysis of Timothy's language sample.

- "Is it easy?" Timothy was holding the picture very close to his eyes because he wasn't sure what the story was about. His behavior is telling us that he isn't sure what the visual patterns on the picture mean. In other words, he does not have a lot of language for the picture. If he does not have the language, he also does not have the concepts that connect the patterns of what he sees in the picture with the language for telling about the concepts.

- "I don't know how to read." This is another way for Timothy to say he doesn't have the concepts for the patterns of the picture. He sees patterns but he doesn't know what they mean. He moves the picture around and he moves his head around looking and looking.

- "Now I can see it." His behavior and language tell us that he learns best by being able to *do* something with what he sees. He moves the picture around until he sorts enough of the visual patterns to see some shapes.

- "Two boys 'en one grandpa, uh, they grabbed the corn. He's holdin' a bak-set for him to put all the stuff in." Timothy labels what he sees. He sees a hand reaching (to pull a corn husk), and to Timothy this looks like a common pattern of "grab." He sees a basket and processes the acoustic pattern as an acoustic misperception, "bak-set," which means he doesn't hear acoustic patterns well. If he doesn't hear acoustic patterns well, he does not learn language from oral speech. He uses an indefinite term, "stuff," for a specific referent. He does not really see how all of the people are working in a garden and how they are helping each other.

Timothy does not understand the language of the picture, but he is learning the pieces of what he sees. He is learning by seeing the shapes of ideas and is producing the shapes of motor movements. In this case, he moved the pictures around to create the shapes of the concepts so he could see the pieces of the picture. Timothy has more structures than he has meaning. His learning for patterns for the pieces or structures of language is greater than his conceptualization of language. Most children with ASD acquire language like Timothy does, with motor acts of what they see. Chapter 5 describes how these types of patterns create visual concepts for using language.

Case Study Three: Mark is a 17-year-old high school student. He functions with a lot of language and has been diagnosed with high-functioning autism. He has received lots of intervention over the years. In response to a question about how he is doing at school, Mark's language sounds like this:

"Well, I am a human being, you know. Well, obviously, I am human. I have strengths, well, we all have strengths, you know what I mean. We all have strengths. We do have, well, I have, uh, I have some things I don't do well. Well, we all do, but I am human, we all here. Like, well, like sometimes I don't do well on every little thing. But, I do know how to write. But, I don't know, well, what does 'windy' mean? Like, well I am really working hard to find words."

Mark wants to talk through all of his activities. He appears to have a lot of language, but his language does not express very many specific ideas. Why is he telling us about being human and having strengths? We were not talking about that! "Windy" is a word he read in an assessment passage; he is still trying to figure out how it relates to the passage. Mark is using the motor patterns of his mouth to try to understand what others say and what he reads. Unfortunately, the sound of his voice interferes with the language development. He would do better writing his ideas down so he could see what he says. Mark has a lot of patterns, even the patterns of rehearsed phrases such as "I am human, you know," but he is struggling to use sound to refine what others say or what he says.

> **Activity: How does the language of the three case studies differ? How is it similar?**

Summary of Language Acquisition

Language represents a person's thoughts or concepts. In order to learn these concepts, input must be such that the child's learning system recognizes patterns that form concepts. When the input is changed to match the child's learning system, language – the symbols to represent concepts – increases along with the underlying cognition. Since 60-80% of the population with autism is also diagnosed with mental retardation (Fombonne, 2003), it is very important to ensure that language develops. Chapters 5-8 discuss how the development of concepts for social, behavioral, and academic development occurs for persons with ASD.

Language Structure

As we have seen, language forms in the way the concepts develop from the recognized patterns. Therefore, different recognized patterns form different characteristics of languages. For example, English is a language that consists of acoustic patterns that interconnect with the visual patterns of seen concepts in the environment. For example, a word in English has both an assumed visual representation, such as what the mother looks like, and an acoustic pattern representing the mother, "mama." The child is looking at the toys and Mom says, "Pick up your toys." The child hears the mother's voice as recognizable acoustic patterns as he also sees the visual patterns of the toys. These acoustic and visual patterns of English create the same type of written English patterns. That is, letters (visual representation) are matched to sounds (acoustic representation or pronunciation) to form the basis for teaching reading and writing of English in the U.S. culture (e.g., see Arwood & Young, 2000; Cooper, 2003; Heilman, 2002; McGuinness, 2005).

In order for acoustic and visual patterns to become intertwined in the neurological learning system, the sound characteristics and visual characteristics must interconnect in the brain stem. This pathway, which allows for the interconnection between sound and sight, is called the auditory pathway (e.g., see Tortora & Anagnostakos, 1990). A child's neurological ability to see and hear input as a mixed set of visual and acoustic patterns forms auditory conceptualization. Figure 4.6 shows how a child can see and hear patterns as auditory concepts.

Figure 4.6. Auditory Patterns Form Auditory Concepts.

A child who can process sight and sound for auditory concepts also thinks in the auditory properties of auditory languages like English. The subtleties of English are easy to understand when a person thinks in the auditory properties of English. Chapter 5 describes all of these properties.

As previously discussed, individuals with ASD have difficulty processing by integrating and inhibiting patterns. Furthermore, they do best with motor patterns forming the shapes of visual concepts. Because auditory patterns require a maximum level of neurological integration of sound and sight, and because persons with ASD have trouble integrating sight or sound patterns for concepts, they are not able to form auditory patterns for auditory concepts. Therefore, a child with ASD who can pick up and use acoustic patterns typically does not think in the sound of his own voice. He may or may not even hear his own voice. If he does hear his voice, he is not using the sound but the motor movement of the mouth for processing language concepts. In other words, individuals with ASD think in a visual-motor form of patterns that are not auditory, even though they may use acoustic patterns very well. While they can learn to match the acoustic patterns of speech for English, their underlying concepts are not auditory.

People with ASD can use the acoustic patterns for speech imitation but acoustic patterns do not form language. And, they can recognize the visual patterns of what they see. These visual patterns form visual concepts, which are thoughts that can be represented by language. Figure 4.7 shows a child with ASD who is able to hear Mom and is able to imitate what Mom says but is not able to follow the auditory instruction of putting away the toys. The child hears Mom. The child looks to see what she says but she is no longer talking. The child waits until someone shows him what the acoustic patterns mean. ***Showing the child allows him to see the patterns of motor actions as visual concepts.***

Figure 4.7. Seeing What Someone Says.

> *Activity: What is the difference between auditory patterns and visual patterns for language?*

Watching motor patterns shows how a visual concept of shape based on movement is developed for the child with ASD. A child can also watch the mouth to create language concepts.

Figure 4.8 shows how a child with ASD watches the hands move the toys.

Figure 4.8. Watching Someone's Hands.

Figure 4.9 shows the movement of the mouth to create an acoustic pattern for speech.

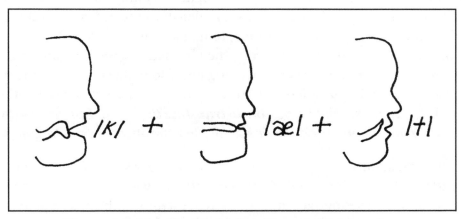

Figure 4.9. The Mouth Makes Shapes for Meaning.

The motor movements create the space of a pattern. The patterns overlap to form visual concepts. So a child with ASD thinks in visual concepts. Figure 4.10 shows how children with ASD acquire a visual form of language.

Watching visual-motor patterns.   Writing or drawing visual-motor patterns.   Visual symbols of language.

Figure 4.10. Acquisition of Visual Language.

Language is a set of symbols that represents the underlying mental concepts. Visual conceptualization is typically represented by the characteristics of "visual languages." Visual languages, such as Mandarin Chinese, ASL, indigenous oral languages such as Chamorran, Polynesian, or Hopi have different properties than auditory or alphabetic languages like English (e.g., see Heilman, 2002; McGuinness, 2005; Ruhlen, 1994). Chapter 5 discusses these components.

Different languages not only have different structures but also different underlying formation of concepts. Individuals with ASD use the underlying visual constructs for language. There are estimated to be thousands of visual languages in the world and many auditory languages. Those that are like English, which uses integrated sound and visual patterns, include Romance languages and Germanic/Slavic languages. They are auditory in nature. So, while thinking in visual concepts, individuals with ASD are expected to process and use English, an auditory language. They must translate the constructs or components, sounds and letters, into visual forms or visual patterns. As a result of this translation, they may lose some of the inferred or idiomatic meanings of the English language. For example, in English we might say, "It's raining cats and dogs!" to mean that the rain is pouring down. A sixth-grade girl diagnosed with AS burst out laughing. I am sure she translated the English words into the pictures of what she heard. In the process, the idiomatic expression was lost. The other students in the classroom understood the visual meaning but also realized that the mental visual picture of cats and dogs raining down is figurative, not literative language. They saw the outburst from the student with AS as inappropriate. ***Not being able to translate the visual language into the auditory meaning often results in miscommunication or socially inappropriate use of language.***

Figure 4.11 shows how an auditory language functions. A stranger says, "What is your dog's name?" The child sees the dog and hears the sound of his own voice answering the question at the same time as he answers the question. The auditory language system integrates the sound patterns of the speaker's voice, "What is your dog's name?," with what the child physically sees. The sound does not come first and then a mental picture, nor does the picture come before the same. The sound and sight patterns integrate and inhibit recognizable patterns to form concepts that are auditory in nature.

Figure 4.11. Auditory Language.

According to Arwood (Lucas, 1980, 1991), who has been collecting language samples and analyzing language function of children and adults for the last 20 years, the majority (about 85%) of learners in the United States develop new concepts with a visual way of thinking. Figure 4.12 shows the child looking at the dog and hearing the adult's voice but not seeing what the adult says. The child asks, "What?" and then looks up at the adult's face to see what the adult says. This is a visual way of thinking and learning language.

Figure 4.12. Visual Language.

Of those who have visual language form and function, approximately 30% do not connect the sound with the visual concepts. Individuals with ASD fit into this group. They connect the motor movements or the shapes of visual concepts with other motor movements. (The reader should be reminded that we are not talking about learning preferences that are educationally taught, but the way a person actually acquires a new concept for language purposes.) Children with ASD are able to hear sound, even develop acoustic patterns for speech, but they learn concepts for language best if they can connect motor patterns to form visual concepts for language use.

Figure 4.13 shows a child with ASD looking away when he is asked a question. Some children do not even know the person spoke to them. Some hear the sound and look to see what the sound means. Others hear the sound patterns and repeat the patterns and may even give back a stereotypical pattern such as "My dog's name is Fido" without thinking in the sound of the concepts.

Figure 4.13. Motor-Access Language Functions Separately from Sound.

Summary

The structure of language development for individuals with ASD is visual in nature, not auditory. The structure is formed from the movement of the shape of what is seen (letters of words, movements of mouth, etc.). Therefore, a child with ASD first recognizes the structure of *shapes* of ideas, not the sounds of ideas. These shapes or structures have the properties of the visual patterns of visual concepts. Therefore, individuals with ASD use the movement of shapes to create visual language structures. Language structure parallels the function of the way the patterns create concepts. So, different neurobiological patterns result in different concepts and different language structures. This means that individuals with ASD create concepts from the motor shapes of patterns. These concepts are visual in nature just like visual languages such as Mandarin Chinese create concepts from visual patterns. Some languages function based on visual properties, and other languages function with auditory properties. Since individuals with ASD use the movement of light for acquiring concepts, they function with mental language that follows the properties of a visual language. To determine if a child is using language that is mentally visual or not, the child's language structures can be assessed using language sampling. The next chapter describes the visual and auditory properties of language.

Concepts for Chapter 5

What are the visual language properties?

What are the auditory language properties?

What is meant by "language context"?

What is meant by the phrase "visual brain in an auditory world"?

CHAPTER 5

The Visual Brain in an Auditory World

I think in shapes of the ideas you see.
I see the shapes of what I say.
My world is a context of shapes of events ...
I am in the shape of my pictured event.

Learner Outcomes: As a result of reading this chapter, the reader should be able to explain the differences between auditory and visual metacognition for linguistic function.

Chapters 1 through 4 described how the neurobiological learning system develops language. According to Arwood's Language Learning Theory (Arwood, 1991; Lucas, 1980), sensory input forms perceptual patterns, which integrate through inhibitory processes to form concepts. Then, language patterns assign meaning to the concepts. The function of language is to represent the development of concepts. Individuals with ASD develop concepts from sensory movement patterns. The shapes of the fine-motor movements store as visual concepts in the visual cortex of the brain. Thus, the child with ASD is said to have a "visual brain."

This chapter will describe the characteristics of visual concepts compared to the characteristics of the auditory concepts used by the dominant auditory U.S. population. These concept characteristics parallel the properties of visual and auditory types of languages, including English.

It should be noted, once again, that we are not talking about modalities used in teaching or about learning styles. *Modalities* refer to how material is presented or taught. For example, a teacher presents a chart for the students to copy. Because the chart can be seen and because the students are to copy it, the modality used is visual. Visual modalities may or may not use the properties of learning systems that must use visual concepts for learning. *Learning styles* refer to the educated preferences of a learner (e.g., Jensen, 1998; Kovalik, 1994). Thus, learning styles can be taught and do not always match a learner's neurobiological way of learning new information. This book is talking about how the neurobiological learning system processes information for acquiring new concepts that language can represent.

Language Representation

Language represents the underlying concepts. And, since concepts are acquired from the integration and inhibition of sensory input, concepts represent the way sensory patterns are organized and recognized by the neurobiological system. As discussed in the earlier chapters, different sensory systems record different types of information. The acoustic system records pitches (how high and low in frequency) of sound, the loudness level of sound (amplitude), and the duration or how much time sounds take to produce a pattern, like the time to say "cat." But the eyes do not record the properties of sound. The eyes record the points of reflected light on planes, and any movement of the eyes or body results in more points of light being recorded.

Since newborn babies do not hear words or see objects, the differences in sensory systems allow the mind to develop different concepts from the baby's many physical experiences (e.g., Greenough et al., 1987). Caregivers use language to assign meaning to the physical entities of what the baby sees and hears. For example, the baby points to a bottle and the mother says, "Do you want your bottle?" Mother's spoken patterns help assign the conventional, agreed-upon language that represents the object, "bottle." "Bottle" is the agreed-upon language for the underlying concept. Thus, the baby's communication is given language by the mother.

Language represents not only ideas or concepts but also the way the concepts develop. The learner's underlying thinking is known as *metacognition*. The learner's underlying way that language functions to represent thinking is *metalinguistic function*. Languages develop parallel to the way people live and think. Thus, if a language develops through patterns of the visual system, then the underlying metacognition or metalinguistic function will relate to the physical properties of the eyes. If a language develops through the auditory system of acoustic and visual patterns (auditory concepts) combined, then the metacognition represents auditory physical properties. Therefore, different languages form to represent differences in thinking (Gil, 2004). Some languages are visual in their characteristics, and some are auditory.

It is not the purpose of this book to explain the ontogeny of these different languages but to point out how differences in language relate to metacognitive and metalinguistic differences for people with ASD. Children with ASD think in the properties of visual metacognition and visual linguistic function. Furthermore, the way they develop visual thinking is not simply a way of seeing ideas; they develop visual concepts through the movement of patterns to form the shapes of ideas. The motor movements that develop visual cognition do not directly transfer to the properties of an auditory language like English. Thus, most individuals with ASD require some form of intervention, treatment, or help with language functioning for social, academic, and/or behavioral purposes. The next section of this chapter describes the differences in linguistic properties that are most noteworthy for individuals with ASD.

> *Activity: What does language represent?*

Language Properties

Languages have different properties related to the way people of a culture think (Arwood, 1991; Gil, 2004; Ruhlen, 1994). The cultural thought or metacognition, in turn, supports the properties of the language that represents cultural conceptualization. Because concepts develop from the underlying pathways of sensory pattern integration, the metacognitive processes of thinking parallel linguistic function. In other words, *language is the way a person thinks.*

Auditory languages like English use the auditory concepts of time to connect spoken ideas, to refine concepts, and to share verbal meaning. Time comes from acoustic patterns integrated with visual patterns. Other languages such as Mandarin Chinese or ASL use the visual concepts of space to relate spoken ideas, to specify concepts, and to convey shared meaning. Space is the plane of sight recoded from integrating visual patterns. Since the language characteristics are different between auditory and visual types of languages, the underlying conceptualization is also different. Remember: *Language is the way a person thinks.*

The assumption that just because a person speaks, reads, or writes an auditory language like English she experiences a parallel auditory metalinguistic function may not be valid. In other words, auditory languages like English developed from the need of people to move locations, and moving into places they could not see, such as the future, required time elements to communicate their actions. Time features come from the acoustic sensory input. One spoken idea is connected to another idea with time structures. For example, "I will see Mary tomorrow" shows time with the verb as well as with the adverb "tomorrow." However, a person can speak or write English, an auditory language, and think with a visual metacognition. In other words, a person can learn to use an auditory language like English but think in a way that has linguistic function properties more like Mandarin Chinese, a visual language.

> **Acoustic patterns do not form language, but acoustic and visual pattern integration creates auditory concepts that show the time connections of language.**

As mentioned, about 60-90% of the pre-K to 12th-grade U.S. population uses visual metacognition for learning new concepts (Arwood, 1991). Yet our culture expects learners to read, write, think, view, listen, calculate, and speak English as if they think in the auditory properties or linguistic function of English. In other words, education for U.S. literacy is based on auditory properties of English even though most children do not think in these properties. And, 100% of individuals diagnosed with ASD use a form of visual conceptualization and metalinguistic function.

The next sections compare the most important properties of auditory languages like English to the most important visual properties of languages like Mandarin Chinese or ASL. The importance of understanding these properties as learning differences rests with the way children with ASD need information presented so that they may acquire visual metacognition as well as a visual linguistic function. Their ability to become literate depends on educators' understanding of how they learn language, the properties of visual metacognition, and visual metalinguistic function.

Context

The first noteworthy property of language is whether or not context is used for assigning meaning. Some languages use a lot of context and some languages use little context. ***Context refers to people, their actions, their objects, and their locations.***

Visual cultures. Thinkers who need a lot of context to understand their world want a story about people, actions, objects, and places to help put new ideas into the "big picture." Cultures characterized by this way of thinking and learning are often referred to as "story-telling cultures" or cultures of oral language tradition in which the history is passed down to other generations by orally relating ideas (e.g., see Portes, 2002). Within these cultures, individuals have specific roles or functions within a group so the whole or collective group is important (Adler & Towne, 2002). In order to acquire the big picture through understanding the whole context, ideas or thinking must coexist side by side or in the space of an event. An event is a linguistic way of relating a person(s) or agent(s) to their actions and the objects.

Neurobiologically, the concepts that allow for events to dominate within collective cultures come from the part of the sensory system that is responsible for space, the visual system of language development. Therefore, these collective, high-context cultures are visual in nature; that is, the thinkers are comfortable connecting themselves to the events or stories that include them in the bigger mental picture. Figure 5.1 shows a visual thinker in his own space.

Figure 5.1. Visual Thinker.

The collective or visual cultures are also "field sensitive" (Friend, 2006). That is, the person needs to see the forest, the big picture, to see the individual trees within the forest. The whole picture tells a story that allows this type of thinker to relate to other agents, actions, and objects. Likewise, as the people of a field-sensitive culture develop concepts through their visual learning systems, they think in the space of an event. They think about how they fit within the activities of other people and their actions.

People with ASD do very well with the whole picture, or having a lot of context. For example, a young man with autism was participating on a high school theater team. One day he was asked by the judge to sit on the other side of the room so he would be able to see his team better since there were some props in the way of his vision. The young man's job was to time the presentation for his team mates and to give them a cue if they were going over the time limit.

One of the authors watched the young man move to the other side of the room and not be able to do the task. After one team presented, the young man literally climbed over others to get to where he had planned to sit. He had to sit where he could mentally see himself do the task just as he had rehearsed. The context was not the same for him when he was on the other side of the room. When asking him to move over, the judge did not give the whole story of why the young man would need to be on the other side of the room, so the judge's words were out of context. The young man had to have the whole story to understand why he needed to move. Back on the side of the room where he had originally planned to be, his team could not see his time signals but the young man gave the signals anyway. He did his role of timekeeper. Fortunately, the team never went over the time limit. The young man was very field sensitive to the context in which he could mentally see himself. His role would continue whether or not others noticed. He did his role as part of the event, the theater act. This young man thought in visual concepts that had the metalinguistic function of the role of a collective culture. The whole story was a picture of him performing his job as part of the event.

Visual languages like ASL or Mandarin expect a lot of context whereas auditory languages such as Romance and Germanic/Slavic languages like German, French, and English do not use much context for communicating. Like the judge's words, speakers of these auditory languages do not tell the whole story and they do not try to assign a role to the listener. Words are given separate from a story or situation. For example, a person in one of these cultures might greet a person on the run – "Hello, how are you?" and then keep walking. The person says these words as a greeting, a linguistic function. The words are in time of the situation – it is time to greet this person – separate from other activities or events that might be happening. Because time comes from the acoustic input, these types of languages are auditory in nature. Words stand independent of the event! Speakers from high-context cultures find these "greetings on the go" rude – words literally flying over someone else's heads. In a collective culture, the person, upon seeing an acquaintance, would stop and create a context by collecting the pieces of a whole picture. "How is your family? Your sister? Your brother? Your mother?" That is, the greeter in a visual culture asks about all of the agents of the person's immediate family to create the context to show the listener how the speaker and listener connect. The context and the event are more important than the words in a visual, collective culture.

Auditory cultures. In contrast to these visual, contextual cultures, the auditory culture uses words to refer to other words. For example, "How are you?" is made of words that refer to another word, in this case "greeting." Or, a person in an auditory culture might assert, "We will be doing Italy." This does not mean that there are events related to Italy. On the contrary, the words refer to the study of what Italy, the country, is all about. This assertion assumes the meaning of other words.

Context is almost nonexistent in auditory cultures. Auditory cultures place an emphasis on the individual, not the group, and are viewed as low-context cultures. There is also little emphasis on the role of the group members or how all members of the culture will relate to one another. Words can be given without events, without people. The auditory culture uses low context and is called non-collective; that is, the role of each person is separate from the words. Likewise, the person in an auditory culture sees the individual trees that make up a forest. Individuals are seen as producers but not necessarily contributing to the whole.

People with ASD are often viewed as being non-field sensitive; they have difficulty understanding the nuances of an auditory culture where context is low and words are fast. For example, a teenager with AS recently wrote an email to one of the authors requesting help with her studies. Instead of quickly saying that she had been referred for some help with her studies, she wrote a very long and "roundabout" letter consisting of redundant types of sentence construction such as "In order to see how I do in my next two years of high school while being a junior at my high school and having one more year, my senior year, after this year to complete, and knowing that this year, my junior year, is to be harder than my sophomore year and that the senior year is also harder than my junior year and so it goes that I have two more years of high school to do that will tax me ..." What would have taken a polite, succinct paragraph to request help took almost three full pages. The writer had to create context and then refer to each piece of the context to tell the story, otherwise her mental pictures were not complete. In other words, her mental pictures would not make a movie. As the writer's request was read, the writing was in English but the grammar or linguistic function was visually spatial. Each idea had to relate to the previous one and then overlap, as if walking through a cartoon strip.

Activity: How does context fit into visual and/or auditory metalinguistic function?

Displacement

Another property of language is displacement. Displacement refers to how far away from a physical location or a physical object communication occurs. In auditory languages, displacement is accomplished with the acoustic properties of "time." In visual languages, displacement is accomplished by the visual properties of the eyes or the "space" in which light or movement forms shapes.

Auditory cultures. Auditory languages such as English use time elements such as verb tenses, prepositional phrases, conjunctions, and adverbs to modify the meaning of ideas. For example, a simple idea such as "We are going to the store to buy groceries" is loaded with time elements: are, -ing, to the, to buy. Remove the time elements, and the utterance is "We go store grocery." Even the plural on groceries implies the time to pick out more than one "grocery." Time develops from the acoustic system of sensory processing, which means that time is inherent in the auditory system of thinking, metacognition, and therefore auditory metalinguistic function.

Visual cultures. Visual languages do not look at time as a continuum into the future. Instead of time, visual cultures use events or assign meaning to activities. For example, a single word, "morning," might be spoken in front of a string of words, and everything after the word would go with that one word, "morning." "Morning" is used to refer to the event of going to the marketplace, the sun coming up, arriving at the factory at a certain time on the clock; events that can be seen. Clocks show the time of the event, not the ongoing process of timing as one moves through time or time moves through the speaker (Arwood, 1991; Lucas, 1980). In other words, a person who thinks with a visual metacognition knows what time it is by looking at a clock or by the event that is occurring. It is 6:00 p.m. or after because my neighbor always comes home right after the evening news on TV starts (6:00) and I just heard my neighbor come home. The truth is that the news could almost be over and the neighbor be 25 minutes later than usual, but a person with a visual way of thinking relates to the event or the clock, not the time.

In most visual cultures an event begins when everyone who is needed for the event (roles) arrives. Times to begin events are given by the measured space that it takes individuals to arrive. This measured space is the displacement. For example, a meeting is arranged for 6:00 p.m. for seven people. All members of this collective culture know where each other lives. So everyone arrives at around 6:40, because it takes 40 minutes for the person who lives the farthest from the meeting to come. The person who lives the farthest away leaves at 6:00, the time posted, and everyone leaves after 6:00 according to how close they live. These individuals are measuring the space it takes on a clock to get from one place to another; they are not anticipating the time that will pass. On the other hand, in an auditory culture, the meeting time of 6:00 p.m. refers to the time at which all people should plan on being at the meeting. It is the individual person's responsibility to arrive "on time." In an auditory culture, the person is expected to predict (future) the amount of time passing through the traveler and/or how quickly the traveler must move to arrive on time.

People with ASD use a visual conceptual system and, therefore, can seem obsessed with looking at a clock and still be very late or early to an activity. Furthermore, many people with ASD have problems with organization and planning, which are also issues of time. For example, a speech and language pathologist worked with an adult, McKenzie, with autism on many of these time issues. One of the first "time" issues that was considered had to do with McKenzie "showing up on time" for her appointment. On some days she would be as much as 1-1/2 hours late. When confronted, she displayed anger and impatience with the expectation of being on time. After all, she was at the appointment when she arrived. She could see herself in her picture. She did not see the speech pathologist sitting and waiting for McKenzie and she did not see that the speech pathologist had other things to do. To try to help McKenzie understand more of the big picture, the speech pathologist drew out the relationships.

Figure 5.2 shows one example of the final product of drawing in real time to help McKenzie understand all of the relationships in the big picture.

The therapist talked while she drew about how she was wondering where McKenzie was and what had happened to her, whether she was coming, if she should leave or stay to wait for McKenzie, and so on. Because McKenzie could not see the therapist until she arrived, she could not be late. They were not in the same picture together until McKenzie could see the therapist. After all, McKenzie always left work or her home at the time of her appointment, not before the appointment.

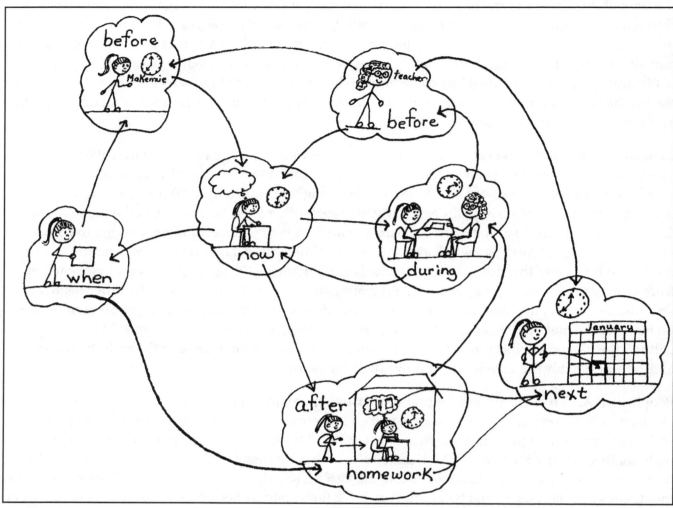

Figure 5.2. An Example of Using a Flowchart to Explain Time.

Classroom teachers complain about students with ASD not finishing work on time or turning work in on time, even when the work is completed before it is due. The work is begun when it is "due." So "doing" an activity is an event that is done when the activity or task is due. "Do" is the same as "due." Chapter 13 introduces strategies for helping people with ASD create the space of events, also known as clock time, to compensate for a lack of internal auditory time. *The space of an event is a visual way of dealing with time in an auditory world. Both internal time and clock time are forms of displacement. Clock time (events) is acquired in a visual system of language, whereas internal time is acquired through the acoustic features of patterns for auditory language.*

Activity: What is displacement? How does displacement work for people who think with visual metacognition? How is thinking different for people who think with an auditory form of displacement?

Semantic Memory

All languages represent underlying concepts. To represent these concepts with language, a speaker or writer must be able to retrieve the meaning of stored concepts. Concepts are most easily retrieved when language is assigned to them. The teacher says, "Write about what you did this summer." The teacher's words are auditory. They are not in context and they use a time reference that is not about what a person sees. The time reference is in the past, but the act is to write about it now. So, the visual writer has to create mental pictures or maps or graphics that represent the meaning of what the teacher instructed as well as the meaning or activities of what the writer did during the summer.

To pull up or retrieve the mental pictures or graphics requires visual semantic memory. The writer must conceptualize what the teacher means and then attach the language to the concepts before he can retrieve concepts to write about. The writer might visually recall what different summer activities looked like and then try to put language to the visual metacognition. The visual thinker must not only be able to retrieve those picture memories but also be able to assign language, preferably a visual form of language, before he can begin to write. One form of visual language would be to draw out a representation of the mental pictures so the writer can look at the drawings while writing. This is a form of visual semantic memory that uses the drawing, a form of language, assigned to the visual metacognition for better retrieval of memories.

The auditory thinker just has to start putting her own self-talk to the teacher's words; such as, "Oh, the teacher wants me to write about what I did during the summer. Hmmm, let's see. I did a lot of things, so I guess I will write about my favorite thing I did during the summer." In other words, the person with auditory metacognitive linguistic function uses words to recall or retrieve concepts, a form of auditory memory.

Both types of memory are meaningful: The visual semantic memory consists of pictures, graphics, mentally seen words, and movements of ideas, whereas the auditory semantic memory consists of the thinker's own sound of his voice in a form of self-talk. These two types of semantic memory are part of the two different forms of language, and are therefore different. A child with ASD will recall and retrieve ideas that are in visual-motor form – he can see the motor, or movement, shape of the speaker's mouth, hands, and so on. The child will make excellent progress in learning as long as educators and parents put the information into the child's system in the way he can process the learning of patterns for concepts. For example, if we use a hand-over-hand approach for printing or manual signing, we will access the child's visual semantic memory easier than through talking or drilling speech. By using the visual semantic memory properties of the language (graphics in context and event-based use of space), the child with visual metacognition will show more cognitive development and language development than when presented material in an auditory way (low context and in time).

Worksheets, for example, are typical school tasks that require the use of auditory memory – completion of tasks by retrieving words out of context. Typical instruction in spelling, reading, and multiplication tables is also auditory – words and numbers out of context. Commands for behavior compliance such as "sit down" are also auditory because they are out of context. Further, paired reinforcers given to increase the likelihood of the behavior "sitting" are also out of context, as are primary reinforcers such as drinks or cereal pieces. (More on behavior may be found in Chapters 7, 11, and 12.) All activities, tasks, and words given without a context are auditory in nature and require an auditory form of semantic memory. The visual metacognitive thinker may sit and stare or try to figure out the task but won't have a way to attach enough meaning to understand when, why, or how to do the task. Likewise, training a person to perform an act such as "sit" in response to a command or directive is sending the input out of context. For a visual metacognitive thinker, this type of training will not go into the semantic memory for later retrieval. Because the training is out of context and the reason for sitting (the language part) is not part of semantic memory, the visual thinker will not be able to do the task except in response to the same training conditions – like matching patterns without conceptualization or language. ***Semantic memory is long-term memory. Therefore, understanding how to reach a learner's semantic memory through the language properties of the thinker or learner is necessary for long-term learning.***

Visual semantic memory can include photographic memory. The learner is able to mentally picture a graphic image and able to pull up that photographed mental image from contextual information. Individuals with ASD have wonderful photographic memories. For example, a person with autism remembers *exactly* where a picture hangs; that is, the metacognitive "picture" is an exact match to what the person saw in the real world. Case in point: An 80-year-old man diagnosed with autism and living in a sheltered home used no speech or written form of communication. As far as the home workers knew, he also read nothing. Whenever he came into the room for therapy, he would go around straightening the pictures, pillows, and chairs, and pick up lint on the floor so that the room would look exactly like it did the time before, even if the time before was weeks prior to his visit.

Many young nonverbal children with autism have shown the exact visual match of the world they see with the exact photographic mental image taken before. One nonverbal child with autism mentally photographed students putting peanuts into a basket during an Easter egg hunt. He moved his head up and down as each peanut was placed in the basket. He was finished watching as soon as he knew all of the peanuts were accounted for and put in the basket. Even though there were other students around who may have had peanuts to contribute, this child jumped up with the actual last peanut. He knew no numbers, said no words, and didn't read, write, or speak, but he saw the whole group of peanuts *once* and therefore knew metacognitively the exact pattern of peanuts to be put into the basket.

A 9-year-old who was being physically managed in a self-contained room for hygiene skills was reported to not be able to read, write, or talk. His behavior was under strict stimulus control, which meant that without the punishers/rewards his behavior was out of control. Yet, he walked into a waiting room and picked up a *TV Guide*, which he thumbed through as if he were reading it. Then he went over to a chair, stood up on the chair, and changed the TV channels until he had found the show he wanted. He then sat and watched the channel he had chosen. He had matched the words to his mental pictures to the channel numbers without reading, writing, or speaking. These types of photographic matches within a context show that the person has good semantic visual memory, which can be used for teaching writing, reading, and oral speech (in that order). A later chapter will be devoted to strategies for using photographic memory.

Only with the use of a visual shape or pattern that taps into the child's visual metacognitive linguistic function will the child learn. It should be noted that some children with visual semantic memory (photographic memory) often appear to obsess on letters. In reality, these learners are looking at the shapes of letters, not the letter names. Shapes are part of the spatial linguistic function of visual metacognition. Even though many find this focus on visual shapes to be unusual, the ability to see the motor movement of how shapes change in space, how they are written, and what they mean conceptually is a strength for a child with autism. Unfortunately, some educators and parents try to hide the letters from the student because they see this focus as hyperlexia or a disability. As part of the linguistic function of the child's visual metacognition, the teacher can use the child's photographic ability to semantically retrieve thousands of shapes of words to teach the child to write, to tell what is written or to read, and to begin speaking with the oral motor patterns of the shapes of movements of letters to form acoustic-motor visual forms on the mouth. Figure 5.3 shows a child looking at the shape of a written idea to form the shape of a concept.

Figure 5.3. Written Ideas Form the Shapes of Visual Metacognition.

The photographic property of being able to retrieve the shape of visual patterns can not only help the person read and write but also create oral-motor patterns that are physical shapes within the mouth. These oral motor patterns become speech. Chapters 9-10 will describe how motor patterns form speech.

Activity: How does semantic memory differ between auditory and visual linguistic function?

Summary

Visual semantic memory retrieves visual metacognitive ideas or concepts. Connecting these visual images with visual-motor patterns (speech or writing) helps students with ASD learn academic, social, and behavioral meaning. On the other hand, teaching children with ASD to be literate through auditory memory tasks such as spelling letters and sounds, producing sounds for speech development, or learning to read with an emphasis on phonics is frustrating to them and often precipitates acting-out or self-destructive types of aggressive behavior.

Linguistic function refers to how a language works to express the properties underlying the metacognition or concepts of a language. Visual languages use high context, space of events, and visual semantic memory whereas auditory languages use little context, time of duration, and auditory semantic memory. ***Children with autism use a visual form of thinking that is usually accessed by the motor movement of the hand, mouth, and so on, so as to create visual mental shapes of ideas.***

Figure 5.4 shows the different types of metacognition and subsequent linguistic functions (adapted from Arwood, Brown, & Robb, 2005) of students in a classroom where the teacher gives an auditory instruction. Note that the child who is making hand movements or motor acts to create visual metacognition or pictures is the child with ASD.

Figure 5.4. Different Thinkers Use Different Concepts for Different Language Functions.

SECTION TWO

Language and Learning

How Does Learning Language Affect Social, Behavioral, and Academic Development?

Chapter 6 – Learning to Be Social

Chapter 7 – Learning to Behave Appropriately

Chapter 8 – Learning to Be Literate

Chapter 9 – Learning to Speak

Concepts for Chapter 6

What is security for a child with ASD?

Why is social maintenance important in learning?

Why does a child with ASD have difficulty with social agency?

How does language development affect social development?

CHAPTER 6

Learning to Be Social

I want to feel safe, but my shirt tag bothers me.

I want to be cool, but my friend's face moves.

I want to be around people, but they change constantly.

I want to be me, but I don't know who I am.

Learner Outcomes: As a result of reading this chapter, the reader should be able to explain the development of security, social maintenance, and social agency.

Children learn to feel socially secure through their neurobiological learning systems. Chapters 1 through 4 described the neurobiological learning system and Chapter 5 explained how language assigns meaning to learning. This section of the book describes how learning language affects social, behavioral, and academic performance for individuals diagnosed with ASD. Of the five developmental domains (social, language, cognitive, physical, and motor), the area of social development is probably the most elusive for children and adults with ASD. As a result of the difficulty that people with ASD have with social development, part of making the diagnosis of ASD necessitates a problem with social development. This chapter will explain how children with ASD have difficulty with social development. Chapter 14 follows up with strategies for helping individuals learn to be socially competent.

Security

One of the earliest and most important social concepts acquired by infants is "security." ***Security is a conceptual product of learning.*** From the input of sight, sound, touch, taste, and smell a child knows if she has been somewhere before, if the place is familiar, if the person's voice is one heard before, if the object is okay to touch, taste, and so forth. Familiarity with past experiences is an early level of learning to feel secure. The child is able to anticipate the familiar sensory input and therefore begins to be secure. Figure 6.1 shows a child learning to be secure by using sensory input.

Figure 6.1. Learning to Be Secure.

When a child is able to take in the sensory input and recognize the patterns from past experiences, his sensory world is familiar. Sensory input records as patterns of information, and the child "knows" the smells, tastes, touches, sights, or sounds. From the past input of sight, sound, touch, taste, and smell, a typical learner feels comfortable, and these familiar feelings or patterns become conceptual. The child is learning to be "secure."

Children with ASD have difficulty making sensory input familiar since their learning systems do not automatically recognize past patterns as meaningful. So, even though the child has experienced the sound input of a fire engine many times before, the sound of a fire engine is heard as an unfamiliar sound – not connected with "security" or any other meaning. The child perceives the sound as loud, even painfully loud. Figure 6.2 shows a child with ASD responding to the sound of a fire engine. The sound is unpleasant, unfamiliar, and makes the child feel insecure.

Figure 6.2. Fire Engine Sound Is Not Meaningful.

Instead of socializing to these sensory inputs, the child with ASD tends to try to sort out or protect herself from the changing patterns of sound input. For example, some children with ASD cover their ears or hide under the furniture to block the ever-changing patterns of their own mom's voice. Or they scream (see Figure 6.3) to block out sound patterns such as the siren of a fire engine.

Mom's voice is painful …

Truck's siren is painful …

Figure 6.3. Screaming Blocks out the Fire Engine Sound.

Sound input changes in patterns of pitch, loudness, and duration. Children with ASD don't recognize the past sensory patterns and therefore do not easily turn the sensory patterns into concepts. As a result, the sensory patterns remain unknown and the child feels insecure with the sensory surroundings. Figure 6.4 shows a comparison between perceiving patterns as concepts and not perceiving patterns as concepts.

Patterns

Concepts

Figure 6.4. Perceiving Perceptual Patterns as Concepts.

Children with ASD often exhibit behavior that shows their lack of ability to make sensory patterns conceptual. For example, Charley, diagnosed with autism, screamed when he walked onto the school bus. The teachers put headphones on him to block out the noises of the bus. The bus driver played the children's favorite music and allowed them to make music selection choices. With the headphones on, Charley could not hear the bus driver's music so he wanted the bus driver to turn up the music. The bus driver explained to Charley that he had to take the headphones off if he wanted to hear his music selection; otherwise, the music would be too loud for everyone who did not have headphones on. The child took off the headphones. Figure 6.5. shows the bus driver scenario.

| Child wears headphones on bus and rocks. | Driver plays music on bus and children listen. | Child asks driver to play the music again. |

Figure 6.5. Bus Driver Adds Meaning.

As the school year progressed, Charley learned to take turns with the other children requesting their favorite music. One day, a fire truck with its siren on came by. The siren seemed to upset Charley, so the bus driver taught the boy the differences among fire truck, ambulance, and police sirens. Charley would ask to go by the fire station to see the fire truck. Since Charley was often the last child on the bus, the bus driver could request a different end of route and take him by the fire station with the school's and his parents' permission. At first, Charley would hold his ears when making the request, but the bus driver vocally produced the fire truck siren, so Charley had to take his hands down to hear him. The bus driver explained how the siren was different from the other sirens and how he would have to listen carefully to determine if it was a fire truck, an ambulance, or a police car. By the end of the year, Charley really enjoyed his bus rides.

The bus driver arranged for Charley to go to the race track and ride in a pace car. The noise at a race track is quite loud and the pace car makes a lot of its own noise. There were no headphones. Before Charley's family took him to the race track, the bus driver explained what Charley would see, what he would hear, what the car going fast would feel like, and so on. Once in the pace car, Charley asked the driver to take another lap and to go faster. His parents and the school personnel were amazed at the progress he made on the bus. In fact, one of the teachers told the bus driver that it was like the student had his own counseling session every day on the bus. In other years, the family and school personnel had always tried to have Charley ride the bus, but after a couple of weeks the parents would have to transport him as Charley's bus rides were too upsetting to him.

In previous academic years, Charley's parents and his school personnel put headphones on him whenever he covered his ears or acted upset with his surroundings. The music in the headphones would block out other input, including the social exchanges of students and the driver. Riding the bus with headphones maintained the uncertainty of the sounds on the bus and the insecurity of other unexpected sounds outside of the bus. Riding the bus did not have enough meaning until the bus driver took the time to explain the ride and set up a reason for the headphones to be replaced by the sound of the boy's favorite music. In this way, the other students were also connected to Charley because they heard his music as well. The bus driver used a lot of gestures and pictures whenever possible to augment his words. Charley learned to feel secure with his bus environment. The bus driver made sure that all the students had opportunities to hear their favorite music and gave consequences to anyone who could not take a turn by eliminating all music for a ride. Charley often requested the same couple of songs and this irritated some of the other riders. The bus driver would give other songs more meaning such as telling Charley to listen for the drums or he would help the other students learn the words of the songs requested by Charley.

The bus driver constantly changed his interpretation of Charley's behavior. Instead of interpreting covering his ears as a problem, he saw it as a student who did not understand his environment, and therefore did not feel comfortable with it. The bus driver wanted Charley to feel comfortable and to fit in with the other students. So he used language to explain the sounds. As a result of the language and the consequences of listening to the sounds, Charley acquired the meaning of what the sounds meant. When this child acquired the meaning for sounds, what had been intense, unrecognizable patterns, even painful sensory input, became meaningful perceptual patterns that he could recognize and therefore conceptually enjoy. Figure 6.6 shows how a child with ASD hears different sounds as intense sensory pieces.

Figure 6.6. Sound Consists of Pieces.

These sensory inputs remain disconcerting until someone assigns meaning to the pieces of sounds. Once the sounds have meaning, they are no longer patterns but concepts. For this young man riding the school bus, the loud sounds were no longer painful or a distraction but meaningful concepts. Charley was comfortable riding the bus. He was even comfortable riding a very fast, loud pace car that he had never seen or experienced in any way because he had the language for what the experience would be like. ***With meaning he was secure in knowing what to expect from his environment!***

This process of putting meaning to the sensory input is opposite of what a typical learning system does (see Chapters 1-3). That is, a typical learner receives the sounds of the environment, and his neurobiological sensory systems integrate the raw input into meaningful patterns. The patterns are meaningful because old patterns are recognizable and new patterns are added so that concepts develop. The typical learner is secure knowing that the sensory input always has meaning. Figure 6.7 shows the typical learner acquiring meaning of sounds as input integrated to form concepts.

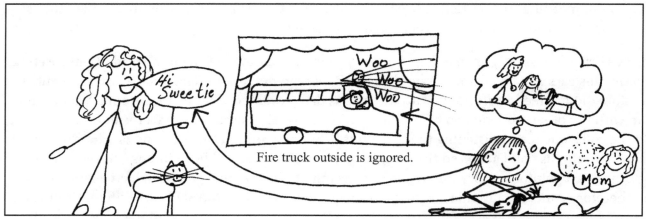

Seeing and hearing Mom feels good.   Touching the family pet feels good.

Figure 6.7. Typical Learning System Makes Meaning out of the Pieces.

For children with ASD, the sensory input does not form meaningful patterns, so educators and parents have to assign meaning to the sensory world for children to develop security. Waiting for the child with ASD to develop meaningful patterns by protecting the input keeps the child from developing a level of comfort or security with her environment. Thus, putting headphones on the child or keeping her from experiencing the usual sounds, tastes, touches, smells, and sights minimizes the learning of concepts. In other words, limiting the sensory input, in essence, limits the child's meaning.

For example, recall the student described in Chapter 4. Jackie was 12 years old. She did not like food with lumps or too much texture. She screamed to the voices of others talking to her. She threw objects she touched and she hit people as if they were objects. She did not have the meaning of these separate sensory experiences. She could not conceptualize the sensory input until someone began to assign meaning to everything she did, kicking, hitting, biting, throwing, tasting, screaming, and so on. They gave her meaning with visual patterns (written words) connected to visual concepts (pictures). Layers of input were given to each act and to every behavior she produced.

Shortly after this therapy started, Jackie began looking at faces, taking hands for help, "reading" words, complying with requests, and so on. Her behavior literally turned around in six weeks – six weeks after years of therapies to deal with unwanted behavior. Using therapy designed to eliminate behavior without giving Jackie meaning for changing her behavior had resulted in protecting her from learning. This type of protection also shielded her from experiencing her world. For example, at mealtime she would wait for someone to set down bowls of pureed, bland food in front of her as if dropped in by helicopter. As Jackie began to acquire meaning for how to fix the food, she could make choices of what she wanted to eat and made choices that would change the textures of acceptable food. Figure 6.8 shows the difference between food having to be the same in sensory input because there is no meaning assigned it and how language allows a person to choose different foods and therefore different textures.

Food must be the same.   Food can have many different textures.

Figure 6.8. Thinking Changes with Conceptual Development.

Language about food gave Jackie the choice of different textures with different meanings. She learned to select from many different foods. Security from sensory input came from the meaning of language assigned to the sensory input by the adults in the girl's environment. Jackie felt secure, not only in her ability to make choices about food, but in her world because the inputs were given meaningful language.

Security is one of the very early concepts of a social world. To assign meaning to one's world, the sensory inputs must have meaning. A typical learning system develops this meaning from neurological integration of input because the system inhibits recognized patterns from the past. Language is then a natural outcome of the learning system. Language represents the conceptual development.

> *Activity: Explain how sensory recognition is the first level of learning to be secure.*

Children with ASD do not have a learning system of sensory security. They cannot count on inhibiting past sensory input to form meaning until language gives the baffling sensory input meaning. Therefore, using language to assign meaning to their unrecognizable sensory patterns works to help them develop socially. Figure 6.9 shows how children with ASD don't perceive the sensory input as a secure environment.

Figure 6.9. Sensory Input Becomes Pleasant with Language Meaning.

The absence of meaning leaves children with ASD feeling insecure to certain sensory input. On the other hand, when language gives meaning in the way a child with ASD learns, the child is able to use his learning system to feel secure. For example, the boy on the bus could understand the association of a sound such as the bus driver imitating sirens with different siren patterns. He could match acoustic patterns. Most children with ASD can match acoustic patterns. The bus driver then added where the siren came from by showing the boy the fire truck. But not all children with ASD can take acoustic patterns and match them to visual patterns. For example, 12-year-old Jackie could not do that. She had to see the picture of the idea, such as a specific food, with a picture of her eating the food paired with other visuals that were acted on or motored, such as eating or drinking. Because she could not put acoustic patterns to her concepts, Jackie also had not learned the acoustic patterns necessary for speech whereas Charley on the bus had begun to develop speech.

The sensory world is different for children with ASD, not only for sound and sight but also for taste, touch, and smell. Children with autism who do not have language often try to use the non-distance senses of taste, touch, and smell to make meaning. For example, they may smell a person's hand, ear lobe, or hair. At first, the smell is separate from the concept of the person. But as these children gain language, the smells become part of their concept for a person or an agent.

Jake, a 6-year-old nonverbal male with autism, always greeted new people by smelling their ear lobes. As his language developed, he would say the person's name such as "Ellyn" and then rub his own ear lobes. On occasion, he would even say, "Ellyn, smell your ear!" as he reached for the lobe without gaze to identify that the ears belonged to a person. Jake had trouble with other sensory systems as well. He often tried to move another person's fingers or feet as if they were not attached to the person. The smell of the ears was probably more constant than that of either hands or feet. Hands and feet, much like faces, constantly change their positions. The different positions make the look of the feet, face, and hands difficult for children with ASD. As Jake's language increased so did his ability to recognize people and to interact with them rather than their ear lobes, their fingers, or their feet. He would wait until he had met the person more than once before he would ask to smell their ears or reach down and move their feet. Finally, with enough language to write his questions and to have written conversations with others as a teenager, he learned why smelling someone's ear is personal and not acceptable in our society.

The security of the sensory system is often baffling and difficult to acquire for a child with ASD. Figure 6.10 shows how even a familiar face can lack the security of meaning.

Figure 6.10. Even Familiar Faces Change the Way They Look.

Children without autism integrate the smells, tastes, sounds, touches, and sights of Mom's face into the concept of "Mom." This concept, "Mom," is language-based. "Mom" represents a lot of different sensory experiences integrated into one concept and then symbolized by the word "Mom." However, the child with ASD may pull away from Mom's arms or look away from her voice and cover his ears when Mom talks. For example, one mom said that her son Ian was so different from her other children. He did not want to cuddle, nurse, or be close to her face. As Ian began to develop language, he began to reach out to get her arms to do things for him, but he still had difficulty relating to ever-changing face postures. Even into his teen years, he positioned his body so that more of his back, not his face, was toward the people who talked to him.

The security of sensory input from sound and sight helps typical learners develop a sensory awareness of their world. Unfortunately, the sensory system for a child with autism does not offer much security. Even the basic pressure of touch can be absent of meaning for a child with ASD. In order to make pressure as intense as possible, and therefore to create as much meaning at the sensory level as possible, children with ASD sometimes resort to self-mutilation; chewing fingers, causing loss of tissue from infection; banging heads; picking at minor cuts; and so on. Hurting oneself provides intense touch without the meaning or conceptualization of the language we refer to as "pain." The reader should be reminded that "meaning" refers to the levels of learning that occur within the neurobiological system (e.g., Arwood, 1991; Carruthers, 1996; DaMasio, 2003; Sylwester, 2003) and that language assigns meaning to the sensory input for concepts to be understood. The concepts of touch are based on pressure. As the child creates intense pressure, the neurological learning system recognizes the sensory input, the lowest level of meaning.

David, a 9-year-old male with autism, stopped picking at his face when his language began to give him meaning as a person. Jeff, an 8-year-old male with autism, chewed off the tissue of five fingers, three on his right hand and two on his left hand. With two thumbs and three fingers left intact, his ability to use his hands had changed, but the chewing did not stop until his speech became meaningful and he began to engage in social interactions with others. *Meaningful speech or language assigns meaning to sensory input so that the world makes more sense.*

In summary, the sensory system of a child diagnosed with ASD lacks perceptual pattern integration to form concepts and, therefore, leaves the child with a sensory-perceptual system that is separate from his environment. Whereas typical learners are connected to their environment through the security of the meaning of their sensory input, children with ASD lack these environmental connections. The sensory input in children with ASD remains separate perceptual patterns until language can assign meaning for concepts to develop.

Activity: How does a child with ASD develop the basis of social development, a feeling of security?

Social Maintenance

As we have just seen, learning the meaning of one's environment is the first step toward social development. However, the early stage of feeling secure in one's everyday environment is far from the goal of being socially competent, the ability to initiate and maintain healthy relationships (e.g., Arwood & Young, 2000; McAfee, 2002). Early progression toward social competence develops from acquiring meaning for social interactions with others' words and actions. For example, a typical baby cries in response to hunger patterns. The parent responds to the cry and tries to figure out what the baby needs. As soon as the parent's actions meet the physical needs of the baby, the baby stops crying.

In a child with autism, the sensory input doesn't develop patterns that are conceptual, so the child may try to repeat the patterns. The child cries and cries and cries and cries. The child repeats these patterns. No matter what Mom does, the crying doesn't seem to stop. Mom's actions do not provide meaningful perceptual patterns, so the baby repeats the patterns of crying as a form of stimulating his learning system. Some children with ASD seem to develop these early patterns from sensory input and therefore appear normal until it is time to turn the perceptual patterns into concepts and the concepts don't develop. Then they may begin to perform unusual behaviors to repeat more advanced patterns. For example, Jenny, a 6-year-old female diagnosed with autism, appeared to have two "normal" years before she began screaming, hitting, not speaking, and so on. She had developed the early patterns of nonverbal interaction, but as she became older, she could not make these early interactive patterns conceptual. For most children the basic give-and-take between child and caretaker becomes more conceptual at around 18-24 months of age. The baby cries and Mom's consistent interactions become the concept of "Mama." Baby fusses and Mama gives the baby her blanket and says, "Do you want your blanket?" So, at around 18 months the child says, "Mama-blankie."

In order to take the basic sensory inputs and turn them into perceptual patterns related to hunger, thirst, comfort, and pain, a child must be able to recognize old sensory input. Then she must be able to take complex patterns of perception such as people's nonverbal gestures and their words and develop concepts. Mom taking care of hunger is the same Mom who takes me to Aunt Jane's house and the same Mom who reads me *Winnie the Pooh*. These more complex concepts are not in the here and now. Knowing that Mom can read the book even though Mom is not in the room and the book is at home, which we will soon return to, requires complex neurological maintenance with the many inputs that are rapidly changing. Children with ASD do not find meaning with maintaining these ever-changing perceptual patterns into concepts of social development. Mom may have provided the bottle and the initial constancy of the environment, but as the child approaches conceptualization of these experiences Mom's face changes, her words change, her voice changes, her smell changes, her touch changes, and so on. Mom is irritating to the child!

The child with ASD can no longer maintain with this irritating input, "Mom." As the child gets older, he kicks, screams, hits, and bites. All of these behaviors are a cry for meaning – make sense out of my world! To make Mom quit moving, the child pulls Mom's lips, takes off her glasses, and scratches her neck. These behaviors are a cry to stop the voices from sailing over the child's head. The child wants the spoken words to quit moving. "Put Mom's words where I can see them." The child wants his world to be meaningful.

We divide the world into pieces and ask the child with ASD to practice these pieces such as practicing sounds, practicing sitting, and practicing pointing to objects on a page. Dividing the world into pieces makes the world more difficult for the child with ASD to understand. *It is the sensory and/or perceptual pieces that the child with ASD cannot make into meaningful concepts. These patterns or pieces do not make concepts, which results in the child not being able to maintain socially.*

A child with autism takes the sensory pieces and repeats them over and over to try to make meaning. Somehow the repetition is supposed to become meaningful. For example, Laurie, a 7-year-old female with autism, would take anything that was made of paper and taste it, tear it, stroke it, chew it, roll it up and put it up by her ear to hear it, and so on. This type of behavior was an attempt to maintain with the paper. Typical learners younger than 3 years of age can often be seen trying to make the same type of meaning from the parts or pieces of an object. For example, an infant tastes paper and then makes a face. The infant tears it and shakes the pieces from her hand. Each act results in new meaning. For the child with ASD, the meaning is not new – just the sensory patterns are new. So, a child like Laurie makes sensory patterns, matches the patterns, and then repeats the patterns over and over. That is, whereas typical learners move to new patterns, children like Laurie try to find the meaning in the old patterns by maintaining with the practice of matching and repeating the old patterns.

If a child cannot recognize the perceptual patterns as meaningful, she will match and repeat the patterns. For example, recognized oral-motor or acoustic patterns are echoed and become echolalia. Figure 6.11 shows a child echoing vocal patterns.

Figure 6.11. Echo Patterns.

The child does not socially maintain with the speaker but maintains with the acoustic patterns by repeating the patterns.

Some children with ASD match and repeat other types of perceptual patterns. For example, some children see light patterns as nonmeaningful, so they flick their fingers in front of their faces to see the patterns over and over in an attempt to make meaning. Or, objects that move easily repeat patterns, so a child may watch a top spin over and over and over. The child will sit patiently watching the top spin with each revolution like a brand-new experience. The child can spend endless hours trying to figure out how objects change. Figure 6.12 depicts some of the many postures of children with ASD trying to make sense out of their sensory environment.

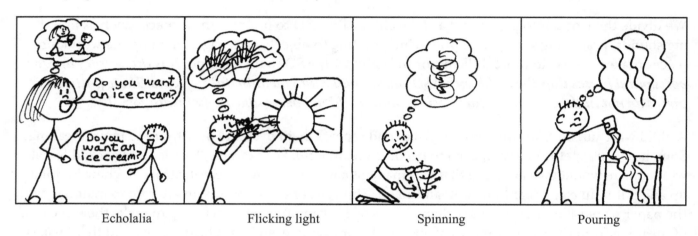

| Echolalia | Flicking light | Spinning | Pouring |

Figure 6.12. The Same Movements Create Different Patterns.

Water and paper are especially intriguing since they create many different types of perceptual patterns. Water can be put in a cup like an object but it runs through your fingers when you try to hold it. Paper makes noise when you roll it up, but when it is flat it makes no noise. Children with ASD maintain activity with these perceptual patterns in trying to conceptualize the meaning. Like water and paper, people are also difficult to understand. People continuously move and are always talking and making sounds. Even their smell and how their skin tastes change with soaps, perfumes, lotions, and so on.

When people relate to other people, the integrated sensory patterns form sets of perceptual patterns that create the concept of who a person or an agent is. Agency consists of a complex set of concepts surrounding who people are. For example, a mother is also someone's daughter, possibly a wife, a neighbor, a friend, and so on. So a child develops these agency concepts by maintaining socially with others. Since children with ASD cannot change the sensory patterns into concepts, they do not develop social concepts such as agency very easily.

Concepts surrounding agency are the basis of social development. Social maintenance is the result of knowing other people (agents), their actions, and their effects on others. A typical learner socially assigns meaning to what others do, just like others assign meaning to the recipient of the interaction. However, many individuals with ASD have difficulty assigning meaning to what others do, resulting in a lack of social maintenance. While people with ASD are given ways to respond, they are often not given the language for why they respond. For example, they learn to get on the bus with headphones, but they do not know how to maintain with the actions of others because they do not have the language for how to take off the headphones and act with others. *Therapy or intervention that does not assign meaning to social behavior does not promote social maintenance.*

Activity: How does a person develop social maintenance?

Social Agency

As we have seen, sensory input provides security. Perceptual patterns from the sensory input provide a child the opportunity to maintain with the objects or people around her. Social maintenance helps develop the concepts of who people are, what they do, and how they act. This basic set of concepts about how people see themselves is called agency.

Understanding what people do allows a child to begin to integrate past sensory input into patterns of meaning, recognizing the speaker's voice, reaching for the mother's hand, smiling at seeing an ice cream cone or hearing the sound of the ice cream truck. Figure 6.13 shows the typical pleasures developed from these sensory inputs that form recognizable patterns which turn into concepts.

Figure 6.13. Typical Sensory Input Creates Patterns for Concepts.

A basic interaction between a child and his parent develops into a social interaction with a person selling ice cream. The buying of the ice cream is a pleasant experience for all the people or agents. Children with ASD lack this same type of pleasant interaction among people as they struggle with the constantly changing features of people, their faces, feet, and hands. Agents move, and with every movement the person with ASD sees a whole new sensory set of imaging. It's like flipping the pages of a book to make a movie or slowing the frames of a movie down to the individual pictures. Agency includes all of the social concepts about people; concepts related to self-esteem, self-awareness, self-concept, and self-image. Because of the struggle with perceiving the visual changes of agents, people with ASD usually lack some development with social agency concepts.

Social competence is the ultimate goal of developing agency. To be socially competent, a person must be able to initiate and maintain healthy relationships (Walker, 2004). But initiating and/or maintaining a healthy relationship with someone requires the ability to see him as an agent and to also understand that other people function as agents. Figure 6.14 shows different types of agency that develop as part of the social process of learning how to initiate and maintain interactions with others.

Self-esteem: I am a good achiever!   Self-concept: I like who I am.   Self-awareness: I can jump over the bar.

Figure 6.14. Different Concepts of Agency.

Four levels of agency development are typically learned as part of social development. Table 6.1 shows these social stages of metacognitive agency cross-referenced with a drawing to depict the types of interactions at each stage.

TABLE 6.1. Different Levels of Cognitive Development.

Sensori-Motor Level Agent is an extension of the environment.	
Preoperational Level Agent is about "me." The big "I."	
Concrete Level Agent is one who relates to others.	
Formal Level Agency is about taking another's perspective.	

Adapted from Arwood, E. (1991). *Semantic and pragmatic language disorders.* Portland, OR: Apricot, Inc. Used with permission.

The four levels of basic agency development parallel the conceptual stages of development. Thus, at each stage of cognitive development, a child should show parallel growth in social development. A child with ASD who has difficulty acquiring the social stages of agency also has problems in cognitively developing concepts about herself and others. For example, a young man diagnosed with high-functioning autism learned the social rules for greeting people. When greeting somebody, he would say "Hello, how are you?" Sometimes this greeting would be on top of the other person's words. He knew the rule, but he didn't understand the other person's role. If the other person stopped to say hello and not to just greet, he would again say "Hello, how are you?" He was not able to see that the other person had changed the role of the interaction from a greeting to something more relational. These social deficits also showed up in the way he walked or moved through space. The trunk of his body was often stiff as if he had a pole down his spine as he tried to physically ground to what he saw while moving through space. *Grounding is a comfortable aligning of one's body in physical space.*

People who use a visual-motor way of thinking use this spatial type of grounding as a way to keep physically connected to the world when sensory input doesn't neurologically integrate patterns into concepts. Typically, people ground to the concepts and not the external world of sensory patterns. Since concepts are difficult to acquire for persons with ASD, they ground more of their own bodies to the physical world. Chapter 5 explained the language properties of visual thinking. Grounding is a property that is part of the spatial characteristic. With auditory thinking, a person grounds to the sound of words, not to the physical space. The person with a motor access to the visual concepts for linguistic function, such as many individuals with ASD, often shows rigidity when relating to the changing movements, roles, and meaning of people. To be socially competent, a person with ASD would have to learn to be at least concrete cognitively in the acquisition of agency. This level of attainment allows the person to develop social rules about how to interact with others. Chapter 14 will discuss some of the strategies used to develop social development for competence.

> ### *Activity: How does social agency become part of social development?*

Summary

Learning to be social requires the development of social concepts from sensory input that forms perceptual patterns. Caregivers and significant others assign meaning to visual patterns to create social concepts of security, maintenance, and agency. Security occurs when the infant or young child feels comfortable in integrating sensory input such as the sound of a siren into the concept of the noise the fire engine makes. Feelings of security allow the child to maintain an interaction between the child and others. When a child maintains an activity, such as both the adult and child taking turns telling a story to a picture, the child begins to show a level of agency. An agent is a person who acts on the environment such as saying, "No, I will do it," showing a level of independence. Since these social concepts are developmental in nature, their acquisition parallels the cognitive stages of development whereby the child acquires more meaning about agency.

Concepts for Chapter 7

How do children learn to behave appropriately?

How does the development of behavior relate to learning?

Why does behavior change?

How does reading and writing affect behavior?

CHAPTER 7

Learning to Behave Appropriately

I can be trained.

I can learn to sit.

I can learn to hit.

I can learn to spit.

So, why don't I learn to behave?

Learner Outcomes: As a result of reading this chapter, the reader should be able explain how a person with ASD learns to behave appropriately. What types of motor intervention can be used so the child acquires behavior concepts?

Behavior is a developmental product of the learning system. The learning system acquires the meaning of behavior. Children *learn* what to expect and how to appropriately respond to environmental input. In the previous chapters, the learning system was described as a set of processes: Receptors take in sensory input. The sensory input overlaps to form perceptual patterns. Old recognizable patterns allow new sets of patterns to integrate to form systems of concepts. People assign language to these concepts as symbols that represent shared meaning. It is through this learning process that a child acquires the meaning of how to behave. If a child has a typical learning system and lives in an environment that provides the meaning of language, his behavior should also be typical. However, children with ASD experience differences in learning and, therefore, often show differences in behavior. The purpose of this chapter is to describe the way a child with autism learns to behave.

Development of Behavior

The ability to walk, run, share, play, and so forth, is the result of the learning system acquiring concepts. A child who walks learned to walk. A child who shares learned to share. Children learn to behave. They learn to recognize the sensory input such as voices, environmental sounds, touches, tastes, smells, and movements of light. These inputs form the patterns of what is okay to do and what is not okay to do. Parents or caregivers provide additional sensory input such as "Amy, sit down on your bottom." As Amy is putting all of this information together neurologically, her parent reaches up and physically helps Amy sit down. Amy is learning to behave. Figure 7.1 shows Amy learning to behave.

Figure 7.1. Amy Learns to Behave.

Amy hears the parent's voice, looks at the parent, and recognizes the tone of the voice and the body postures. Amy follows the parent's eye gaze that looks at the seat. Figure 7.2 shows Amy complying with the parent's command to sit down.

Figure 7.2. Mom Helps Amy Learn to Behave.

Because Amy can neurologically integrate the various sensory inputs into recognizable patterns, she is developing concepts about sitting down. Examples of recognizable patterns include her mother's voice, the chair's surface, the parent's touch of her arm, and so on. As these types of patterns increase in meaning, the number of concepts increases. Concepts include Amy's understanding of the voice pattern "sit down" to mean bend her knees and put her bottom on the chair. Amy begins to think in concepts. Eventually, she uses these concepts to learn to behave. Amy's development is following an expected pattern of learning.

Children with ASD can hear and see and can develop the patterns of sight and sound. When they hear sounds, their learning systems can match the individual pieces of those sound patterns. Figure 7.3 shows how a child with ASD matches the sounds of music patterns. The child is learning the sound patterns, but not necessarily what the concepts of these patterns mean.

Figure 7.3. Matching Sound Patterns.

Figure 7.4. Matching Written Patterns.

Adapted from Arwood, E., & Brown, M. (2002). *Balanced literacy: Phonics, viconics, kinesics.* Portland, OR: APRICOT, Inc. Used with permission.

Activity: How does a child learn to behave?

We have seen that children with ASD cannot always integrate perceptual patterns into concepts. So, instead of being like Amy who is learning the concepts of behavior such as how to sit when told to sit, a child with ASD may be learning the sensory patterns to produce nonmeaningful behaviors such as hitting, kicking, screaming, or biting. A child with ASD who hits and kicks or screams and bites has learned to hit, kick, scream, or bite. But why does the child learn these nonmeaningful behaviors when no one else acts this way?

A child does not learn the meaning of behavior from watching what someone else does. A child's behavior is based on conceptual understanding. For example, a newborn baby responds to the sensory input with a basic movement or motor response. With sufficient sensory input over time, the child develops larger patterns of movement such as walking. Most children with autism develop the basic gross-motor act of walking since they can develop basic patterns of sensory-motor integration. The next level of development requires the patterns to be organized into concepts that can be assigned symbolic or language-based meanings. However, a child with ASD does not automatically make meaningful patterns into concepts. For example, in Figure 7.5 Mom reaches for Erin. Erin sees the movement of Mom's arms but does not recognize the meaning of the movement. Erin pulls back, looking away from the source of the movement. Erin flails her arm at the moving object.

Figure 7.5. Erin Protects Herself by Flailing Her Arm.

Activity: Why does Erin seem to be hitting?

Mom thinks that Erin is "hitting." At a sensory level of pattern organization, Erin is moving the unknown object, Mom's arm, away from Erin's space. Because Mom believes that Erin is hitting, Mom wants to try to control Erin's behavior. Mom might say "No hitting," hold Erin's arm and say "no," or put Erin in her own chair. These attempts to control Erin's unwanted behavior assume that Erin understands what she did with her body that Mom did not like.

Trying to control Erin's behavior through trying to stop the behavior with the use of punishment only makes the event more difficult for Erin to understand. Over time punishment, if the meaning of punishment is not known, usually escalates the aggressiveness of behavior. Because adults want to avoid the aggressive behavior, most adults turn to a form of reinforcement of desired behaviors. So, Mom works hard at telling Erin what she is doing that Mom likes. "Erin, I like the way you are sitting." This also assumes that Erin understands the language of Mom's voice.

However, without conceptualizing the meaning of behavior, Erin is not choosing to stop flailing or hitting. Her unwanted behavior, hitting, is not really replaced by an appropriate behavior such as, "Mom, don't pick me up. I can walk by myself."

Using either verbal punishment or verbal reinforcement of behavior assumes that the child has the adult language to understand the reason for the punishment or the reinforcement. More about how to reinforce behavior will be provided later in this book. For now, it should be noted that learning to behave requires conceptualization that language assigns meaning to.

Concepts develop across four stages (e.g., Piaget, 1971) (also see Chapter 3). Figure 7.6 shows the four stages of conceptual development.

| Sensori-Motor Development | Preoperational Development | Concrete Development | Formal Development |

Figure 7.6. Stages of Concept Development.

Activity: How is learning to behave related to conceptual development?

Due to their difficulty forming concepts from typical environmental input, children with ASD sometimes do not show behavior that is progressing developmentally as expected. Remember from Chapter 6 that children with ASD have difficulty acquiring social concepts because people constantly move. Learning to behave is part of learning to be social. The behavior of children with ASD is often socially inappropriate. For a child with ASD, people movements create individual movie frames. With each movement, a new picture is formed. Instead of seeing an arm conceptually reach for Erin, Erin sees the pieces of the movement as if there were multiple objects coming toward her. In order to organize the meaning of a movement such as an arm reaching, the individual frames of movement can be drawn for children with ASD. Figure 7.7 shows a cartoon of Erin sitting down.

Figure 7.7. Cartoon of How to Behave.

These cartoons (Arwood & Brown, 1999) take a child developmentally through the frames of what a particular behavior looks like. In essence, the child is put into the behavior by being drawn into the picture. In other words, first the child is part of the picture as the picture of the child doing the act is drawn. Meaning is assigned to the pictures, not only with oral words but also with print. The child learns the rules about people who are in the picture. Finally, the child can use his own language to tell about what he sees in the cartoon. Literally, the child is in the picture. Figure 7.8 shows stages of visual conceptualization or thought.

I am the picture.　　I am in the picture.　　The rules are about others I know.　　I can think in visual mental symbols.

Figure 7.8. Drawing the Child Helps Him See His Own Behavior.

> ## Activity: How does drawing the child as part of a cartoon help the child learn to behave?

When the child is drawn into a cartoon, he can see himself move through space, from one place or frame to another place or frame. Literally, the drawing of the child in the cartoon shows what a behavior looks like; more specifically, what the child looks like doing the behavior. The drawing takes the child out of the auditory world of non-understanding of the adult's voice to seeing the world. Some children with ASD need even more visual-motor patterns for the language of behavior to develop. So, the written words with the cartoon may be even more important. As the child is drawn into the pictures, he has more language for the world around him, and he begins to see the world more constant. For example, individuals with high-functioning autism (e.g., Grandin, 1995, 2005; Grandin & Barron, 2005; Grandin & Scariano, 1986) or with Asperger Syndrome often talk about trying to hold themselves constant or imagining themselves held constant so that the world doesn't move too much. Figure 7.9 shows this type of thinking.

I like to feel physically grounded.   I like sitting in the corner.

Figure 7.9. Holding the World Conceptually Constant.

By being part of a set of pictures in a cartoon, or by staying still or imagining being held tight, the person cannot move but the world can move. The child or adult can think about the outward movement because his or her own movement is still. However, when the child begins to move, so do her mental pictures. With each motor movement, the child's visual thoughts change.

Activity: Cartoon strips of a child engaged in a particular behavior help a child see the behavior, see himself engaged in the behavior, and hold the movement of the world still. Why does this help a child learn to behave?

Most children learn to behave by the adults using sound to tell them what to do and how to do it. But as we have seen, children with ASD do not learn behavior from auditory language. They do much better with a visual-motor form of language such as cartooning and writing. Since they have difficulty holding the movement of objects and people cognitively still for conceptualization, this means that these motor movements are strengths: The child with ASD learns best through the access of motor patterns. In other words, *children and adults with ASD have a motor access to their visual concepts. Any type of movement changes their visual thoughts. The development of visual concepts only occurs when appropriate motor movements overlap into concepts.*

Activity: What type of patterns does a person with ASD use for learning concepts?

In an auditory world, most of the sensory input is not motor- or visual-motor-based but vocal or acoustic. To teach behavior, parents and educators use oral language commands out of context, such as "John, sit down." "Isaac, put your toys away." "Sarah, put your crayons in the box." "Glenda, don't pick your nose." "Shelley, eat your food." These types of commands are auditory in their language function (see Chapters 4 and 5) and therefore difficult for individuals with ASD to understand. Furthermore, children with ASD have difficulty making meaning out of constantly changing input such as the mouth speaking. To hold the mental thoughts constant, the adult can draw the child into pictures and then into cartoon strips to show the meaning of words moving from the adult's lips. Figures 7.10 and 7.11 show these types of pictures.

Figure 7.10. Single Picture of Child Not Doing Behavior.

Figure 7.10 shows a child in a single picture after a particular behavior happens. In Figure 7.11 the same child is in a cartoon that shows her how she looks doing the expected behavior.

| Sarah sees Katie. Katie sees Sarah. | Sarah hits Katie. | Katie says, "Don't hit!" Katie thinks that she does not want to be Sarah's friend. |

Figure 7.11. A Cartoon of Expected Behavior.

The language of the cartoons is used to replace the child's inappropriate behavior with expected behavior. In this way, the child can see herself. The cartoon holds the world still from moving and helps assign language to what the child sees.

Since people's mouths and bodies move and children with ASD learn by being able to visually conceptualize meaning from the overlap of movement, keeping the pictures still helps the child acquire concepts. However, the pictures give the visual meaning of words. The words are still oral and spoken. To hold the spoken words still, the written ideas that go with the pictures also have to be present. In Figure 7.11, notice that words are written to match each of the pictures. To a child who does not read or write, these written words are patterns. The shapes or patterns of the words look the same when the print is the same. Therefore, for some children, typed words are more meaningful since they do not change shapes like a person's print.

The child learns the shape of the word while watching the hand move to write the idea. Some children do better if they feel the educator's or parent's hand move to trace over the words, in a hand-over-hand way. (More about using hand-over-hand methods in Chapter 8.) An adult's hand over a child's hand printing the motor patterns of words matched with the pictures of the concepts of the wanted behavior helps a child with ASD begin to develop meaningful concepts of behavior. *Conceptual meaning has to have a motor access for people with ASD. However, movement also affects the way a child with ASD views his world.*

Activity: How does movement help a child with ASD learn concepts of behavior?

Developing behavior through the learning system means that the child must develop the concepts of what the behavior means. Language assigns meaning to the behavior in the way that the child's world interprets. Creating the meaning of behavior for children with ASD requires either a visual-motor representation, such as drawing, and/or a motor representation, such as writing of the concepts that go with an activity or the picture.

Visual-Motor System

To learn to behave appropriately, the child with ASD must form visual concepts. These visual concepts of what "sitting," "standing," "helping" look like must also have a way for the child to retrieve the meaning later. Thus, the child needs to see the visual meaning as with drawing the concept, as well as be able to hold the meaning of the activity still. In other words, when a child with ASD moves, the child's visual mental concepts also move. To keep the internal pictures from moving at the same time the child is moving, the child with ASD will try to "ground" to physical properties of the world around him. Grounding also follows the stages of conceptual development. Figure 7.12 shows the child in his own picture (lowest level of conceptual meaning) grounding or "sliming" along the wall.

Figure 7.12. Grounding Along the Wall.

The child tries to keep as much of his body along the wall as possible as he moves. This physical "attachment" to the wall helps the child move vertically to the ground by being parallel to the wall. In other words, the child is a horizontal extension of the wall. To the observer the child looks like he is standing. To the child, he is *cognitively* lying on the wall. In this way, he is part of the space of the wall. Figure 7.13 shows a child sitting in the space of a bean bag chair.

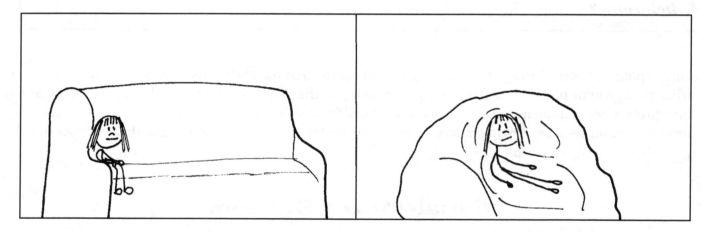

Children always sits inside arm of sofa.   Child is part of bean bag chair.

Figure 7.13. Child Sitting in the Space of a Bean Bag Chair.

Some children and adults with ASD always sit in a particular place like the end of a sofa, in a bean bag chair, or a car seat. These types of spaces allow them to ground more of their bodies to the space that they are physically in.

When the child is drawn into the space of a picture and then sequenced through the space of a cartoon, she is learning to separate from being on the picture (like being on the wall) to being a part of movement through the pictures. This change in thinking about being separate from the objects means that the child's conceptualization increases. Figure 7.14 shows a cartoon drawn by Kitty Mulkey, a speech and language pathologist. This drawing is of a child learning to go to the toilet (Arwood & Brown, 1999). Notice how the pictures all go in the same direction. Each frame has three thought bubbles: one shows the previous frame, one shows the present thoughts, and the third shows the next ideas. With the thought bubbles drawn, the child as well his thoughts are in the same space. The cartoon is providing the visual language for the child to learn to behave. Conceptually, the child is learning the behaviors that go with the language "going to the bathroom."

Pictures overlap by using thought bubbles.

Figure 7.14. Learning to Think About Behavior.
Adapted from Arwood, E., & Brown, M. (1999). *A guide to cartooning and flowcharting.* Portland, OR: APRICOT, Inc. Used with permission.

A child with ASD who is learning to behave is also learning to move through space. As such the child must make mental concepts that relate to spatial movement. As the child develops more mental concepts about moving through space, she does not have to ground physically but can begin to ground to the internal pictures. The external drawings in cartoon form help the child acquire these concepts of space. Figures 7.15-7.18 show the development of learning to move through space for a child with ASD.

Figure 7.15. The Child's Movements Are an Extension of Mom.

Figure 7.16. The Child's Movements Are Separate from Others.

Figure 7.17. The Child's Movements Follow the Rules of Others.

Figure 7.18. The Child's Movements Follow Others' Expectations.

In Figure 7.18, the child is learning to think about what she will do when the bell rings and she has to leave the room and go to her locker to get her things and then walk to the bus so that she can go home. She can plan her use of space in her head.

A child who is diagnosed with ASD and is learning to behave is also developing a way of thinking about moving in space. The child prefers the world to be held still to make sense out of the input. If she cannot make sense of her own movement in space or others' moving hands, bodies, and so on, she will move a part of her body in an attempt to make meaningful patterns (see Chapter 6). To try to limit the variety of input, the child will either try to stay grounded in a space or repeat the incoming input over and over. In the first situation, the child is not moving into space where the sensory input is new. In the second type of grounding, the child repeats input so as to block out new input. Remember from previous chapters, the child with ASD is trying to make sense out of the sensory-formed perceptual patterns. Because she cannot make concepts automatically from auditory perceptual patterns, she tries to control these patterns so as to make meaningful visual concepts. Repeating motor patterns creates new sensory input that is familiar – flicking, bonking, echoing, banging, twirling. Figure 7.19 shows these different types of motor repetitions as learning to behave in repetitive ways to block out nonmeaningful input.

Figure 7.19. Repeating Voices, Hand Movements, and Body Movements.

When a person with ASD limits movement by grounding to a chair or wall or imagining a body restriction such as an animal harness, these external restrictions keep the child's concepts from moving in response to input. Both types of grounding help the child to create motor movements that are more socially acceptable. Appropriate motor movements are appropriate behaviors. Behavior consists of multiple actions in context. *The development of appropriate behavior is learning to move with acts that are meaningful across time.*

> **Activity: How does a visual-motor way of learning to behave help a child with ASD develop appropriate behaviors?**

Meaningful Behavior

To be appropriate, behavior must be meaningful. Meaningful behavior uses more than perceptual patterns. It must be conceptual. Conceptual development of behavior is arranged from the child being in his own picture to being outside pictures of others' activities. Figures 7.20-7.22 show the hierarchy of development of the child with ASD who is trying to acquire visual meaning of behavioral concepts such as following someone else's directions.

Figure 7.20. Who Is That?

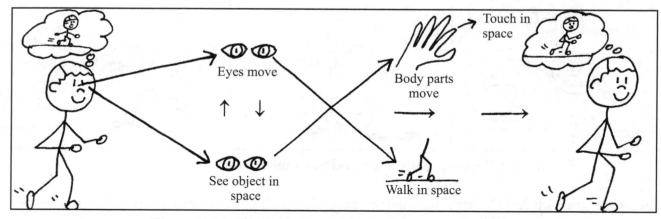

Figure 7.21. The Body Parts Move, Creating Concepts.

Learning with a Visual Brain in an Auditory World
124

Figure 7.22. The Child Matches Body Movements with Meaning of Pictures.

Children with ASD often show gross-motor development for behaviors such as walking, hitting, and sitting down at a level greater than their conceptualization. The conceptual meaning of behavior follows the four stages of cognitive development.

Developing Conceptual Meaning of Behavior – Level 1

At the first level where the child is in her own picture and trying to limit the input to make more meaning, the child often looks rigid in movement, much as if she has a pole down the spine and rotates on that pole. When the space is not restricted and she lacks conceptual meaning, the child will literally fall through space. This type of falling looks like the child is bolting or running away. For example, when a child with ASD has limited conceptual development and is walked into a gym without any physical grounding (another person's hand or body, for example), she will fall forward as if running. Figure 7.23 shows the child moving through space as if falling.

Figure 7.23. Falling Through Space.

The child is up on her toes and vertically moving, but is literally falling. When the child gets to something that is meaningful enough to stop the movement or when the child falls into something that stops the movement such as a wall, the movement stops. Cartoon strips can be laminated and carried along so the child can make meaning out of walking in big open spaces such as hallways and gyms. Figure 7.24 shows an example of such a cartoon.

When I walk to Sue's classroom, I will move my body slowly and keep my hands down by my body.

When I get to Sue's classroom, I will knock on the door and wait for Sue to open the door.

While I am visiting Sue's classroom, I will move my body slowly and only touch Sue and the students on the arm or hand.

When I am done visiting Sue's classroom, I will slowly walk back to my classroom.

Figure 7.24. Child Learns to Walk in Open Spaces.

In these big open spaces, the space is so big the child has no place to physically ground, so she falls through space until grounded. By seeing herself drawn in her own picture moving through space, the child learns to ground to the meaning of the pictures. In this way, the child with ASD can begin to be in the pictures and not just be an extension of her physical space or of her movements in space.

Sandra was a 12-year-old nonverbal child diagnosed with autism. She did not read, write, or talk. She had limited hygiene skills and was physically aggressive by hitting, biting, and throwing objects. (Remember these acts of behavior represent her ability to use patterns instead of conceptual meanings. If she sees an object, she moves the object. If someone reaches toward her, she moves her arm in the same direction, hitting the object [the person's arm].) Sandra was isolated with a full-time aide so that she could not hurt other students or staff. To create meaning conceptually for Sandra, she was moved (motor movement) through all daily activities. Figure 7.25 shows a person helping Sandra hand-over-hand pick up a book of pictures that Sandra knocked onto the floor.

Figure 7.25. Learning to Behave with Someone Else's Physical Help.

For Sandra, voices were assigned meaning with hand-over-hand pointing to pictures that sequenced the day's events (see Figure 7.26).

Figure 7.26. Voices Become Pictures, Become Pointing.

Then pictures of the activities were assigned meaning with print as in Figure 7.27.

Figure 7.27. Activities Become Printed Words.

All activities of daily living were assigned meaning with natural consequences, pictures, hand-over-hand movements, and print (see Figure 7.28).

Figure 7.28. Hand-over-Hand Activities of Daily Living.

Learning to Behave Appropriately

For Sandra, for every act, movement, vocalization, and eye gaze, a picture was assigned meaning in context so that she could create concepts of acceptable behavior from her unacceptable patterns of movement. The pictures were lined up so that she could see her day. Within four weeks she had 60 pictures that she would do in a hand-over-hand method with an adult to see her day, before the day, during the day, and at the end of the day. Her choices at each activity were lined up so she could see the choices within each activity. For example, she had about 30 different choices she could make in response to mealtime. All of the pictures had print and were produced as hand-over-hand activities.

The more severe the level of disability, the less information the person acquires conceptually. Figure 7.29 shows John unable to see the concepts from the patterns.

Figure 7.29. John Does Not Create Concepts from the Patterns.

John is not learning the concepts of how to behave. While he can hear and see, he cannot make meaning out of what others say or do. He needs to see the meaning of the overlapping motor patterns, which does not happen frequently in a typical environment. Remember the nonverbal 9-year-old male discussed previously, who would sit down in a chair in the waiting room and thumb through the pages of a *TV Guide* as if he could read, even though he had shown no signs of understanding any print. (He was in a learning skills classroom where no reading skills had been introduced and his parents had never read to him.) After thumbing through the *TV Guide*, he climbed up onto a chair and changed the TV channel to match something he saw in the guide. He had learned the conceptual meaning of the relationship between the TV and the written patterns of the shows and their times, even though he could not "read," "write," or "speak." In this task, he looked very well behaved. (Keep in mind he did not ask anyone else if they were watching a program before he changed channels and he climbed up on the chair to change the channels.) Figure 7.30 shows him learning the concepts of how to watch TV – he would match his mental concepts with what he could see himself do even though he could *not* understand the meaningfulness of spoken and written patterns because letters have sounds. Remember he *could* match the visual patterns of the print on the page against the concepts of the pictures on the TV.

Figure 7.30. Learning the Patterns to Watching TV.

This same 9-year-old was then brought into a clinical room that had very little meaning for him. His behavior consisted of hitting, standing on the table, making faces into the two-way glass, and screaming. The initial clinician was terrified and was soon replaced by someone who understood that these behaviors meant that the child lacked meaning. The new clinician assigned meaning through the use of print paired with pictures and manual signs (no letters or sounds) to the activity within the classroom. The student, respectively, learned to write, read, and speak. As his learning of concepts increased, his behavior became meaningful and therefore acceptable. He would come into the clinic room and sit down, read the print, sign the meaning, and then speak the concept. These were all in context of events – people doing things in situations where objects and the place overlapped, such as stories about boys playing football. Figure 7.31 shows this boy learning to conceptualize behavior.

Figure 7.31. Learning to Conceptualize Behavior.

Developing Conceptual Meaning of Behavior – Level 2

Once a person begins to develop concepts from overlapping movements such as from writing, he can begin to separate himself from being in the picture. This is the second stage of developing the meaning of behavior. For example, a high school student with autism would burn the skin on his arms for his friends to watch. He could see the fire. He could smell the skin burn. And he could see the wound afterwards. He was told not to light the skin, but he did not comply. He could see the exaggerated expressions on the boys' faces as they watched in amazement. He could not feel the pain until someone drew for him the way the fire burned his skin and how that felt. Once the concepts were introduced through writing with pictures, he could feel the pain. The concepts showed him how to assign meaning to *feeling* pain.

To learn to behave differently, this youth had to learn the specific concepts of the sensory input to recognize the meaning of the patterns, the relationship between what he could see or smell and the motor movement of the hand writing the meaning of pain. Figure 7.32 shows this youth trying to make meaning out of behavior.

Figure 7.32. Making Meaning out of Behavior.

He was no longer at the first level of being an extension of the environment, so he did not hit, bite, or scream. At the second level of conceptual development, he was no longer in the picture, so he could watch his skin burn without pain. By adding the language to what happens when the skin burns and by putting him back into the picture as feeling pain, he could use those concepts to behave differently.

Developing Conceptual Meaning of Behavior – Level 3

At the third stage of developing concepts to behave appropriately, the learner follows the language rules for behavior. For example, a 13-year-old nonverbal male, Chad, diagnosed with autism, had become increasingly more violent as he became older. By ninth grade (13 years old), he weighed over 200 pounds and was close to 6 feet tall. He did not talk, read, or write. By writing the concepts for drawn pictures of everything he did in a day, he quickly began to talk and write. He picked up the movement of the mouth from watching people write the words. His own mouth movements had meaning to him, but the adults talking to him had no meaning.

For example, a discussion about appropriate behavior did not work. His aide would draw the concepts and then write the words used for talking, conversing, and explaining behavior, academic concepts, social skills, and so on. The aide would draw out behavior and then write about it. Chad would pick up the movement of the written patterns as speech and would try to talk about the situation, but until he wrote, his behavior did not change. For example, he knew what the rule was for walking down the hall.

As he walked, his pants would start to slide down, so he would reach around the back of his pants and give himself a "wedgie." The girls would giggle and the boys would not want to walk with him. Chad asked why the boys did not like him and why he did not have a girlfriend. His aide drew out the scenario – what others saw and thought. See Figure 7.33 for an example of what would be drawn.

Figure 7.33. Rules About Walking Down the Hall.

Chad was shown what others thought and then the ideas would be written. "If Chad does not want others to see the pants wedged in his bottom, he should pull up the pants from the side and wear a belt so the pants don't slide down." Hundreds of concepts like this had to be drawn. If he began to orally argue, he was told to write. As soon as he wrote the meaning of the concepts, he no longer argued. Through writing he acquired the concepts for the rules of behavior that most children learn through the spoken words of others. These rules are the third level of learning to conceptualize behavior.

Developing Conceptual Meaning of Behavior – Level 4

At the fourth or final level of conceptualizing behavior, a person uses multiple forms of sensory patterns to form concepts that symbolize the meaning of concepts. For example, on the higher end of the autism spectrum, individuals have more sensory integration and therefore more information. They have more ways to acquire concepts and therefore acquire concepts more easily. For example, individuals with AS can use patterns that they can hear, see, or touch as long as there is a motor connection. Figure 7.34 shows how these motor connections work to create concepts.

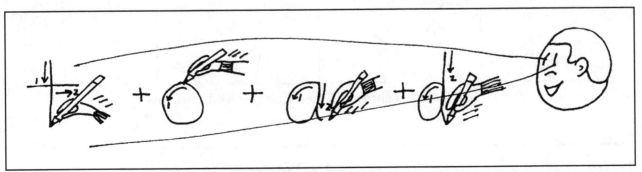

Figure 7.34. Motor Connections Form Concepts.

Learning to Behave Appropriately

Motor connections include patterns for speech, acting on tasks, moving the mouth, watching others' mouths move, and then overlapping these different types of motor patterns. Often individuals who can overlap these patterns talk a lot. For example, Chad never talked until he was in ninth grade. Once writing was used to access his visual thinking, he was always talking. Others perceive this constant speaking or motor mouth moving as annoying at best. Figure 7.35 shows the motor mouth process. Moving the mouth creates motor patterns that are connected to what individuals with ASD see. They see it; they talk about it. They think it; they talk about it. When they write, they write pages and pages and pages.

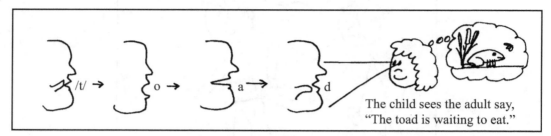

The child sees the adult say, "The toad is waiting to eat."

Figure 7.35. Motor Mouth Movements.

For example, one professional adult complained that she knew she drove everyone crazy with her talking but she could not talk less. She felt she wasn't through talking until all the ideas she had in her head had been talked about.

But moving and talking can be difficult. A college student diagnosed with AS had to learn all of the concepts about what the campus looked like, who was in his class, what they looked like, what his professors looked like and talked like, what the rules were for the coursework, and so on, before he could walk across campus and speak to others. As long as he was moving or thinking, he had to talk only about what he saw or was thinking about. He ignored others' voices until he had acquired all of the concepts for attending college. Then he would walk up to a person he knew and say, "How are you?" He then would back up and move forward repetitively while the person responded. As long as the conversation was focused on the greeting or his words ("How are you?"), he could talk. As soon as the greeting extended beyond the basics, he would walk away. Figure 7.36 shows this young man trying to organize the meaning of how to behave on a college campus when he sees others.

Figure 7.36. Learning to Cross Campus and also Talk.

Activity: How do individuals with ASD learn to behave?

Summary

Learning the concepts of how to behave follows the cognitive stages of development from the lowest sensory level of being an extension of basic sensory input, to being in the picture acting on the world, to understanding rules of behavior to learning social concepts of cultural expectations of behavior. The more meaning that is assigned to behavior, the more conceptual the behavior, and the higher the level of understanding how to behave.

Concepts for Chapter 8

How do patterns and concepts relate to reading and writing?

What is a definition of literacy?

Why do children with ASD sometimes have difficulty
with literacy?

Can learning to read and write be a visual-motor language task?

CHAPTER 8
Learning to Be Literate

Each letter is the shape of a puzzle piece.
These shapes have a meaning that I can see.
When I write, I create the shapes of the hand movements
To the pictures that dance in my head!

Learner Outcomes: As a result of reading this chapter, the reader should be able to explain how language mediates all aspects of learning to be literate and how learning affects the development of literacy.

Literacy refers to learning to read, write, think, view, calculate, listen, and speak (Cooper, 2003). The purpose of this chapter is to show how gaining literacy for a person with ASD is the result of being able to use motor movements as visual shapes stored in memory as visual concepts. Language represents the concepts. The products or artifacts of language include the acts of reading, writing, speaking, and calculating. So, the development of language is the result of learning to be literate. ***Learning to be literate for children with ASD is a visual-motor process of overlapping hand and mouth movements into shapes that store meanings as visual concepts.***

Reading

The typical approach to teaching reading is based on an auditory way of putting sounds (acoustic patterns) with letters (visual patterns) to form the usual auditory concepts or words of English. Remember from Chapters 3 and 5, auditory patterns are a combination of visual and acoustic input. And auditory languages like English use words as a basic unit of thinking (Chapter 5). So, if a child can sound out the visual pattern, it is assumed he will recognize the meaning of the "word." This approach to reading also assumes that the person learning to read is able to interpret the meaning of the word when he hears the word spoken. The final assumption is that the child can interpret the collected meaning of all the words. Therefore, many educators assume that oral fluent reading is a measure of understanding. The spoken word is the basis of reading fluently and of understanding the material read. In other words, this approach to reading is auditory in its assumptions. It assumes that the reader thinks with auditory concepts; that is, the child can hear his own voice interpreting the meaning while orally reading or saying the sound patterns that match to the visual patterns.

But as we have seen, children with ASD do not think in the sounds of self-spoken words. Instead, they see the pictures of language mentally. Furthermore, these mental pictures often go away when there is sound, including the child's own voice orally reading. Therefore, reading with sound for a child with ASD does not provide for comprehension.

Activity: Why is the typical way of teaching reading an auditory language task?

To read with comprehension, a child must develop concepts along with the representative language to interpret the meaning of the print on the page. Many children with ASD must first acquire the visual concepts to be able to read. These mental concepts are often developed through the movement of hands, eyes, mouths, and so forth. Later in this chapter, we will discuss how these movements form visual mental concepts. The point here is that the usual auditory approach to reading does not work well for children and adults with ASD. Figure 8.1 shows the difference between the visual conceptualization of seeing the idea on the page and being able to hear the concept.

Figure 8.1. Visual Recognition and Auditory Recognition of an Idea.

Reading with the Eyes, Not the Ears

Individuals with ASD think with visual language. Figure 8.2 shows a child with ASD looking at a page of letters and turning those letters into shapes like pieces of a puzzle.

Figure 8.2. Letters Are Shapes Similar to Puzzle Pieces.

This is the first stage of reading for a child with ASD: The child sees the letters as puzzle pieces. While some see this ability as too much attention to the letters, or "hyperlexia," the authors see this ability as a gift. The ability to see the shapes of letters offers the child the opportunity to also see the shape of the meaning of a group of letters that we call a word. Figure 8.3 shows a picture dictionary where the child sees the words to a story as shapes.

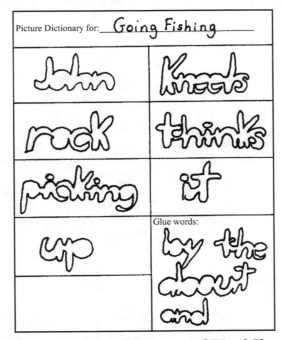

Figure 8.3. Picture Dictionary of Word Shapes.

The second step of reading for a child with ASD is to attach meaning to the shapes. Since the child sees the shape of the letters and the letters can combine to form a "whole meaning," which is also a shape, it is important to assign meaning to these shapes. Meaning is not in the form of letter names for children with ASD. Letters have no meaning, and their shapes do not need to be given geometric names like "rhombus." The shapes have the meaning of the mental idea. Figure 8.4 shows the progression of meaning of these shapes for a child with ASD.

Figure 8.4. Shapes Become Visual Concepts.

Since children with ASD do not have an auditory way of processing language, it is O.K. to bypass teaching letters. Learning letter names requires the child to say the name (acoustic pattern) of the letter (visual pattern), which is an auditory task. Instead of letter names or identification of the puzzle pieces (letters), the child can see the shape of the puzzle or word (see Figure 8.3). But the child with ASD may not have meaning for that shape. So, the meanings must be taught!

To teach the meanings of the shape, put the meaning into even a bigger puzzle, a whole event. An event is someone who does something such as "John bounces the ball." To make this event a visual situation, draw the event or show a picture of the event. Figure 8.5 shows an event type (Arwood & Unruh, 2000) of picture.

Figure 8.5. Event-Based Picture.
From Arwood, E. (1985). *APRICOT I kit*. Portland, OR: APRICOT, Inc. Reprinted with permission.

This picture shows complete people, their actions with feet and hands, all on one plane. Not all children can see the meaning of what is in the picture because they may not have enough language. Language fills in the meaning. Remember the brain sees the light points on a plane and movement only. But in a picture, there is no movement, so the child is left to see only two dimensions of light. Figure 8.6 shows what a child with ASD might see.

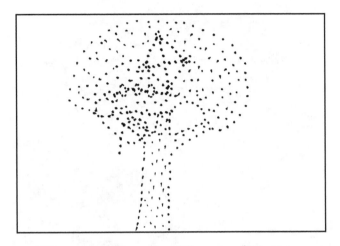

Figure 8.6. Perceived Image of Picture.

Notice that the child may not have enough meaning to see the "complete" picture. Seeing the complete picture as a typical adult sees it is the result of language development. For a child with ASD, the process of seeing the language of a picture is like this:

1. The child looks at the picture and the eyes see points of light.

2. With enough overlap of these light patterns, the brain begins to see shapes. The shapes might be of a person, an object, or a piece of a person or object.

3. Each shape is a concept.

4. The child sees as many of the concepts of the "complete" picture as she or he has language for.

For the child to see the whole picture, *language of the mind represents a perceived third dimension. The more language the child has, the more of the picture she will have meaning for.*

Activity: Why does the shape of a word have more meaning than the letter names or the sound of a word for a child with ASD?

For children with ASD, mental concepts are visual shapes. Seeing a picture is the result of being able to create shapes for the concepts. When the parent or educator shapes the words (e.g., Figure 8.3), the child begins to see the shapes of words with or without language. If the child does not have the language for the printed word, then the shape of the word has to be paired with the shape of the concept. This pairing of shapes of words with pictured concepts begins to develop the language or meaning of the ideas. Figure 8.7 shows a picture with the printed labels on the picture. In this way, the child is beginning to see the concepts, not hear them.

Figure 8.7. Pairing the Shape of the Words with the Meaning.
From Arwood, E. (1985). *APRICOT I kit*. Portland, OR: APRICOT, Inc. Reprinted with permission.

When a child can see the concepts, he will begin to learn the meaning of the concepts. The next section explains how the print becomes a shape in the mind that can be paired with the concept to develop language for literacy.

Working Hand-over-Hand

A child with ASD will not attend to the picture or the print unless she has adequate conceptual meaning for language. But many children with ASD do not develop language unless pictures and print provide visual meaning. So, the child must be able to develop motor-based language through movement. To connect the child's motor-based language learning system with the visual print on a page, the educator or parent pairs the shapes of the hand writing the words with concepts. Figure 8.8 shows a picture dictionary of the labels from Figure 8.7.

Picture Dictionary for: The Kite in the Tree

Dad | climbed
ladder | take
stuck | Kite
Out | Glue words: the, to, of
tree |

Figure 8.8. Picture Dictionary of Hand-over-Hand Word Patterns or Labels.

The labels were put on the picture while a person told the story of the pictured event. When the person said "tree," the person also labeled the parts of the picture with the spoken words. For many children with ASD, this labeling is done hand-over-hand.

To create a hand-over-hand pattern, the adult places a regular-size pencil in the child's hand for writing. Then the adult places her hand on the back of the child's hand and guides the child's hand through the writing of the pattern (word). Figure 8.9 shows a hand-over-hand placement.

Figure 8.9. Hand-over-Hand Writing.

When the adult touches the child's hand, the child often pulls back because of what some refer to as "tactile defensiveness." Actually, the child pulls back because her brain records the intensity of the sensory pressure on the hand instead of the language of the meaning of the concepts about working hand-over-hand. In other words, the pulling back is a response (sensory input) to the pressure of touch. Once a child's learning system functions at a higher cognitive level, the child has more choices in how to respond. For example, the child could say, "Please don't touch me" or "I don't like the touch." Again, the child's ability to conceptualize the touch requires her learning system to form perceptual patterns that will create the concepts that language represents (see Chapters 1-3).

When you take the child's hand, be sure to firmly grasp the hand like taking an object. Do not look at the child but look at the child's hand and hold on tight. If necessary, just write one or two labels with the child. Once the child recognizes the meaning of the word, he will no longer pull back. In fact, some children actually begin to reach for the hand soon after the hand-over-hand process begins.

If a child with ASD does not have sufficient language to talk about the picture, he will not see the concepts of the pictures, just patterns. The print on the pictures helps put a name or tag to the concept. Many children with ASD do not cognitively pair the visual shape of a word or tag with the underlying pictured concept because they do not have the language for the pictured concepts. And many children also do not make meaning from the spoken patterns (acoustic) of telling the story while labeling the picture. But almost all children with ASD can mentally record the writing or movement of the hand as mental shapes. *Movements make shapes. Shapes of movements make pictures. Pictures are concepts. Language refers to these concepts! The child with ASD can learn language through writing.*

Activity: How does a child with ASD develop language through the motor process of writing?

Figure 8.10 shows the sequence of mental development of the movements into shapes, concepts, and language.

Figure 8.10. Motor Process of Writing.

Each movement of the hand becomes a visual pattern that creates the shape of an idea. When the written word shapes are put onto the picture, the child can begin to see the concept that is labeled. This labeling is called marking. The label *marks* the concept with the shape of the idea or word. This shape of the word becomes a mental shape. The shape of the word is printed with the concept so the shape marks or represents the concept. The child begins to see the concept as part of the shape (see Figure 8.4).

Overlapping the Patterns with the Concepts

A child's brain is searching for patterns, so there must be plenty of patterns for the child to cognitively experience. The event of people doing actions with objects in relationship to one another (e.g., Figure 8.8) provides the child with the opportunity to have many patterns. Each idea in the picture requires several patterns. Since a child's brain develops with the stimulation of many patterns, the more patterns there are, the more the child develops. On the other hand, when the number of patterns is controlled so that there are only a few concepts developing, the child's cognition also is controlled and cognition does not develop. There are many variations from what is expected to be normal development of reading and writing. Figures 8.11 through 8.14 show some of them. More about reading and writing concepts will be discussed in later chapters.

Figure 8.11 shows how a child sees the mental concept in response to viewing the pattern. Many children with ASD develop silent reading or visual-motor movements of the eyes to create visual concepts long before they word call or read aloud with sound.

Figure 8.11. The Child Looks at a Shape and Thinks of the Concept.

Some children with ASD actually learn to write before they can draw, and some children never like to draw because the drawing involves too much language while the writing is of the recognizable motor patterns of visual concepts. Figure 8.12 shows a child who writes before she draws.

Figure 8.12. Writing Before Drawing.

Some children with ASD prefer to write instead of talking or listening to others talk. This type of motor work on a computer or keyboard allows the child to feel the motor patterns of the shape of the words and to relate to the visual concepts. Figure 8.13 shows a person who prefers to write on a computer over talking or listening.

Figure 8.13. This Person Prefers to Write.

For many, the way to the acoustic-motor patterns of speech is through the overlap of motor patterns. Figure 8.14 shows a child learning to write to create enough overlap of patterns to also be able to speak.

Figure 8.14. Overlap of Motor Patterns Helps Develop Speech.

As the patterns overlap to form concepts, the child also begins to develop cognition. *Language represents the cognition.*

> ### Activity: How does the overlap of motor patterns help a child diagnosed with ASD become literate?

Cognitive Development

A child with ASD uses visual concepts for cognition. But in a society that provides constant auditory stimulation for thinking, reading, writing, and so on, the child will not develop the visual concepts. Some researchers (e.g., Sturmey & Sevin, 1994) estimate that as many as 80% of children diagnosed with autism also are diagnosed with mental retardation, a disability that suggests there is a limit on cognitive development. However, most children with ASD who have access to visual concepts develop normal or above-average cognition. The authors have worked with many children who are severely impacted by autism who did not show cognitive development until they were able to access motor patterns of ideas in order to create shapes of the meaning of written words in context of activities and events to represent their visual cognition.

Activities of daily living (ADL) can also work to provide hand-over-hand opportunities for the child with ASD to "read" the environment. The caregiver or educator takes the child's hand and assists the child to feed herself, to make her bed, to dress herself, to put objects away, and so on. These activities are then labeled or marked with the written words that connect the shape of the printed word with the concept of the activity. The hand-over-hand actions impose agency on the child (see Chapter 3 for an explanation of social development or agency), and the child sees the shape of the pattern that creates the meaning for the actions or concepts. The adult pairs the written words with the activities and draws a two-dimensional stick figure of the concept that goes with the word. Figure 8.15 shows a sequence of these pictures of a child learning the routine of the classroom. Specifically, it shows a child how to walk into the room and what to do.

| After walking into the classroom, Sally walks to the cubby area and hangs up her backpack. | Next, Sally walks to her desk while thinking about the book she is going to take out of her desk. | When Sally is at her desk, she sits down and takes out her book so she can look at the ideas in it. | While looking at her book, Sally thinks about what she sees on the page. |

Figure 8.15. Hand-over-Hand Drawing of Activities.

The hand-over-hand drawing of the activity coupled with the hand-over-hand labeling of the meaning of the words helps develop cognition. Most children with ASD attend to the print more than the picture of the activity because the print is a puzzle of shapes that doesn't change shape, and therefore doesn't change meaning. That is, the print remains constant in the way the shape feels and looks. The meaning of pictures comes from the person who drew them, not the person looking at them. In other words, pictures are not conventional or shared concepts. For example, give 10 teachers the task of drawing "Christopher Columbus," and the result is 10 different pictures. But the written label "Christopher Columbus" retains the same shape on any of the drawings. The written words attach the visual shape of an idea to the picture so the child can see the concepts of the pictures and then see the meaning of the shapes of the words. Hand-over-hand labeling helps develop these visual concepts so the child's cognition also develops as one shape adds to another shape.

Children with ASD often have difficulty in new situations and in transitions because they do not have the language to be flexible. This type of drawing and writing with attention to the child making the motor movements of the ideas (hand-over-hand) helps the child acquire the language for such transitions. Since language assigns meaning to the underlying mental concepts, children with ASD need to mentally be able to see themselves move through the shapes or frames of the pictures to create the movement of a transition. Figure 8.15 not only showed the labeling with drawing and writing but also the transitioning. In other words, the child moves from picture to picture, and each picture is a piece of the transition. When a sufficient number of visual shapes or pieces of the transition are in place, the child is able to see himself move. This is much like building all of the pictures of a hand-held cartoon. The pictures of the cartoon are flipped, and the static drawings turn into a hand-held movie.

Other motor movements also develop cognition. For example, a child who is able to type ideas on an old-fashioned typewriter is able to see the patterns of the strike of keys, which can't be seen on a computer. A child who is able to write his ideas is also developing cognition. These other motor accesses to cognition will be discussed later.

Activity: How do motor movements create cognition?

Reading Comprehension

If a child with ASD is able to see the shape of written words, he may see all print as a series of puzzles. As the child moves through the day, these puzzles (shapes of words) become a part of what the child "knows." For example, one of the authors, Arwood, supervised work with a 10-year-old male, Jake, diagnosed with autism. Jake did not talk, read, or write. He was "spending time" in a class for children who were severely impacted by a variety of developmental delays. There were no academic components to the class curriculum. The school's responsibility was to feed, diaper, and protect the safety of these children. Jake's parents lived in a rural area and they did not read to him. They spent their days making a living and taking care of the basic needs of their children. There were no books in the home.

The school transported Jake to the nearby university twice a week for "academics." The first day, he came into the university therapy room and began screaming, throwing objects, and making faces in the two-way window. He then jumped up on the table and made all sorts of kicking, screaming, and arm-swinging types of movements while he watched himself in a the window. Arwood assigned a therapist who could use ASL — a language that depends on motor movements to create shapes on the hand. She then paired the hand movements with written words that were put on pictures. The child came into the room, sat down, and worked on the shapes of the hands (hand-over-hand) with the words. The clinician would point to the printed word, "jump," for example, and the therapist would sign the concept. The child's face was touched and he was stimulated to say the word as he signed it. When the sign movement and the mouth movement occurred at the same time, he could plainly say the word.

Not long after this process began, it became clear that Jake "knew" the printed patterns of many more concepts than this process could assess. In other words, he could "read" or recognize the visual patterns of many more words than he could sign or say. Even though no one had ever worked on letters or reading with him or had read to him, he had learned the shapes of the words much like the shapes of a puzzle. It was unclear where he had picked up the patterns. Within two semesters, this child's behavior looked very different than during the first week. He would walk directly to the room, sit down, and begin to sign and say every written pattern or word he could find.

A videotape showing Jake doing this process was presented at the American Speech and Hearing Association Convention to a room of about 300 people. The response by the crowd may be summarized by the comments of the lady who raised her hand and said, "This boy doesn't have autism. He is socially interacting — reading, writing, and talking." What this lady and others did not understand was that a child with ASD learns to be social (Chapter 3), learns to behave (Chapter 7), and learns to read, write, and talk through the visual meaning of shapes of ideas. Just like other children learn to be social, behave, and do academics with the spoken words paired with the written words, children with ASD will socialize and behave and read and write if we provide meaningful input that matches the way they learn language for thinking. Chapter 9 describes how motor overlap of patterns for visual conceptualization enables many children severely impacted by autism to speak.

How much a child with ASD understands depends on how much meaning we can provide by attaching patterns and concepts for visual cognition. The pattern is the motor movement of the hand or mouth making a shape of an idea and then attaching the visual patterns of an activity or event to create a concept that goes with the printed pattern. Once a child with ASD is able to see the shapes of words, he often has many more patterns than concepts for ideas. It becomes the educator's job to help attach the print of the pattern to concepts in context for visual concepts to be glued together with language. Once the child understands the concepts and has language to represent them, comprehension occurs. *A child's comprehension is as good as his language development.*

Activity: How does motor overlap of patterns create meaning conceptualization and subsequent language?

Angie, a 6-year-old female with autism, did not speak, read, or write. She did not draw, was not toilet trained, and the behavior program set up by her school only worked for repeated sequences of activities. If her schedule was exactly the same day after day, she followed the patterns of the sequence, but if people tried to engage her in any way other than the repetition of tasks, she did not behave well. For example, if Mom wanted to take her to the doctor or someone new came to the home, Angie screamed undifferentiated sounds (e.g., eeeeeeee) and kicked, bit, and scratched. When a typewriter was offered to her, she typed patterns of words that she saw – flamingo, Toyota, twinkle. These words were in context but without meaning, so the therapist paired hand-over-hand print and pictures to the typed words to create meaning. It soon became clear that Angie's comprehension of the patterns of words was greater than her understanding of the meaning of the words. Children with ASD may be able to recognize hundreds of patterns of printed words but have little meaning for them. *Creating the connection between these patterns and their concepts, and then putting the concepts into language for later understanding takes time.*

Even though it was difficult to determine how many patterns Jake could understand or how many patterns Angie could type, it was apparent that the meaning for these patterns was as good as we could provide the connection between the pattern and the concept. We had to provide the language for Jake and Angie to develop the meaning of the patterns to be able to comprehend or conceptualize the print. Language glues the patterns and concepts together for children with ASD (Lucas, 1976, 1977).

Writing to Read

Reading for a child with ASD is really writing and recognizing the patterns, and then pairing the shape of the written patterns with their concepts. The child then must be given ways to represent or use the concepts. The child has to use the concepts so that language represents the child's conceptualization. Several types of motor acts can represent the concepts; speaking, signing, and writing are the most common and therefore the most conventional. The following list summarizes the stages of reading up to this point.

1. Provide a context, either with an ADL or with an event-based picture (Arwood, 1985; Lucas, 1977).

2. Label or assign meaning to the activity by printing the labels on the picture or drawing the parts of the activity and putting the labels on the pictures (Arwood & McInroy, 1994).

3. Use hand-over-hand to point to the activity parts and to the specific words spoken with the picture (Arwood, 1985).

4. Use hand-over-hand for writing the labels on the picture or series of pictures that go with the ADL (Lucas, 1976).

Once the labels mark the specific ideas or concepts within the ADL or the picture, the labels are put into a picture dictionary (Arwood & Brown, 2002). Figure 8.3 showed how the entries in a picture dictionary might look. The shape of the idea replaces the individual letters and the child with ASD sees the shape as a puzzle piece of the bigger picture. The picture dictionary holds all of the pieces just like a box. The child can take the pieces out and rearrange them to make a new sentence. Bubbling of the words and writing the words in the picture dictionary requires a hand-over-hand methodology for most children who are learning to read and write. After the words are in the picture dictionary, they are put into sentences that go with drawings about the ADL or the event-based picture. Figure 8.16 shows the drawing of a story about a pictured event, the picture dictionary, and the writing for a very low level of language functioning or a very young child.

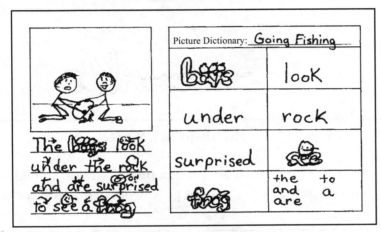

Figure 8.16. Writing for a Young Child.

Pictographs or iconic drawings are put with the bubbled words so that the patterns and concepts have meaning (Arwood & Unruh, 1997). Once the writing is complete – either by an adult-child hand-over-hand method or independently by the child – the adult uses the child's hand to point to what is written and either sign or say the word. By having the child tell what she wrote, the child is using her own speech or motor movements of the mouth to say what she writes. Sometimes, as previously described, by overlapping these motor patterns, the child's speech can become intelligible. (More about how to facilitate speech will be provided in Chapter 9 about learning to speak.)

By using this process, the child first reads words that are the shapes of patterns that label ADLs or an event-based picture by producing the shape of the printed idea and then saying the idea printed. The printed word is a pattern. The picture attached to the bubble of the printed word pairs the pattern and concept for language development. *Writing the ideas on the picture dictionary into a story creates visual language. Reading is the art of being able to understand the print of visual language.*

Activity: Why is writing so important in the process of learning to read for a child with a motor access to the visual language system?

Writing

The most important element in learning to be literate for children with ASD is writing. Writing is conventional! It is a motor process that can communicate with others. Writing shows a child the movements of the mouth and, when paired with the meaning or concept, the child learns concepts and improves cognitively. Writing can be taught much like a jigsaw puzzle. Each pattern is a shape that fits into the context. Even though pieces may have similar shapes, only one piece fits the context. So a child with ASD can learn to write the shapes.

To learn to write the shapes, most children with ASD need to be able to make the movement of the shape. For example, if the child wanted to write "twinkle," he needs to see the shape. To see the shape most children need to bubble the pattern in context. Figure 8.17 shows the written word "twinkle" in a bubble shape (Arwood & Brown, 2001; Arwood et al., 2005).

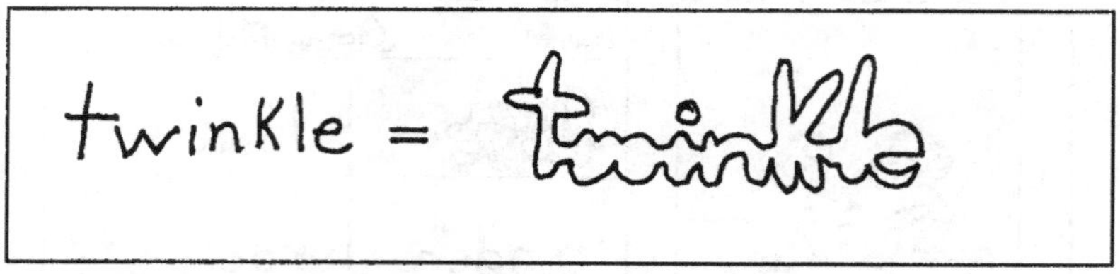

Figure 8.17. The Shape of a Written Idea.

The idea must be connected to an event such as "Glenda sings 'Twinkle, twinkle little star'." Better yet, the bubbling of words occurs as part of a story about people or agents within a context or an event.

Activity: What is the relationship between reading and writing for a child with ASD?

Speaking

Speech consists of acoustic-motor patterns, movement, and sound. Speech is without meaning. When these spoken patterns create meaning, it is because they represent language symbols. Language symbols represent the underlying concepts or ideas. The child's thinking or cognition is the same as the child's conceptualization. Without language, speech is meaningless. Working on speech without language also suggests that the time is spent on empty patterns. No matter how many vocal, spoken patterns a child can produce, the development of language is a different process. On the other hand, working on language so a child can produce the acoustic-motor patterns that represent his cognition results in speech. The next chapter describes how a child with ASD learns to speak and to use speech.

Activity: Why is speech without language meaningless?

Calculating

Learning to perform mathematic operations can occur at two levels of learning: the pattern level and/or the conceptual level (e.g., Countryman, 1992; Dethlefs, 1989; Hart, 1992). If a child is learning patterns only, she looks at the numbers and signs that represent operations and immediately provides a response. For example, 2+2=4 is a particular pattern. It does not represent two objects added with two more objects to result in a sum total of four objects; it is just a pattern. Some adults with ASD can fill in a whole page of college-level math like Calculus II based on patterns only, but with no conceptualization of what the patterns mean. A child can learn to perform math operations as a visual recognition of completing a pattern.

However, some children cannot physically see the numbers because there is not enough of the right type of sensory input to form visible patterns that have language attached. These children need the meaning or conceptualization of the math operations to be able to recognize the patterns. For example, one 8-year-old male screamed every time a sheet with numbers was placed in front of him. When he was told to just tell what he saw on the paper, he used a monotone, robot-like voice to call out random numbers. He knew that numbers were the answers but he could not *cognitively see* the numbers on the page. Language symbols name the patterns that one sees on a page. So, for example, if a person is looking at a number on a page, there is only a difference in the light points that he sees. To identify the differences in input as a pattern, the person has to be able to process the input as a pattern. Once the pattern is visible, a person can put a name, such as "5," to the pattern. Figure 8.18 shows this process.

Figure 8.18. The Child Does Not "See" the Numbers.

In this figure, the child does not really see the numbers, which is why his thought bubble is empty. The teacher asks for the numbers and the child spews back number names that are just speech patterns without concepts. The teacher then takes the child's hand and moves it to form the shape of the number "5." The child now has the motor pattern for "5" as a concept. What does "5" mean? The child does not know the concept yet. Figure 8.19 shows the child gaining the concept to go with the motor pattern.

Figure 8.19. Learning the Concepts of Numbers.

Once the motor patterns are paired with the concept or the meaning of "5," the child can begin to perform operations such as adding, subtracting, and so forth. Without the language or name of the number, such as "5," to go with the concept of quantity of the number, such as five pennies, many children cannot see the numerals or patterns on the page. Further, some children, even if they do see the numerals or patterns, do not know the label or name of the "number" because they do not have the language of the concept to associate with the pattern of what they see. For example, the child looks at the page and does not see anything that he can recognize; therefore, he has no name or language for the numbers on the page. But sometimes children can name the numbers (patterns) even though they do not know what the numeral or number "stands for" in terms of meaning. In such cases, they have speech patterns without language.

Hand-over-hand printing of the numbers helps develop the motor patterns but does not create the language meaning of the number. For example, the pattern "5" is paired with the number of fingers on a hand. Figure 8.20 shows how this pairing between pattern and concept or meaning might look for numbers.

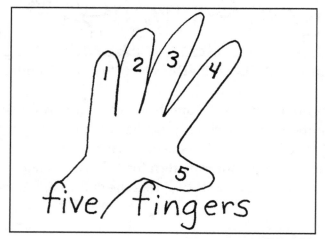

Figure 8.20. Learning the Language of Numbers.

Math should be considered a set of symbols – language – that, when written as an event, creates sufficient context to make the numbers come to life. For example, "Yesterday, I (I story) went to the bakery to buy some cookies for my family. In my family, there is my husband, my two daughters, my son, and me. Each of us wants a cookie to eat. How many cookies will I need to buy so that each of us has one cookie to eat?" Figure 8.21 shows how the problem is drawn out conceptually.

| one cookie | and | one cookie | and | one cookie | and | one cookie | and | one cookie | = five cookies |
| Dad | | Mom | | me | | sister | | brother | for the family |

Figure 8.21. The Language Event of Numbers.

Just as in the process of writing, the child with ASD may need to say the language of the written words of the math problem in order to create the overlap of visual motor patterns (hand, mouth, eyes) necessary to acquire the conceptual meaning of the numbers and operations.

Some children with ASD are able to translate the pictures of math concepts such as a hand with five fingers for the number 5. This ability is sometimes so fast that the child can calculate faster than most children can calculate using the numbers.

One child, age 7, was not allowed to stay in the first-grade classroom because he threw objects. However, with the assistance of one of the authors, he was allowed to re-enter. His first day back was also the day of a field trip for the students to collect Easter eggs that the high school students hid. The student was told to walk behind the others so he could watch their feet move. He was given g-signs (gestural signs) to guide him in watching the other children's feet. At the back of the line, he was able to follow the footsteps in front of him, carefully putting his feet down to exactly match what he saw. When the feet of the people in front of him stopped, he stopped. Once into the field, the children stood and waited for the egg hiding to stop. The author used g-signs and told the boy to watch the basket for the eggs. The children began to hunt eggs. He grabbed two eggs close by and put them into the basket as egg number one and two. Then he began to stare. With each additional egg that a child put into the basket, he would nod his head. Faster and faster the children came with their eggs. This child's head moved up and down once as his eyes focused on each egg. With the last egg, he proclaimed that there were 62 eggs, and he was right! Each head move matched the next number. Even though he had virtually no language, he had the ability to watch each child put an egg in the basket. His eye movements matched his head movements. Cognitively, he was counting the repetition of the pattern – someone putting an egg into the basket so that when the last egg went into the basket, he vocalized the last number, "62."

Activity: How does math represent the properties of language, a set of symbols?

Listening, Viewing, and Thinking

Reading, writing, speaking, and calculating provide a child with the symbol systems usually associated with literacy. However, there are other important cognitive processes – listening, viewing, and thinking. Typically, listening is a form of hearing sound that is meaningful. When a child hears a person say the child's name, she is to respond. This response tells the speaker that the child is listening. However, acoustic patterns have virtually no cognitive meaning, so a child with ASD does not typically respond to her own spoken name any better than to the sound of a squeaky door. These children do not make sound into meaningful concepts (see Chapter 3) but do make visual-motor patterns into meaningful concepts (Chapters 4 and 5). So, instead of listening, a child with ASD watches.

Watching does not mean that the child with ASD looks at the people and what they are doing. The child sees every little puzzle piece or shape that makes up a whole event. In fact, many children with ASD are so good at seeing the pieces that they cannot see how the trees make up a whole event. In other words, they can see everyone's shape, hair shapes, hand shapes, and so on, but they are not able to tell you why the people are in the room together. This means that *children with ASD view the world from seeing the pieces of the whole.* They have the sensory features of the patterns but not necessarily the concepts or the language for the concepts. Because they see the shapes or pieces, they also may have difficulty inferring the meaning or language from the whole, or picking out the significance of the whole. Thus, the child with ASD builds his language world from seeing the visual pieces put together into meaningful whole ideas. In other words, a child with ASD thinks in a form of visual language, a language in context (Chapter 5).

Since a child with ASD watches instead of listens, views the meaningful details and not the whole story, and sees the idea instead of hearing the spoken, oral language, strategies for cuing the child into the process of literacy must follow these abilities.

In an auditory setting (most classrooms and the way most education is set up in the United States), teachers and parents tell children to listen, to wait, to not interrupt when someone else is speaking, to take a turn, and to be quiet. All of these directives are auditory ways to try to make a child behave a certain way. But what does listening look like? What does waiting or turn taking look like? What do I *do* when I am not interrupting? How do I be quiet?

The auditory messages are easily given in an auditory culture. Everyone knows how to tell a child to listen. But if a child does not listen with sound, we must translate auditory messages such as "listen" into visual-motor messages (Arwood & Young, 2000; Arwood et al., 2005). For example, "Mike, watch my hand write the words on the board," "Mike, watch my lips move as I talk and make pictures of the lip movements in your head," or "Mike, watch the shapes my hand makes while I write." Even telling the child what to do when others are listening helps. "Mike, while the teacher moves her mouth to tell the students what to do, you are to make pictures of what she says in your head." Figure 8.22 shows Mike making pictures in his head for the activity of listening. This cartoon would be drawn in real time with the child watching the hand move (Arwood & Brown, 1999).

Figure 8.22. Learning to Listen.

Oral language should be visual and specific to what the child sees. For example, we often want to know how a child views the world, so we ask for feelings or thoughts. "Cara, how do you think Marla felt when you hit her?" Feelings equal the sensory level of learning, and emotions require language at the formal (11+ years with good language) level of learning, making it difficult for individuals with ASD to respond. However, a child with ASD can learn to see how her actions affect another person. The language might sound like this: "Cara, when your hand (point to hand) touched or hit Marla's face, we see Marla has tears. Marla's tears mean that your hand hurt her. When your hand hurts Marla, you "make" Marla cry." As you talk about the event, draw and point to the changes in Marla's facial postures.

Figure 8.23 shows an example of a drawing already completed that illustrates how to assign meaning to actions that hurt others. This type of drawing also shows what the meaning is for others' facial postures, tears, and so on. Whereas feelings are preoperational and emotions are formal, this type of language gives the rules for the concrete level of understanding, which connects the feelings and the emotions.

Figure 8.23. Learning Emotions.

As the child begins to replace hitting with more acceptable behaviors, it is important to also include the consequences of hitting. "Cara, see how Marla makes a face and thinks that you will hit her and she does not want to be with you? If Marla does not want to be with you, then she also does not want to play with you. If she does not want to play with you, then she does not want to be your friend. If you want Marla to play games with you on the playground or to play board games in the classroom, then you do not want to hit her. And if you don't hit her, then Marla will think you are her friend."

This type of oral language is oral cartooning, which we also call Mabel Mini-Lectures, and can be used on a one-to-one basis or with a whole classroom since most students in U.S. classrooms think in visual language (Arwood et al., 2005).

Many people think that these types of explanations are too long. However, the length of the information actually provides more concepts or meaning so that the child has sufficient meaning to make mental pictures for visual language comprehension. In this way, the child begins to view the world not just in terms of his own actions, but in terms of the effects of his actions on other people as well as the consequences of his actions on himself (Lucas, 1977). Thus, the child's thinking is also improved so that he functions at a higher cognitive level of development (Arwood et al., 2005). The more visual language the speaker utters, the clearer the child's pictures of what is said becomes. The faster these oral pictures overlap, the easier it is for the child to understand the speech acts. Oral assignment of meaning to what a child sees and does is rooted in how well the speaker provides language that overlaps (Arwood & Young, 2000). A child can comprehend and therefore listen to oral visual language.

Activity: How is listening related to the way the words are spoken?

Summary

Literacy is the development of learning to read, write, think, view, speak, listen, and calculate. Children with ASD learn these developmental products through a process of seeing the shapes of ideas from the movement of the hands, mouth, and body. As a child becomes more literate, her language and cognition increase and the child's behavior becomes more developmentally appropriate. Chapter 9 presents the complex process of learning to speak for children with ASD.

Concepts for Chapter 9

What is speech perception?

Why is speech difficult for some children with autism?

What is natural speech?

What is echolalic speech?

CHAPTER 9

Learning to Speak

Blah, blah, blah.
Don't you have anything to say?
I hear you, but you say nothing.
I speak, and no one understands.

Learner Outcomes: As a result of reading this chapter, the reader should be able to define speech, and explain how speech perception affects learning concepts and the relationship between speech and language. The learner should also be able to explain why language therapy is more important for a child with autism who does not talk.

Speech is a set of acoustic motor patterns used in the structure of oral language expression such as for English. These acoustic motor patterns are specific to those found in a learner's environment. For example, children hearing English speak in the patterns of English. The ability to produce such patterns lies within the anatomy and physiology of the human being. The ability to make these patterns meaningfully represents underlying concepts within the neurology of the human brain. The purpose of this chapter is to explain how speech is developed and why some children with ASD do not develop speech in a typical developmental way.

Definition of Speech

Speech consists of acoustic patterns or sounds arranged in a sequence. The sequence matches patterns spoken by others in the same environment. The patterns are learned by speakers as representing ideas or concepts. So, when a person says "cow" in an English-speaking culture, usually "cow" refers to the concept of a four-legged farm animal that gives milk. However, without the underlying meanings or concepts, spoken patterns are jargon and do not represent meaningful ideas. These jargon-like patterns are utterance acts but do not form speech acts. To be speech acts (Searle, 1969), the patterns must include the meaning of the concepts represented by the spoken patterns as well as the utterance act. In other words, a person cannot have "speech" as we know it without concepts representing language. But a person can make speech-like sounds or even produce utterance acts that "sound like" English without the underlying meaning of language. For example, a child might say "ga-ba-dat," and someone might interpret the utterance as "give me that." It is not really an English utterance act even though someone interprets the meaning. So the child in this example has utterance acts but not really speech. A child may also be able to produce speech without language. For example, a child might produce an exact replication of a sound pattern that he has previously heard. The child hears someone say, "She flew on a 747." Later, in a relevant or nonrelevant context, the child says "She flew on a 747." The child has speech, but because the utterance act lacks appropriate meaning, he doesn't have language.

Many children with ASD have difficulty developing acoustic-motor patterns and, therefore, do not develop "speech" without intensive intervention. Many children also have difficulty sorting the patterns to form the concepts for language acquisition. Some of these children can produce perfect speech but without the underlying language. These perfectly produced utterances represent the imitation of others' productions. Such imitation or echoed utterances, called echolalia, lack the underlying conceptualization or meaning of the utterances.

In order to learn "to speak" a language such as English, the child must not only be developing the concepts underlying the spoken utterances, but also be able to hear and speak the patterns of the language such as English. *Speech consists of acoustic patterns or utterances that represent the shared meanings of other communicators within the same culture.* So, if the primary language is English, most of the speakers raised in that community speak English. The speech represents the oral conventions of the language. Speech does not represent the way a person thinks. In other words, the child with ASD may be able to talk in English but not think in the constructs of English.

Since speech represents conceptual language, it makes sense to increase language before working on the properties of speech. Some children with ASD do not even develop the types of jargon utterances that some young children are able to develop. In these cases, it is often assumed that the child does not have the speech structures to produce the sound patterns or that she does not have the sounds of speech to string the produced sounds into words. The next section will discuss the anatomy needed for speaking.

Activity: What is speech?

Anatomy of Speech

The anatomy for speech consists of the trachea or windpipe for air to pass through the larynx. The larynx opens and closes to allow the air to move the laryngeal folds (larynx) so that the air waves are vibrated or phonated for sound. This pattern of air is then broken up by the articulators – teeth, lips, jaws, tongue, palates, and nose – in order to produce a variety of sounds. Figure 9.1 shows the phonation tube or resonator to produce the vibrations for sound, resonance, and the articulators for changing sound into specific speech elements. Formal types of content can also be drawn. Several university professors (e.g., Arwood et al., 2002) draw formal concepts in real time to help students to quickly understand how spoken concepts match the visual mental cognition.

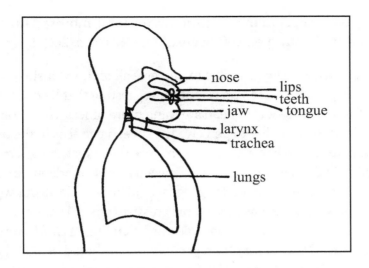

Figure 9.1. The Speech System.

The air from the lungs passes up the trachea through the larynx to the articulators. If the articulators move without the larynx vibrating, we get the shape of a sound but no sound. For example, put your lips together. Now open the lips and let a breath of air escape. There is air but no real sound. Now put your lips together and open up the lips as you say "bee." The shape of the mouth is the same, but the larynx is vibrating and there is sound. Put your hand on your neck near the "Adam's apple" and you will feel the vibration or production of sound called phonation.

The anatomy of the human vocal system produces vocalized and nonvocalized patterns. English is arranged so that there are consonant-vowel-consonant (CVC) patterns. The vowels always have sound or vibration when they are produced. The vowels carry the energy of the sound. Meanwhile consonants help produce differences in sounds such as /f/ and /p/ (International Phonetic Alphabet has one written sound for each produced sound). The /f/, as in the word "fish," is a consonant that is produced differently with the lips than /p/ as in the word "pish" for "pish-posh." The word sounds rhyme, but the words have different meanings. The different consonants "carry" the difference in meaning, or what is called discrimination, while the vowels carry the energy of the sound.

Activity: What is the anatomy of the speech system?

Speech Perception

Perception is part of the learning system. The learner receives the sensory input through the receptor organs, which accept information in the way they function. That is, the eyes accept light and movement whereas the ears accept the properties of sound (see Chapter 3). New input that is similar to past input forms a pattern of perception. These perceptual patterns continue to organize by inhibition of old patterns with integration of new input, ultimately creating concepts. *The way a child perceives speech determines how well she can produce sound for sound production.* It should be noted in this connection that speech refers to the acoustic-motor (oral-motor) patterns, not the content or ideas of the language produced with speech (Owens, Metz, & Haas, 2007).

A child who produces exactly what he hears is able to perceive all of the acoustic properties of sound for speech. The child hears a story that he later says verbatim, suggesting that he can perceive the sounds of the patterns of the story. The ability does not mean anything more or less. Imitation of speech production means that the child has the acoustic ability to perceive the speech patterns in the order and sequence produced and to repeat those patterns. When a child can produce these speech patterns, there is no reason to work on speech. The child has adequate production of speech as well as adequate speech perception. This child is missing language, not speech. Work on language would be beneficial, but work on saying words or phrases, or practicing parts of words such as present progressive tenses, is not necessary and will not ultimately make this child use oral language that is natural and functional. *A child who can imitate someone else's speech does not need speech therapy for sound production.* It should be noted in this connection that speech refers to the acoustic-motor (oral-motor) patterns, not the content or ideas of the language produced with speech (Owens, Metz, & Haas, 2007).

What if a child does not imitate speech patterns in any form and, therefore, is not developing speech? Does this child have adequate speech perception? Some people would argue that a child might be able to perceive the sounds and still not produce them. If this were the case, the child would develop normally in other areas. For example, the child would learn to do any task that was shown to her such as dressing, feeding, putting away toys, and toilet training. The child would also show normal social development such as gazing, turn taking, hugging, and so on. The child would understand the language of what is in her environment.

Unfortunately, this is not what we see with children with ASD. When children with ASD cannot develop speech patterns, it is usually not because they can perceive the sounds but just not produce the sound patterns. It is because they cannot perceive the sound and, therefore, cannot organize the sounds to form patterns of concepts. Therefore, speech work does not develop speech.

Instead of working on speech sounds and speech perception, the intervention should work on helping the child form concepts in a way that matches the child's learning system. Since sound is not forming patterns, another sensory system must be considered. Vision is the other distance sense. So does working on visual patterns that represent the meaning of concepts develop speech, an acoustic-motor form of production? The answer is a resounding "YES!"

Speech is an acoustic form of perception that is produced by the motor system. Speech production represents the underlying development of the conceptual system. Therefore, developing the concepts will help the child acquire the meaning to support the speech system. The more concepts the child develops, the more meaning the child has to understand what people say. If the concepts are developed through a motor set of patterns such as the hand movements of writing, the child's brain can record these movements as shapes, similar to the movements seen or produced on the mouth. Even though a child is not able to perceive the sound of speech, the child can learn to match written shapes to visual shapes of the mouth. The written words show a visual pattern that is motor produced (just like speech). So, when a child writes an idea, she can literally feel the shape of the written word matched to the meaning of the visual concept. In this way, she learns to say the motor pattern of speech through the motor pattern of the hand writing the ideas. So speech perception can be developed through writing. How to develop speech through writing will be discussed later in this chapter.

Speech Production

Learning to speak is like putting the finishing touches on an orchestral masterpiece. First there must be the individual pieces such as the ability to produce sounds, the ability to perceive the sounds that others produce, and the ability to know what the meaning is of the idea that one wants to produce. The brain orchestrates all of these individual pieces to produce speech. When a child can imitate acoustic patterns, she can produce speech and, therefore, does not need work on speech production. When a child with ASD doesn't produce the sounds, she needs to see the language of what others say. Again, the child does not need work with speech production as much as work on learning the patterns of the concepts for language purposes.

To produce speech means to learn the language of the sound patterns in a way that matches how the child learns concepts. So, if a child can't use the acoustic sensory input for speech, the visual-motor elements of writing should be used. Write everything the child sees, needs, uses, wants, desires, and so forth. Each written pattern is a diagram of what those movements on the mouth really say. In addition to writing everything so the child can see the spoken patterns, use the child's hand to produce the concepts. Hand-over-hand writing (introduced in Chapter 8) is like a map for how to make the hands speak the sound patterns. Every time the child's hand moves under the hand of the adult to produce a correct pattern of meaning, the child's learning system records the pattern of the idea. These motor movements of the hand are shapes that represent the concepts.

Children who learn the meaning of these visual-motor patterns are acquiring the language concepts. Figure 9.2 shows the process of speaking from learning to write.

Figure 9.2. Writing to Speak.

Learning to speak through the process of writing follows a set of principles based on Arwood's Language Learning Theory (Arwood, 1991). First, the adult shows the child the visual-motor pattern that represents an idea or concept, "basket," for example. Then the adult assists the child, usually hand-over-hand, in writing the pattern of the idea, which is a conceptual shape to the child. The child now matches the motor movement of the hand with the motor movement of the mouth along with the meaning of the concept, and the child's speech becomes intelligible. The speech is produced as a motor pattern connected to another motor pattern. For some children with ASD, the motor patterns must overlap exactly at the same time for the child's oral motor to be intelligible. In other words, if either the hand or the mouth moves before the other, the two motor patterns do not overlap neurologically to create the correct motor shape of the mouth. The correct motor shape of the word produces the sounds that we recognize as the word the child "should" say. Some children need many overlapping layers of motor patterns to acquire the acoustic motor patterns of speech.

An 8-year-old male, diagnosed with autism, did not speak. In order to develop speech the child needed many overlapping sets of motor patterns. The educator would draw out the events of each one-on-one session. The steps of the session included the following:

- Draw out what it looked like to sit down.

- Point to the elements of the event-based picture. Adult talks about it and draws each of the elements. Adult points to the drawn elements and tells the story.

- Use the picture dictionary (PD) to pattern the individual words of the picture story, they would …
    1. H/H (hand-over-hand) fingerspell a word
    2. H/H write the word in the PD box while the teacher finger spells the word
    3. H/H bubble around the word
    4. H/H pictograph the meaning above the word
    5. Point, sign (ASL) while saying the word
    6. Repeat these steps until all words in the story are on the picture dictionary.

- When all of the PD words are completed, use the words to write sentence(s) about the story:
    1. H/H finger spell the word
    2. H/H print the word on the line while the teacher finger spells the word
    3. H/H bubble around each word written
    4. H/H pictograph the meaning above each word
    5. Point, sign (ASL) as saying each word … this is where the speech begins.

- When the sentences or session is over (whichever comes first), point to each written word and say each word again and then review the events for the next session.

The story for the intervention was an event-based picture. The adult and child did a hand-over-hand pointing to the elements of the picture as the adult talked about a story with the constituents of "who," "what," "where," and "when." They also developed a picture dictionary (see Chapter 8), and the adult did a hand-in-hand fingerspelling of a word. (The adult used ASL fingerspelling as the shape of the word in the child's hand so the child could feel the motor movements of the letters.) Then, hand-in-hand, they wrote the word in a picture dictionary box while the teacher finger-spelled the word. Next, they, hand-over-hand, bubbled (see Chapter 8) the word and added a hand-over-hand pictograph. The teacher would then point and sign the meaning in ASL while saying the word. This process was repeated until all the words that went to the story of the event-based picture were complete in the picture dictionary.

When all of the picture dictionary words were completed, the adult helped the child use the words to write a sentence about the story. First the teacher, hand-over-hand, finger spelled the word to write. Then the teacher, hand-over-hand, printed the word on the line followed by another finger spelling by the teacher. They also hand-over-hand bubbled each word and pictographed the meaning (hand-over-hand) above each word. Then they read and signed the word as they read the sentence back. At this point, the child began to be able to say the words for which he had produced the motor patterns. His speech was perfectly clear. This boy had received speech therapy for several years without success. All his utterance acts prior to this intervention lacked sufficient articulation to be understood by a listener.

> ### *Activity: How does speech develop from writing?*

Speech Therapy

One of the first types of therapies that children diagnosed with autism often experience is speech therapy. Speech therapy is classically designed to produce speech. Since speech consists of motor-sound patterns, the speech therapist or speech and language pathologist (SLP) designs a lesson plan to work on these patterns. The SLP helps the child move the articulators (teeth, lips, jaws, palate) through the movements or in the manner necessary to produce sounds. Developmentally, the visible sounds such as /p/ and /b/ might first be practiced. The SLP shows the child how to put the lips together and blow and the child practices articulation exercises such as blowing bubbles or blowing through a straw so as to develop the manner of producing certain patterns of sound. The anticipated hierarchy of developing speech goes in this order: place of articulators along with manner or movements for sounds, sounds put together into words, words into phrases, phrases into sentences, and so on.

Unfortunately, adding all of the sounds of a language together into a developmental hierarchy does not produce language. As mentioned in an earlier chapter, language is not just a string of letters and sounds. *Language consists of symbols that represent the concepts or meanings of ideas.* So instead of offering speech therapy first to children with ASD, we need to concentrate on language therapy. Language therapy will provide the child with the meaning of ideas or concepts so that the acoustic-motor patterns or speech can represent the child's ideas or thoughts.

Some people argue that you have to understand a child's speech before you can work on language. This is a valid argument for someone, like an adult, who already shows a lot of language. But a child who is developing language through a learning system that must first create the concepts must be provided with intervention for language before speech.

In addition to sound production for better speech, there are other types of speech therapy such as therapy for fluency or voice or for swallowing. Most children with ASD do not need therapy for their vocal qualities until after they are speaking with lots of language, and many never need voice therapy. A few children who are on the high end of the spectrum demonstrate fluency issues. Again, developing the process of fluently writing also allows these children to be more fluent orally because of the motor connection of writing to their oral motor speech patterns. Some children with a gag reflex that prevents them from swallowing thicker textures of food receive some swallowing types of therapy. Sometimes this helps with the swallowing but without the language for eating, the child may still prefer pureed food. Once the child develops language about choosing different foods, preparing the food, and so on, the child will be able to swallow better so that thicker consistency is tolerated. Remember, *language is the highest cortical function, overriding lower sets of patterns or pattern production.*

Activity: Why would language therapy be more important than speech therapy for most children with ASD?

Speech Segmentation

In the development of the learning system, the sensory input forms overlapping patterns of perception. Perception allows the speaker to manipulate the sensory input. The input in speech is traditionally in the form of sounds. If the child hears the pattern "cake," she is supposed to be able to say "cake." Some children with ASD find it difficult to tell where one set of sounds begins and another set of sounds ends. The child hears a string of sounds that do not separate into sound patterns. This is much like a newborn baby who hears the strings of sounds but cannot tell who is talking or what is said. In fact, a newborn might hear a sentence like a string of undifferentiated sound "zhzhzhzhzhzhzhzhzhzh-zhzhzhzhzhzhzhzhzhzhzhzhzh." This noise is uninterrupted because all environmental sounds such as the buzz of lights are heard as equally important as speech patterns. Whereas most children learn to hear separate patterns, such as the difference between the washing machine noise and Grandpa's voice, some children with ASD cannot develop these differentiated patterns and, therefore, still hear sound as continuous white noise like the static on a radio that is not tuned to a station.

Children who are not able to separate out the sounds into patterns to form speech or to represent concepts of spoken language must learn to see the different patterns by using visual-motor types of strategies. For example, a child may not be able to hear where one idea begins and another ends, much like the preschooler who thinks the alphabet letters "l,m,n,o,p" are one idea. Therefore, learning what sets of sounds "stand for" or represent an idea is almost impossible. But seeing the ideas attached to their meanings *segments* one pattern from another. Figure 9.3 shows a picture drawn hand-over-hand with a child and then labeled.

Figure 9.3. Hand-over-Hand Picture.

This type of hand-over-hand drawing and labeling helps sort the spoken patterns into written patterns or motor shapes for visual concepts. Figure 9.4 shows how the child's first drawings develop meaning as the adult assigns meaning to the drawing.

Figure 9.4. The Words Represent the Concepts of the Drawing.

Figure 9.5 shows how the child scribbled hand-over-hand after he was told a story to a picture. This is one of the first steps of language intervention. The scribbling is a motoric conceptual representation of early concepts. These motor patterns can be modified to show meaningful concepts so that the child can learn language.

Figure 9.5. Child's Drawing.

The adult held the pencil and the child's hand as the adult assigned meaning orally. Hand-over-hand, the adult can shape the child's scribbles into forms that represent more meaning. To these drawn concepts the adult helps write the word forms, again hand-over-hand. The written label that is attached to the picture is the concept. This label, which is the language, is then put into a picture dictionary (see Figure 9.6), bubbled to form the shapes of the words hand-over-hand. Iconic pictures (icons are pictures that match the meaning of the word) are put on top of the words (see Figure 9.6) so that, once again, the concepts are matched to the patterns of the visual motor idea, or printed word.

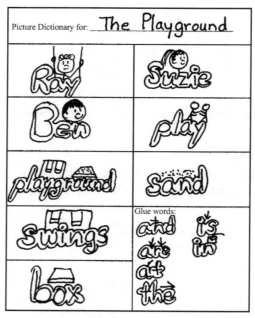

Figure 9.6. Picture Dictionary.

This process of creating motor patterns or shapes of ideas matched to the meaning of ideas helps children with ASD to begin to segment speech. *Segmentation of speech is the ability to hear the pattern that represents one idea from the pattern that represents another idea.* For example, the "boyis" is not one word but two words, "boy is." Once some children with ASD can *see* the strings of visual-motor patterns that match the meanings of the ideas, they can begin to pull out the sound patterns they hear and match those sound patterns to the written patterns. ***Writing is one of the fastest ways to help children with ASD develop speech.***

Sometimes older children with lots of acoustic-motor speech patterns talk a lot. But their talking is not always clear, and sometimes it seems clear or intelligible but then becomes unintelligible; for example, "She brought him some cake and then he left _____ and he so he stood and was like that." These unintelligible utterances occur when the speaker is not able to segment the sounds. An inability to segment occurs when the speaker is trying to produce an idea that is a little higher than his current language level. In the previous example, the child was trying to say that "the lady brought some cake, so he decided to take the cake to his homeroom where he could sit down and eat it." Even though this child talks a lot, the concepts he was trying to convey were very difficult. He was trying to express a situation that was not "black and white." The situation called for him to explain how the lady's behavior changed his behavior. That is, as a result of her actions, he did something that he normally doesn't do. This language is very complex in terms of time as the time elements are conditional. Children with ASD do not understand time as a conditional concept but as an event "marked" by the clock or a visual piece of the event. More about time concepts is found in a later chapter. Because this child wanted to talk about a conditional situation, his language production was too high for his ability to represent his ideas, so the form of his ideas became less conventional. In fact, he became unintelligible.

Another way to look at segmentation is to realize that a child can only process the elements of speech as well as he understands what the elements of speech stand for. That is, if the child has the language for the speech elements, his speech is much more intelligible. Production increases when the ideas are more meaningful to the speaker. The form of an idea, such as the sounds of speech, is more intelligible when the child understands the underlying meaning.

When a higher-end child with ASD becomes unintelligible or cannot write an idea, it is because his ideas are not clearly known to him. When a child with ASD writes all of the letters on top of each other without spaces, it shows that the child is writing patterns but doesn't know what the visual concept looks like. This is also a problem of segmentation. As soon as the word's written shape is paired with the meaning, many children with ASD are able to see the idea as a concept (see Figure 9.7).

Figure 9.7. Meaning Cleans up the Form of Writing.

When a child uses concepts for speech or writing, the patterns are no longer confusing. When the patterns are not confusing, the child separates one concept from another, and the patterns are automatically written and spoken as individual ideas. In other words, the child segments the patterns into concepts. The concepts do not overlap because the meanings are separate. Because the meanings are separate, the oral or written patterns are distinctly separate or clear. The child is able to separate concepts by meaning and patterns by concept. This process is different for a typical learner, who uses the spoken patterns to help establish the meaning of the concepts. Children with ASD do not typically use others' spoken patterns for meaning; instead, they use the visual motor patterns of shape and light to create concepts. In an auditory culture, the shape of writing concepts or the shape of speaking helps a child with ASD to learn.

Echolalia

Speech patterns that a child repeats with little or no meaning are echolalic in nature. Since speech patterns consist of acoustic-motor patterns, a child who repeats these patterns is generating a type of pattern that will not form language. As you probably remember from earlier chapters, acoustic-motor patterns do not form a type of language. So, increasing the number or quantity of echoed utterances will not assist a child with ASD in developing language.

Echolalia is different than normal spontaneous imitation. Many people hear a typical learner use a form of imitation known as "spontaneous imitation" around 2 to 3 years of age. This period of spontaneous imitation usually lasts from a day to about six months. This type of spontaneous imitation has a natural sound to it and a developmental quality specific to the child's level of language development. For example, an adult says, "Let's go see Daddy," and the 26-month typical learner might say, "Go see Daddy?" There is often a modification of the adult's language structures to a level of language that the child is comfortable with accompanied by a rising intonation at the end of the child's utterance. The language structures are not beyond the child's typical language level. But with a child with ASD who is able to repeat **exactly** what the child hears, there is little, if any, natural inflection.

With exact imitation or echolalia, the child is not processing the language of the utterance, so there is no reduction or naturalizing of the language structure to fit with the child's typical language level. Instead, the child produces the adult's language level with a lack of prosody or natural intonation. This type of repetition is not natural or spontaneous. Most spontaneous imitation in typical development does not continue for more than six months. If the child continues to repeat utterances longer than six months, the utterances begin to lose their natural sound and the child appears to be "cycling" patterns. This cycling of patterns results in other input not integrating to form concepts (Arwood, 1991). And, as we have seen, as long as sensory patterns do not form patterns of integrated and inhibited meaningfulness, concepts do not form.

Sometimes, as we have also seen, a child with ASD who produces some natural-sounding words and phrases continues to repeat longer utterances. As more repetition occurs, the few natural ideas begin to be replaced with even more echolalia. On the other hand, a child who has some echolalia who begins to produce more natural-sounding language begins to drop the echolalic utterances. This reciprocal relationship is important in planning speech intervention. Speech intervention that focuses on the natural properties of language rather than the spoken products results in more natural language and, therefore, more natural speech. On the other hand, speech therapy aimed at helping a child produce isolated sounds or words under an imitation format sometimes assist in making the child's speech more echoic. Such echolalia will take the place of natural language. Natural oral language provides a child with everyday functional speech. Chapter 10 discusses the development of natural language for better speech production.

> *Activity: Why does the imitation of speech patterns take the place of natural language acquisition?*

Summary

Speech is the result of having something to say; having a concept to express. Because speech represents concepts, speech intervention for children with ASD should focus on the properties of language. Language properties related to speech intervention for children and adults with ASD will be discussed in Chapter 10. Natural patterns of speech are acoustic-motor in nature and represent the underlying sensory properties of the way a child learns new concepts. Since children with ASD learn new concepts with visual-motor patterns, their visual concepts are in shapes with pictures, movies, multiple mental movies creating concepts for language production. Speech is an acoustic way of representing the visual concepts; therefore, the focus of "speech therapy" should be on creating visual mental language from the motor patterns of visual concepts, rather than on the production of speech sounds. In this way, language provides the foundation for more complex speech production.

SECTION THREE

Language-Based Learning Strategies: Strategies and Interventions for the Visual Brain

Chapter 10 – Communication Intervention and Strategies

Chapter 11 – Behavior Intervention

Chapter 12 – Behavior Support Through Language Strategies

Chapter 13 – Strategies for Creating and Organizing Space

Chapter 14 – Social Intervention Strategies

Chapter 15 – Family Intervention and Support

Concepts for Chapter 10

How does a person assign meaning to a behavior?

How does assigning meaning establish language?

Why does assigning meaning have to be in the form of patterns the child uses to learn concepts?

How does creating a sabotage of the environment help to assign meaning?

CHAPTER 10

Communication Intervention and Strategies

Every move, flip, twist of the body says something!

Every bonk, shake, hit, and spit shows something!

What I say and what I mean is for me to communicate,

And for you to interpret!

> ***Learner Outcomes:*** As a result of reading this chapter, the reader should be able to explain how to assign meaning as a communicative act for different levels of language function.

Communication is for the recipient to interpret. In other words, any behavior can communicate something if the person who sees the behavior wants to assign a meaning. For example, a child vomits. The adult says, "He doesn't like pudding. Every time, I give him pudding, he throws up." The adult assigns meaning to the child's behavior according to what the adult feels about *why* the child vomits. This interpretation of the child's behavior completes the communication act. The adult believes the child's behavior communicates the notion that the child does not like pudding. But the child may have had other meanings for the behavior such as "I don't like the texture of the pudding, but I like the flavor." Or the child may not like the way the adult puts the spoon in the child's mouth. Or perhaps the child is full. The child's intent to communicate depends on the meaning assigned to the child's behavior by the adult. To be communicatively competent the child must be able to interpret the adult's behavior as well.

Communication requires both the sender and the recipient in a reciprocal set of behaviors. The purpose of this chapter is to define communication as a set of acts between two or more people, to explain the role communication plays with individuals diagnosed with ASD, and to provide suggestions for ways to improve communication.

Assigning Meaning

When a person communicates an idea, the communicative act is as meaningful as the person who receives it and assigns meaning to it. Meaning occurs at several levels of learning: sensory, perceptual, conceptual, and language based. These four learning levels increase in complexity beginning with the lowest level, sensory input, and moving to the organized perceptual patterns that form concepts, and finally to the most complex level of language. A person may communicate and receive the meaning of another's communication act at any or all of these levels. For example, a child recognizes the streaming of light through the window and tries to catch the light in his fingers. The child's flicking of his fingers in front of his eyes can be interpreted at any one of the four levels. At the lowest level, *the sensory level*, the adult looks at the child's behavior and thinks that the child understands something about the sensory input. At *the perceptual level*, the adult says the child is having trouble seeing because the light is in the child's eyes. At *the conceptual level*, the adult says the child doesn't like the light. Finally, at *the language level*, the adult says the child wants you to move him to another part of the room that doesn't have light shining on him. This last level is powerful enough in meaning so that the interpretation becomes an expectation and, consequently, every time the child begins to flick his fingers, the caregivers move him.

The interpretation of the meaning of the child's behavior may or may not be at the child's level of understanding. For example, a preschool child suddenly tantrummed every time he was put down for a nap. The parents interpreted this behavior as meaning that the child did not want to take naps any more because he did not tantrum at night when he was put to bed. One day, about three months after the parents had quit putting the child down for a nap, he asked his mom, "Where did the ants go?" The mom asked him about the ants. After many questions, she figured out that during the summer they had been on a picnic and she had said "Watch out for the ants" as she showed him a line of ants headed toward their picnic blanket. A few days later, when she put the child down for a nap, he saw the stream of light coming through the edge of the curtains and thought that he needed to "watch out for the ants." His tantrum had to do with the ants getting on his face since the light fell in a stream down on his face. When the earth shifted and the sun no longer would shine through the edge of the curtain, the boy wanted to know where the ants were. The child had a perceptual meaning for the ants, not a conceptual or language level of meaning.

Any behavior, which is a series of acts, is a response to "some" level of meaning within the communicator's learning system. In the case of the child trying to use his fingers to catch the light, the child appears to be responding to the meaning of sensory input, the first level of meaning. Any additional meaning that the adult wants to assign to the child's behavior is a form of interpretation by the adult. From the previous examples, it is apparent that adults can interpret these nonverbal behaviors at any level of their knowledge or meaning. For example, the adult might say, "Oh, those photons streaming in on electromagnetic waves cannot be caught by the human hand." Or, "those small black insects moving toward our blanket are called ants and they want to eat our picnic sandwiches." The parent may even interpret her own language assignment of meaning by turning to someone watching this interplay of communication and add, "My child is fascinated with hands-on science." The parent feels that the child's various body responses to the environmental lights, sounds, and so on, are meaningful at an adult level of language. The parent is assigning language to the child's nonverbal behavior, language that the child has not yet developed.

Parents sometimes over-assign meaning to a child's behavior but that does not suggest that assigning meaning is not important. On the contrary, ***assigning meaning is very important to the process of communication.*** The child does something and then the adult assigns meaning. The child then does something in response to the assigned meaning, so the adult does something else. This dyadic process between the two parties continues with meaning being assigned after each other's actions. In this way, the child builds meaning from receiving feedback from the parent as well as others in his environment. The building of meaning helps the child build his learning system. The learning system is building sensory input to form more perceptual meanings that become conceptualized and then represented with language. This typical development of the learning system assumes that the child can learn from the adult's actions, spoken words, and so on. Unfortunately, the typical way of assigning meaning to a child to build his learning system does not work in the same way with a child with ASD.

Activity: Why is assigning meaning important to building a child's learning system?

Assigning Meaning to a Child with ASD

A child with ASD does not receive meaning from the same sensory patterns as a typical learner. Remember from the discussion in Chapter 3, a child with ASD learns concepts for language best from motor patterns, not the visual and spoken patterns usually given as communicative feedback. As a result of the difference in learning, a child with ASD does not benefit from some of the same types of assigned meanings as other children do. Furthermore, because the child with ASD does not acquire the concepts for language in the same way, caregivers must rethink the way they assign meaning to behavior.

Because the child with ASD does not learn the meaning of the typical nonverbal and verbal forms of communication, the communication often becomes one-directional. The child does an act and the adult interprets the action. The child does another act and the adult assigns meaning. In other words, for most children with ASD, the give-and-take interplay between the child and the adult does not naturally progress from sensory feedback to perceptual feedback to conceptual feedback, and eventually language feedback.

This lack of interplay becomes obvious at about 18-24 months when the child begins to produce unfamiliar types of behavior in an attempt to gain more meaning from sensory levels of communication acts. For example, the child with ASD *seems* to be developing normally. The child produces infant-like behaviors that the adult assigns meaning to, such as the child cries and the parent soothes the child by feeding her, giving her water, changing her diaper, and so on. The child's learning system for motor development is progressing. As the adult interacts with the child's motor system by carrying the child, feeding and diapering her, and so forth, the child begins to walk, respond to the parent's motor play, and even match some of the motor movements of the mouth to form behavior that the parent interprets as words. After all, this is the way learning systems develop. And because the child is so young, the parents are helping the child's motor system develop. For example, the infant is screaming so the parents pick him up and put him in a place where the child can see, but the child needs help sitting, exploring, and so on, so the parents provide hand-over-hand motor assistance. The child with ASD learns from these motor patterns of communication to sit, walk, and so on.

Unfortunately, for many children with ASD who are developing gross-motor acts, their learning systems are forming systems of concepts from the perceptual clusters of patterns. The early motor responses such as picking the child up in response to the child's physical needs developed the motor interplay. But by about 18-24 months, the child's motor movement or ability to walk away from the parent creates a need for communication interplay that is based on a distance input. Sound and sight allow for distance input but motor input does not allow distance input to be meaningful. The parent can show a child what to do – which is visual; and, in our auditory culture, the parent can tell the child what to do – which is sound given to what the child sees. Either showing or telling the child gives a verbal form of feedback that does not match the motor patterns needed by many children with ASD to acquire or learn concepts. ***Most children with ASD learn concepts from motor patterns not from acoustic-visual or oral language patterns.***

Typically, if a child is able to learn from verbal input, she develops the social concept of agency expressed by the child throwing a slight tantrum along with phrases such as "me do it." A child with ASD does not create this social concept of agency in this way (see Chapter 6), but begins to use more physical ways to communicate to the caregivers that he needs more, not less input. These physical ways to communicate are motor in nature, which should tell the adults that the child is using his motor system to communicate his learning. Unfortunately, adults tend to interpret the behaviors with a language level of meaning such as "The child is hitting."

Activity: What are the four levels of learning that also give four levels of behavior that can be interpreted as meaningful?

The child's use of physical behaviors communicates at a sensory level. Any physical nonconventional behavior tells us that the child needs more input, organized in a different way, to be able to make adequate meaning to communicate at the next level. In other words, we need to assign meaning in a way that helps the child learn at a more complex level. The following are sensory levels of meaning for children with ASD:

1. A child who physically pushes away from a parent's arms needs more meaning assigned to touch, so more pressure when touched actually helps. Hold the child in more of a fetal position up close to the chest as if swaddled. This type of swaddling allows the child to acquire more sensory input so that he receives additional physical stimulation. Remember that this child is not using language to express higher levels of complex cognition such as being able to say to the parent, "I don't want to be held." We are talking about the child who does not possess that more advanced level of learning. This is the child whose only form of communication is a reflexive type of motor response such as pushing away from the parent. Without additional input, the child will not move to those higher levels of communication (see Chapters 1-3 for how the child with autism learns best).

2. A child who screams or yells without words needs more language given in a motor pattern form, such as hand-over-hand fingerspelling, ASL signing in the hand, typing, hand-over-hand writing, and so on.

3. A child who scratches or pinches someone else or him/herself needs hand-over-hand writing and drawing to create more meaning for what to do with the hands.

4. A child who shuts out sound by holding her ears needs more meaning assigned to sounds through actions, consequences, drawing, words, etc.

5. A child who shuts out light by climbing under furniture needs more meaning assigned to the context about the activity, and so on.

6. A child who kicks off her shoes needs more meaning assigned to why she wears the shoes such as to go outdoors for a walk.

7. A child who is repeating a behavior (bonking, flicking, flipping, spinning, etc.) needs more conceptual meaning through layers of motor overlap (example in Chapters 8 and 9).

8. A child who throws toys needs more meaning about the activity such as, "You can raise your hand if you need help" (instead of throwing the toy).

9. A child who tears up all of the papers needs more meaning assigned to the papers and the activities using the papers ("when we tear up the paper, we make a mess that someone else has to clean up," etc.; or "you can ask for help with your juice" [instead of tearing up the paper]).

10. A child who spits out food needs more meaning for the foods so the foods have language assigned to them and are not purely a sensory experience.

The list could go on and on. The following points help us determine what is most meaningful and, therefore, provide some guidelines for assessment and intervention.

- **Assign more meaning by offering more of what a child doesn't appear to like and then check to see if the additional input adds meaning.** For example, the child says he doesn't like soup, but he does like meat and vegetables. Add more water to the meat and vegetables but don't call it soup. Remember, with a motor or physical response to sensory input, the adults are assigning the meaning of the child "liking" or "not liking" something. The more meaning that is assigned, the more the child is able to understand.

- **The child's response to sensory input tells us how the child learns.** If a child is able to walk, then the child's walking behavior tells the adult that the child can learn motor acts. So, the child should be able to develop motor acts commensurate with walking such as sign language or speech representing basic concepts. Or, if the oral language is not developing past a few sentences, phrases, or even words or just sounds, the child needs a non-distance way to learn concepts such as hand-over-hand writing rather than speaking (distance- and sound-based) for communication.

- **When a child responds to a sensory input, that input has meaning to the child.** For example, the child pushes away from the parent holding him. Holding the child had some meaning for the child or the child would not have pushed away. Assigning the meaning that the child doesn't want to be held would be assigning a meaning for a child with lots of language. Unless the child has sufficient language to be able to adequately protest, the parent or caregiver needs to assign meaning to the sensory level of pushing away. Sufficient language would sound something like this, "Mom, when you hold me like that I feel I am going to fall, so please hold me tighter or put me down so I don't have the feeling like I am going to fall out of your arms onto the kitchen floor." Since the child probably does not have that much language, assign the meaning that the child needs more touch, so firmly hold the child and assign as much verbal meaning to being held as possible. For example, the child pushes away and you pull the child closer and say, "Oh, you want a hug; let me hug you and tickle you and roll you into a ball," and so on. Increase the meaning so that the child has a choice of pushing away or not.

- **When you increase the meaning, use multiple modalities.** No child learns by one form of input, and children with ASD need motor input added to more motor input added to visual input, so the more you say, touch, physically move, draw, write, and so on, the more meaning the child will receive. For example, if the child begins to grab your neck, lean forward into the pulling. (The child can't pull your neck backward if you are leaning into the child.) Then hug the child and physically provide a lot of appropriate touch while saying "Oh, you want a hug. Let me hug you." Then you might want to show the communication with a hand-over-hand picture of how to give a hug. Figure 10.1 shows an example of drawing with the written words. Notice that we did not draw the behavior we did not want.

Figure 10.1. Giving a Meaningful Hug.

Chapter 11 explains why we assign meaning to the wanted behavior, not the unwanted behavior. You may also want to write hand-over-hand what the picture about hugging means. Remember the meaning is assigned in real time; that is, while you are drawing the picture. The figure here shows the final product.

- **Assign the meaning that you want**. Obviously, you don't know what the nonverbal behavior *really* means to the child, so assign a meaning that makes sense to you. Until the child can tell you with full language what she intends, you can assign any meaning you want. Let's say the child throws a toy. You take the child's hand and, using the child's hand like an instrument, you help the child pick up the toy and put the toy on the shelf while you assign verbal meaning such as, "Since you are through playing with your toy, we need to put the toy on the shelf so the toy is kept safe so that we can play with it the next time." This may seem like a lot of language, but the words in combinations form patterns for the child. Remember that a simple sentence such as "Put the toy on the shelf" may provide for a response such as the child putting the toy on the shelf, but this simple sentence will not create enough overlap for the child to learn the language concepts. In fact, for many children, this simple sentence only provides meaning for compliance when paired and trained as a stimulus. When spoken in a natural setting, the limited number of ideas in a simple sentence will not create a mental picture of the event and are, therefore, very difficult to understand. Thus, a simple sentence requires the listener to infer the meaning surrounding the sentence, making simple sentences more formal cognitively. For example, "Put the toy on the shelf" implies that the child knows how to put the toy on the shelf, which toy to put on the shelf, which shelf to put it on, when to put the toy up on the shelf, why the child should put the toy away, etc. But with more relational language, the child is able to gain more information, making the task easier. The child participates in the behavior of picking up the toy at the same time the adult speaks the language patterns. Again, for a child with ASD who is not developing spoken language, draw out what you did with the toy and hand-over-hand write the word patterns using the same complete language that will relate the picture with the spoken words. Figure 10.2 shows a picture that was produced in real time with the child and adult writing the words together.

John is through playing with the airplane.

John puts the plane away on the shelf to play with it later.

Figure 10.2. Helping Assign Meaning to a Child's Behavior.

- **Meaning is acquired through any motor act.** It does not matter if the child is watching your hands as you hand-over-hand help him write the words or draw the picture or physically carry the toy to a shelf. A child with ASD is able to quickly see all details because he has more patterns than concepts or language. When the adult assigns meaning by physically performing a motor act with the child, the child is acquiring a motor, spatial form of visual concepts or language (see Chapter 5). The child may be looking off into space as if he is not attending or he may close his eyes or even screech, but the motor acts do create meaning that is conceptual.

- **Appropriate meaning must continue to be assigned no matter what the child's response is.** For example, you take the back of a child's hand to write the words and the child pulls back. The child pulls back because taking her hand does not have enough meaning to conceptualize why you are "taking the hand." Hang on tight and continue to write the words. It is amazing how many children who initially pull back are reaching to take the adult's arm or hand within a few hours. Ian was a 6-year-old male who was undergoing testing for a possible diagnosis of autism. His parents reported normal development until he was 28 months old and then he began to regress. By the time Ian was 6, he was not toilet trained and avoided all kinds of people contact. In kindergarten he was allowed to roam the room. As long he was not physically hurting himself or anyone else, he was allowed to stay in the classroom. Whenever anyone tried to interact with him or expected anything of him, they received unwanted behaviors, screaming, hitting, biting, and so on. When the classroom routine changed, he often left the room so his parents would be called and he would go home where he was allowed to roam his house.

  Without "interference" from outside, Ian was not developing. People needed to assign meaning that would interfere with his perceptual routine so that he could gain new meaning and increase his understanding of his environment so that the repetitious patterns of a routine would yield to meaningful concepts of language. As long as everyone followed his lead, he did not learn. The first day of first grade was different. An adult trained in assigning meaning to children was volunteering in the room. She immediately began to take his hand and draw and write what everyone was doing and what he was expected to do. By lunch that morning, Ian was seeking out the volunteer. Without gaze or verbal requests, he would reach for her arm and manipulate her arm or hand to write with him. Ian began to learn concepts.

- **Assigned meaning should match the normal expectation.** For example, a child would respond to the music on a radio. So the caregivers used the radio to soothe the child. Whether the child was throwing a tantrum when fed or sitting in a corner flicking fingers, the adults would turn on the radio. However, listening to a radio does not have the appropriate meaning of how to eat or how to do an activity in the classroom. The child got bigger and more and more dependent on the presence of the radio. Instead of learning to develop new concepts and more flexible ways of acting, he showed less flexibility and more inappropriate behavior. Rather than giving the child the radio when he threw a tantrum during eating, the adults should have given him more meaning about "eating." The adults might have provided the child with meaning by hand-over-hand making choices of food or hand-over-hand food preparation or hand-over-hand drawing and writing about food preparation. Even if the child could only scribble while staring into space, the hand-over-hand patterns provide meaning spatially for visual concepts for language.

- **Meanings can be assigned in lots of different ways.** The more ways that meaning is assigned to a child's behavior, the more ways the child might be able to develop perceptual patterns that become concepts. For example, the child tears down a plant. The adult tells her about the plant, draws about what the child could do instead of tearing the plant, cartoons out what to do instead of tearing the plant, writes about it, makes a picture dictionary, then draws and writes hand-over-hand, and so on.

- **Be consistent!** Consistency refers to assigning meaning to *each* behavior. If the child wiggles a finger, assign meaning. If the child verbalizes, assign meaning! If the child cries, assign a meaning! For *each and every* behavior assign a meaning. That is consistency! Consistency is not assigning the same meaning to a behavior. For example, a child spits, so every time she spits, you say, "Don't spit!" This provides routine patterns of input that do not have more meaning than spitting. So, rather than stopping the behavior, the child is more likely to spit more (see Chapter 12). Instead of saying the same thing to the same behavior each time, consistency means assigning meaning each time. For example, "Ishmal, when you spit, you spit saliva. Saliva has germs in it, and those germs can make you sick," and so on. The next time Ishmal spits, then hand-over-hand draw the picture with the words of what is appropriate (see Figure 10.3).

Ishmal can spit into the toilet.

Figure 10.3. Meaning of Behavior Is Assigned Through Drawing.

Physically escort Ishmal to the toilet and show him how to spit into the toilet. Or redirect the spitting by taking a tissue and covering the child's mouth and assigning a meaning to the activity. Ishmal starts to spit and you grab the Kleenex and put it over his mouth and tell him he can spit into the tissue and, without any fanfare, immediately redirect him to the task that he was supposed to do before he started to spit.

In summary, assign meaning in multiple ways after every behavior and as often as possible for maximum consistency and learning. Assign meanings that make sense and are different for the same behavior. Use as many different motor patterns as possible such as hand-over-hand writing to go with drawings, speaking, physical redirection, and so on.

"Sabotaging" the Environment to Assign Meaning

For some children with ASD, "sabotaging" the environment actually creates social opportunities for communicating appropriately. Lucas (1977, 1980) provided a description of how to sabotage the child's environment in order to provide a variety of assigned meanings to everyday social contexts, especially for children functioning on the high end of the spectrum. Lucas and Hoag (1976) based their work on the theory of speech acts (Searle, 1969), which suggests that the speaker and hearer enter into a shared act. Lucas (1997) used the term "sabotage" to refer to what the adult has to do to change the environ-ment for the child to experience more opportunities for positive social interaction. By creating simple problems within the context of activities of daily living, the adult provides the child with positive feed-back on how to respond to certain situations in an appropriate way. This interaction becomes a model for the child to gain effective social functioning. (Chapter 13 provides a more thorough description of how to create a social context that functions for a child's intended meaning – pragmatics of language.)

The following section focuses on how to create appropriate changes in the context to provide opportuni-ties to assign meaning. These suggestions are especially useful for children who are acquiring language but are not always appropriate in the way they use language for communication. For example, the child has a lot of language but walks up to a teacher and asks her why she smells. The child is communicating in a way that offends the teacher. The child needs more meaning about what is an appropriate personal question to ask a teacher and what is not. The following is a list of ways to assign meaning to help a child acquire appropriate forms of communication by changing the context and the meaning of the context.

- **Assign a meaning that is different from what the child might expect.** For example, a child is standing posed over her coat waiting for you to put the coat on her. Instead of putting the coat on her, assign a new meaning. Say, "Oh, you want me to put the coat on" and then begin to struggle to pretend like you are putting on the coat. The child will respond! The response may or may not be appropriate, but any behavior gives you the opportunity to assign another meaning. Perhaps the child grabs for the coat and you say, "Oh, let me hang it up!" If the child's behavior is becoming more aggressive or escalating, then bail the child out by saying, "Oh, you want me to help you put on the coat ... say, help me!" *Any* behavior the child produces can be assigned a meaning to help the child complete the task. Immediately help the child put on the coat – that way you give the child no more opportunity to fuss. Using this approach, the child is given three messages: (a) Unless you tell me what you mean, I may not respond the way you want; (b) When you want someone to help with your coat, you can say "help me;" and (c) When you say and act in a way that is expected, you get your needs met.

- **Assign a meaning that may change from time to time.** Every time a 4-year-old has to take a bath, the child fusses about getting water on his face. The child might sound like this. "I don't want to take a bath. I get water on my face. I don't like water. I don't want to take a bath," etc., etc., etc. You could cartoon out getting ready for a bath, followed by cartooning taking a bath, and then cartoon out getting ready for bed after taking a bath with the written words that go with the cartoons (see Figure 10.4).

| Mary takes off her clothes before climbing into the tub to take a bath. | After Mary climbs into the tub, she sits down and begins to wash her body with a washcloth. | When Mary finishes washing, she steps out of the bath and dries off her body with a bath towel. | Once Mary dries off her body, she puts on her pajamas so she can walk to her room and then climb into bed. |

Figure 10.4. Getting Ready for Bed.

For some higher-functioning children, you could also assign a different meaning verbally. Here is the scenario: The child is fussing about getting water on his face. So, while the child is bathing, you take a wash rag with plenty of warm (non-soapy) water on it and rub it all over the child's face while laughing and saying, "Oh, you don't want a little water, so let's do lots of water ... feels so good." Then you can say, "Let's do that again!" You can even put water all over your own face. Be sure it is playful and not mean-spirited and that you are assigning a positive meaning to having water on the face. Swim instructors sometimes use this method to help children get used to water on the face. It is a game! When the child realizes that the sensation doesn't hurt and that a positive meaning is assigned to the sensation, then the child doesn't fuss about water on the face. In other situations, water on the face does not evoke a feeling of fear but of joy. It is all about how you assign the meaning.

- **Create needs for the child.** Many higher-functioning children can meet most of their daily needs by doing for themselves or relying on the structure of the day. For example, when presenting on this topic, the authors show a videotape of a nonverbal adolescent and how to be successful with therapy so that instead of yelling, pushing, scratching, and so on, the adolescent is gazing, completing activities, reaching for help, and beginning to use language choices. When this tape is shown, there is almost always one member of the audience who asks, "Did he act this way at home?" And the answer is, "No." At home, the environment provides a routine of structure that allows him to repeat the patterns of behavior so that there is never a need for him to act out. Therefore, there is never a need for him to change his behavior, for better or worse. In this way, the youth does not need to ask for help or initiate any type of relationship.

Remember that social competence is the ability to initiate and maintain healthy relationships. So, a child who can function to meet her own needs does not have the opportunity to need others.

A child's needs may be created through sabotaging the environment. The following examples of sabotage create the need to communicate with others. Take any object and turn it into something the child can't use unless he seeks help, such as turning the sleeves of a coat the wrong side out, taping the scissors closed, limiting the amount of drink put into a cup or the amount of food on a plate, turning the water off under the sink, emptying the ice tray, hiding a shoe, tying a shirt into a knot, and so on.

When these objects are sabotaged, be ready to assist the child who tries to use a given object. For example, a child goes to get a drink but there is no water coming out of the faucet. Stand right behind the child to talk him through the situation. "Oh, there isn't any water. (pause) I wonder what we need to do to turn the water on. (pause) Maybe we could ask Dad what we need to do. (pause) You could say to Dad, 'Will you help me turn the water on?' (pause) You could ask me, 'Mom, why isn't the water on'?" and so forth. Again, you are there to immediately solve the problem if the child's behavior becomes aggressive or escalates. It is okay for the child to try different solutions and to even ignore your utterances. It is okay to continue to give the child hints, cues to help solve the problem. It is okay to draw out what the solution might be. The purpose for the sabotage is to allow you to model ways to solve problems.

- **Repeat situations and provide alternative solutions.** For example, the child expects you to solve the problem. After giving many prompts and suggesting options for solutions such as asking dad or mom for help, you might have to say, "See, I turned off the water under the sink" as you reach down and turn the water back on and show the child that the water is running. The next time when you set up a situation so the water doesn't run, turn it off at a central location, not just under the sink. This creates the opportunity to once again go through a problem-solving process but with a variety of solutions. Other examples include looking for a key to open a door; finding missing information by asking others, looking on the web, going to the library, getting ready to do a task such as making a bed but not having any clean sheets, and so on.

Activity: How does sabotaging the child's environment help the child create the need for someone to assign meaning?

Assigning Meaning with Oral Language

Assigning meaning allows all behavior to become meaningful. By assigning multiple meanings to the same behavior, in multiple ways, in context, through the way a child learns, the child will develop the concepts for more cognition and ultimately the form of expression or language needed to represent the increase in cognition. Even though many children with ASD need a written, drawn way to understand communication, some children benefit by the adult using the specific elements of the way oral language functions, also known as speech acts. Since assigning meaning involves language, using the rules of how to perform specific speech acts helps set up the type of language that creates the mental visual pictures of the communication acts. Arwood (Lucas, 1977) did her dissertation on how to assign meaning with speech act rules (Searle, 1969) to create adequate meaning of communicative acts for children who were diagnosed with autism. These rules created the type of overlapping language needed to assign meaning to social, academic, and behavioral situations in a narrative form. When these communicative acts are put together with the properties of visual language (Chapter 5), the language sounds like this: "John, when you yell across the room, your mouth opens wide and your words fall out of your mouth filling the space of the room. When your words fill the space, you fill the space that others are in. Since the words fill the room, others' pictures go away and they can only see your words. Because their pictures go away, they cannot do their work. So, if you do not want your mouth to be open so the words fall out and fill everyone's space so their pictures go away and they can't do their work, you will want to raise your hand so the teacher can call on you." This type of assigning meaning is language-based and meets the needs of the communicator as well as the understanding of the listener. Furthermore, it provides a sequence of visual language (Arwood, 1991) that connects the child's behavior with the meaning of the communication of the behavior. Chapters 11 and 12 will make the function of behavior more meaningful.

Language that overlaps contextually to assign meaning to the child's behavior and what is expected of the child connects the child's understanding of his behavior to the meaning assigned by the adult. These types of assigned meanings can occur orally as shown in the previous paragraph, or they can be drawn as a cartoon (Arwood & Brown, 1999) or written. This type of language usage is richer and, therefore, gives the child more information than teaching specific rules of what the adult expects the child's behavior to be. Teaching the social rules from an adult's language level works for many students who are mildly impacted by autism or diagnosed with AS because they have enough language to interpret the adult's assignment of meaning at the language level. However, children who do not have the adult's level of language cannot interpret oral or written narratives about social, academic, or behavioral acts without the richer visual language (Arwood, 1991; Lucas, 1977) that matches the way children learn best. Oral language or drawn language that follows the speech act rules coupled with attention to creating visual language provides the necessary richness of meaning for all learners.

The following example was taken from a teacher who uses a language-based approach in her classroom. She assigns meaning to what the students do all day long by using speech acts with rich language.

Assigning Meaning by Using Speech Acts with Rich Language

After gym class the first-grade students can choose to get a drink of water from the water fountain in the hall before lining up by the wall to walk back to their classroom. As the students are getting ready, the teacher is busy discussing afternoon plans with a volunteer adult. Suddenly the teacher and the other adult hear a "thunk" and turn around to see one of the students, Lisa, with a look of surprise on her face, lying on the floor about a foot away from the first four students in line. The first person in line, Jeff, has a large grin on his face and a twinkle in his eye while the next three students in line have a look of "uh-oh-someone-is-going-to-get-in-trouble" and then turn and look directly at Jeff. The volunteer, Sally, immediately sizes up the situation, places her hands on her hips, puts on her "teacher face," and opens her mouth to begin scolding Jeff.

The teacher, Monica, also sizes up the situation, but instead of giving all of the attention to the victimizer, Jeff, she turns and looks knowingly at the volunteer to hold back for a moment and then focuses on the victim, Lisa, saying, *"Oh ... Lisa are you OK?"* Without giving Lisa time to respond, she continues to say, *"Here, let me help you up and give you a hug. Wow ... that must*

---

have hurt to be touched in such a way that you fell on the floor." As the teacher talks to Lisa, she puts her backside to Jeff so that he won't receive any attention from her, while continuing to hug Lisa and talk to her. The teacher explains to Lisa how to tell if someone is a friend or not. *"Lisa, someone who puts their hands on you so that you fall down is not a friend. A friend is someone who looks out for you and treats you nicely. A friend lets you stand beside them and respects you by not doing anything that would hurt you. Lisa, if I were you, I would look for a place in line where I can stand by a friend, someone who won't hurt me. I would want to stand by someone who greets me warmly, treats me nicely, and touches me gently ... someone who is a friend."*

As the teacher explains the relationships of friends and lining up and making good choices, she is talking loudly enough for Jeff and the other students at the front of the line to hear. When the teacher wonders out loud where Lisa could find a safe place in line to stand, the three students standing behind Jeff all step to one side or the other while keeping their arms close to their bodies so that they can make room for Lisa to stand by any one of them. As these students make space for Lisa, they are telling her with words and actions that they will treat her nicely, that they will look out for her and keep her safe, using some of the language that the teacher has just explained to the group. Meanwhile, no attention has been directed to Jeff, but because he was allowed to remain with the group, he has taken in the entire situation. He sees Lisa getting attention, he sees the boys next to him making room for Lisa by holding their arms tight to their bodies so that she has space, and he has heard the teacher's definition of "friend."

Jeff's face is now red with assumed embarrassment and he looks as though he were chastised, which he was not. He is very quiet and appears to be thinking. He, too, moves down so that Lisa has space in line and he is also holding his arms close to his body to make more space. However, by now, the teacher has already ushered Lisa into one of the spaces that was first made for her by the other boys in line while remarking to all of the students what great friends they are being by making sure that Lisa has space for her body and by treating her so nicely with their kind words requesting that she join them in line. The rest of the students are now in line and the group quietly and carefully walks down the hallway back to their classroom.

The teacher assigned oral language to the concepts of friends, being kind, being helpful, standing in line, and so on, without having to use negative types of language. This teacher also was using positive speech acts. She made several statements of information so that the students learned about how to stand and respect others. She made assertions to Lisa so that she would know the rules for how to expect to be treated. This assertion type of speech act was extremely important since Lisa has a history of emotional and physical abuse. By supporting Lisa, the teacher did not allow her to be objectified.

The teacher also made requests for help that showed students how to ask to find a safe place to stand. This last speech act helped all the students learn about how to create a positive environment for others. The children's behavior that followed this oral assignment of meaning provided great pictures for the students to remember how to look when waiting in line, when finding a place to stand in line, and in walking down the hallway.

> **Activity:** *Why does oral assigning of meaning need to be in a rich, visual form of language that creates mental pictures for the students?*

Summary

Communication consists of nonverbally as well as verbally assigning meaning to others' behaviors. The level at which you assign meaning should be dependent on the level of verbal language a child can produce to explain his intended meaning. If the child does not have the language to explain intended meanings, assign a variety of meanings in consistent ways to help develop his learning system. As the child begins to develop language, sabotage the environment so he has to use a variety of ways to communicate intended needs.

Concepts for Chapter 11

What is behavior modification?

What are some approaches to behavior modification?

How does social learning affect behavior?

How does cognitive learning affect behavior?

Behavior Intervention

I sit and say the names of the cards.

The tree is sitting.

The tree is green.

The green tree is sitting.

Why does this behavior not seem right?

Learner Outcomes: As a result of reading this chapter, the reader should be able to explain the contributions of the various approaches to dealing with behavior for a child diagnosed with ASD.

The first sign that a child may have autism is often recognizing that the child does not behave the way most children behave. A child with an ASD may not engage in social behavior that signals another person to interact. Or the child may repeat behaviors, be behaviorally aggressive, or even self-abusive. A child with ASD may perseverate on some behaviors such as spinning or repeating the exact words that others communicate. Chapter 7 discussed how children with ASD learn to behave appropriately. Chapter 9 provided an explanation of how children with ASD learn to speak, and Chapter 10 described how to provide children with ASD ways to communicate. The purpose of this chapter is to discuss how to treat the behavior of a child with ASD through various forms of intervention.

Behavior Modification

If a child is aggressive towards him- or herself or towards another human being, the first thing that most of us want to do is to modify the child's behavior. It is not okay to hurt someone! It is not okay to hit, bite, scratch, and so forth. The most effective way of modifying the behavior is through the use of principles of operant conditioning. Operant conditioning includes a set of methods that stem from a philosophy of behaviorism (e.g., see Walker et al., 2004). A behavior occurs, and then something happens. Whatever happens when the behavior occurs either increases the likelihood of the behavior happening again or stops the behavior from immediately happening again. If the response to the behavior increases the likelihood of the behavior occurring again, the response acts as a "reinforcer." If the response to the behavior stops the behavior from immediately happening again, the response is a "punisher." *The use of reinforcers increases the likelihood of a behavior occurring whereas punishers suppress a behavior from immediately occurring.*

For example, a child bites his hand, and as the child raises his hand to bite it, an adult says a sharp and louder-than-usual "No!" This parent's loud voice and words act as a punisher, and the child puts his hand down, at least for a short time. Punishers are good at briefly suppressing or stopping the behavior from occurring. Or a child may have his hands folded and resting on his lap and the teacher smiles and says, "Chuck, I am glad to see that you have your hands in your lap," or the adult might simply say, "Nice hands." If the child understands these words, the likelihood of increasing the time the child has his hands on his lap suggests that these words reinforced his hand-folding behavior.

The basic tenets of behaviorism suggest that you find a behavior you like and reinforce it and/or you find a behavior you don't like and punish it. Finding behaviors you like and doing something to increase the likelihood of them occurring again or eliminating the behaviors you don't like creates a chain of behaviors linked by reinforcers and/or punishers. This chain of events works well for children with enough language to understand the relationship between the punisher or reinforcer and the behavior. Basically, the child does something and the adult reinforces or punishes. The child's response provides the opportunity for the adult to respond again. Each behavior is in effect creating the opportunity for the occurrence of a reinforcer or punisher. This opportunity for an occurrence of a reinforcer or punisher is called a stimulus. For example, the child says, "tree" and points to a picture of a tree. The picture is a stimulus for the child to say "tree" and to point to tree. S represents stimulus and R represents the response. Given a Picture (S) ⟶ the Child points (R). The adult says yes or gives a smile or check. The adult's response (R) is a reinforcer (Rf) to increase the likelihood of the child pointing again the next time the picture is shown to the child.

$$S \longrightarrow R\ (RF) \longrightarrow R$$
Stimulus gets a response that is reinforced and increases the likelihood of response occurring again.

The child's pointing behavior and speaking behavior is assigned meaning by the adult such as "good." The adult's response of "good" suggests the child gave the adult's desired response to the picture stimulus. The child's spoken "tree" along with the pointing behavior to the picture is another stimulus for the adult's response, "good." In other words, whether it is the child responding to what the adult gave or the adult responding to the child's behavior, there is a series of stimuli followed by a series of responses. Each response is also a reinforcer or punisher for the continuation of the chain between stimuli and responses.

Activity: What is a stimulus? What is a reinforcer? What is a punisher? Give some examples of each.

All responses are stimuli for the next behavior or response. The adult's response of "good" is a stimulus for the child's next behavior. If, in response to "good," the child's behavior is more pointing to pictures of objects, then the "good" acts as a verbal reward that reinforces the behavior of folding hands. If the "good" does not lead to an increase of folding hands in the lap behavior, the spoken "good" is either neutral or a punisher. ***All rewards can become punishers and all punishers can become rewards.*** For example, a P.E. teacher passes out a sticker that says "I did my personal best" to one student each day. There are 60 students in each P.E. class. If one student is recognized for doing his or her personal best, what about the other students who felt they also did their personal best? For the students who did not receive the reward, the absence of the reward may be a punisher for trying to do your personal best when you do not receive recognition and someone else does. On the other hand, there may be students in the same class who see the sticker given to someone else as a reason to try harder. The absence of such a reward acts as a reinforcer for the students who try harder to do their personal best. Therefore, the same sticker becomes a reward for some students, a reinforcer for some, and a punisher for others.

The absence or removal of a reward that causes the likelihood of a behavior occurring again is called a ***negative reinforcer.*** Whether or not something is viewed as a reward, punisher, or reinforcer depends on the situation and the person. For example, a child draws a picture and then holds up the drawing for the adult to see. The adult says, "Good job." The child begins to cry. After some discussion, it turns out that the child wanted to show the adult that there were some crayons missing and that, therefore, the child could not color the picture the way he wanted. The adult's "good job" was meant as a verbal reward to reinforce the child's act of drawing, but from the child's perspective, the adult punished the child.

In order to try to make sure a response is a reward for increasing a desired behavior instead of being a punisher, follow these guidelines:

- **Pair the response of a reward with a specific behavior so that the response is a *discriminative stimulus* (SD).** A discriminative stimulus is very specific and, therefore, is meant to elicit a very specific response. For example, every time a child is shown a picture of a tree on a specific set of cards, the child is to say "tree." When the child says "tree," the adult says "good." The use of the specific card in a particular task means that when the child is shown the card, the card becomes a discriminative stimulus that only allows a specific response for a reward. However, just because the child says "tree" every time he sees the card does not mean that he will say "tree" when he sees a real tree.

Activity: Describe how to make a stimulus more discriminative.

- **Increase the value of rewards as the behavior occurs.** Rewards that do not increase the likelihood of a desired behavior do not have sufficient value, so the value of the reward should be increased if you want the behavior to occur more often. One option is to change from a nontangible to a tangible reward. For example, a verbal "good" may not mean enough to a child to motivate her to do the behavior again, so give her a sticker instead. But remember, the sticker will only work if the child has the need to have a sticker. ***The reward is valued only if there is a need.***

- **Use tangible rewards that have language value for most effectiveness.** Tangible rewards like stickers have language value. If a child collects stickers and has the language to want another sticker because the sticker represents how well he is doing, giving a sticker will work. The child has to be able to "say" or think in his head this type of language: "Gee, every time I do a job that the teacher wants, the teacher will give me a sticker. So, if I want a lot of stickers, then I keep doing what the teacher wants and I will keep getting stickers." In other words, these types of tangible rewards work best when the child is able to use lots of language to make the mental connection between a reward like a sticker and the task the teacher gives the reward for.

  It should be noted that there is a difference between reinforcement of a behavior that is linked to a response, such as a pigeon pecking a light for more food and a child being given a tangible reward such as a sticker for working on a task. The pigeon has no language but is being conditioned to operate on the light in order to get a basic need (hunger) met while the only way a child can connect the stickers to the work is through making a cognitive language connection that the two events are somehow connected. The pigeon's reward is actually a primary reinforcer, not a tangible reward. In other words, stickers do not reinforce work. The act of receiving a sticker is reinforcing IF the child makes the cognitive connection that positively increases the likelihood of doing the work because the child wants to please the sticker giver, wants to receive the stickers, likes the nonverbals of parents who smile when they see the stickers, and so on. There is no physical connection between stickers and doing the work unless a cognitive connection is made with language.

- **Increase the physical need for a reward to increase the personal value of a reward if the child does not have the language for the reward.** For example, a child who is thirsty may want water, so water could be a reward that would have a lot of strength or primary value. Primary reinforcers include drink, food, and sleep. Many educators use cereal, for example, to pair "sitting down" and "pointing to a card" behaviors together. The child sits and points to a card and the adult gives the child a piece of dry cereal or a taste of pureed cereal. *These primary reinforcers work well for accumulating behaviors that are basic to one's needs.*

  For example, many researchers have been able to show how children with ASD can sit during a task by pairing the sitting with a wanted primary reinforcer such as cereal or juice. Some programs may ask parents not to feed their child in the morning in order to be able to use primary reinforcers at school to help a child comply. In this way, the child is not overfed. The bottom line is that a wanted primary reinforcer is a powerful way to gain compliance of behaviors, but it may challenge some ethical and moral values if carried too far, such as depriving a child of sleep. Furthermore, there may be more cognitive ways of gaining compliance that also increase a child's thinking about the situation, which provides the child with empowered choices based on an increase in thinking and language.

  The purpose behind pairing a wanted behavior with a primary reinforcer has been to gain compliance and to stop the unwanted behaviors such as hitting, slapping, and so on (e.g., Lovaas, 1987).

  The child is given specific training that occurs through discrete trials of using a discriminative stimulus, also called a prompt, such as "Sit down," paired with a reinforcer that acts as a reward. As soon as the pairing of the wanted behavior with the reward does not happen, the child may go back to the same unwanted behaviors or more severe behaviors. For example, Arwood worked in several model programs where behaviorism principles were used to obtain desired physical behaviors such as appropriate sitting, standing, eating, and so on. Primary reinforcers always created more desired behaviors. But the same children with behavior controlled during discrete trials of paired stimulus and response acts often came to school and went into a free play room where they would exhibit a whole range of undesirable and inappropriate behaviors such as repetitive flapping of the arms, bonking the head with a tight fist, hitting objects and people, rocking the body back and forth, flipping objects around the room, biting objects and people, flicking light with fingers, and so on. Then someone would give a specific stimulus such as "Time for academics." The children who were under the control of the stimulus (SD), "Time for academics," would go and sit. Once sitting, each child would be *trained* using primary reinforcers to do a variety of tasks.

The process by which the children were trained to perform a variety of tasks was the same discrete pairing of stimuli with reinforcers. For example, a child is wandering around the room and using a closed fist to hit the side of his head or bonking. At first the child would be physically guided by the arm to a chair and assisted to sit. As soon as the child sat, the adult would give the child a primary reinforcer. Since the value of a primary reinforcer is based on need, the children would often be given a very small breakfast so that they would eat enough primary reinforcers to be full. As the children got bigger, the number of stimuli and paired activities increased.

Some people object to the notion that food is withheld and then used as a reinforcer because food should be paired with a physical need of hunger. When food is paired with the successful completion of a task, it rewards the task so that the child may need to eat whenever she does the task at a later time.

- **Pair wanted behaviors with reinforcers, such as discriminative stimuli with primary reinforcers (RF+), to obtain basic compliance behavior.** The more stimuli you pair, the more discriminative responses to the same RF+ you will notice. For example, you can get a child to sit and look at a variety of different objects drawn on cards and the child will give different words to the many different pictures all for the same RF+. In this way, the child's desirable behaviors are growing in number. Even though the behaviors are growing in number, the language for the meaning or conceptualization of the meaning of the cards may not be increasing, however.

Activity: Why does the pairing of a discriminative stimulus with a primary reinforcer increase the likelihood of specific behavior occurring?

- **Use many different objects and people for the stimulus.** At some point, parents and educators want the child to sit down when other people ask him to sit, with or without a reinforcer. One option is to have multiple people give the SD to reinforce the child when the child sits. The child's behavior in response to the SD is *generalized* to other people and to other settings. For example, a child from New York, Jimmy, came to Oregon for an evaluation. He walked into the clinic with his mother and father. They opened the door and the child fell through space (remember that when a child fills his space by grounding, the child looks like he is falling through space; see Chapter 6) as he bolted across the waiting room and into the work room where he saw a table and a chair, in the same visual form as the one he had in New York. He sat down and with an open hand began to slap the table. The clinician, who is trained in a behaviorism format, recognized his slap as "let's work" and went over to work with him. Mom immediately pulled out his activity cards and said, "He is ready to work." The child's slap was a discriminative stimulus for Mom. He was given a stack of paired cards on a ring. The educator or Jimmy could turn either card. On the left side the cards were all colors. On the right side, the cards were all objects. Jimmy would say the left card and then the right card (see Figure 11.1).

Figure 11.1. Paired Colors with Objects.
The picture cards on the left were in color. The card on the right was a black-and-white line drawing.

Some of the pairs made sense: "green tree," "yellow ball," or "blue water." Other pairings did not make sense: "black tree," "red girl," or "purple eye." From what we know about learning, the child is learning patterns (see Chapter 2 for a review of how a child learns). Jimmy could produce the name of the colors with more than 50 objects. He had more word patterns than a typical learner of language would have at 2 years of age when two-word utterances are expected. So, the clinician pulled out a picture of a boy and a girl playing ball together in an event (park context with others playing games). She pointed to the girl, but Jimmy began to rock and then to wring his hands. She said, "Say girl." Jimmy could imitate, so he said "girl." Jimmy did not know what the acoustic pattern of "girl" meant, he had just been trained with patterns. (It should be noted that his spoken patterns sounded artificial and lacking of meaning.)

Any behavior or skill can be analyzed and paired with a valuable reward so that it is reinforced and produced. A child expects a specific response on the part of the adult when the child produces a behavior under a specific condition. The child is trained through a form of conditioning that operates on these principles, also known as operant conditioning. So, desired behaviors can be paired with a reinforcer to obtain a behavior on command, but the same behaviors may not occur in a natural setting or under other circumstances, or show an underlying conceptual development.

Activity: What is operant conditioning?

Modification of behavior is relatively simple. Pair a need with a desired behavior, and every time the need is present, the wanted behavior will be present. The authors have 60 years of combined experience working with children with ASD, and they have seen children trained to do many, many types of skills and tasks. Many children who are trained to respond grow to be physically bigger and often more aggressive but still lack the natural development of speech, language, or conceptual understanding of behavior.

Language and cognition do not consist of developmental behaviors and skills and, therefore, function naturally, when not trained but acquired. Remember that language represents cognition, and cognition consists of concepts that are acquired. As educators we often look at the products of language such as the use of the concept "dog" as a developmental product, but, in reality, the use of "dog" is a neurobiological process of learning the concept, not being trained in the production of the concept. (See Chapters 3 and 4 for an explanation of the relationship between cognition and language.) Understanding how to do a behavior analysis or a task analysis helps us know when to use operant conditioning to produce desired behaviors that are trained. But training a child to produce desired behaviors in response to specific stimuli does not replace unwanted behavior with more language for more developed cognition for behavioral choices. *Learning to think and problem solve requires more than "training." Learning to think requires the acquisition of concepts, and being able to use the concepts requires the acquisition of language.*

> ## Activity: What is behavior modification?

Behavior Analysis

The key to effective behavior modification as described in the previous section is that the "trainer" is able to analyze behavior. To analyze behavior, the trainer must see the child's individual motor acts separate from any interpretation by an observer. For example, a child has an open hand and flails the arm. The arm lands on the adult. The adult interprets the behavior as "hitting." In a good analysis of the child's motor act, the adult will see that there are several movements: the open hand, the elbow bending backwards as the arm moves back toward the shoulder, the arm going forward, the hand landing on the shoulder. Figure 11.2 shows how these separate acts might look when cartooned.

| Hand is open. | Elbow is bent back. | As elbow is bent back, hand and forearm come back. | Arm's weight pulls arm forward, and hand lands on adult's shoulder. |

Figure 11.2. Acts Form a Behavior.

So, did the child in Figure 11.2 hit the adult? If the child hit the adult, the child would need this much language: "I see the adult. I can raise my hand and when I do I can swing my hand. And when I swing my hand so that it lands on the adult, then I will hit the adult. The adult will not like me to hit. Hitting a person hurts." For most children who don't have this much natural language, the child is really not hitting. But when the child's hand rests hard on the adult, the adult gives an immediate response that the child can see. The adult flinches with eyes open wide, which pairs the adult's reaction, a reinforcer, with the child's behavior, hitting.

The adult can see the child's movements as acts that form a behavior, which the adult interprets with language as "hitting." If the adult sees the motor acts as hitting, she must stop the behavior. To stop the behavior, the adult has to punish or oppress the unwanted behavior and/or reinforce a desired behavior that will ultimately be incompatible with hitting. However, the adult could see the behavior as unwanted movement rather than hitting. The choice is up to the adult. If the behavior is unskilled, the adult has the option to redirect the motor movement into something more meaningful.

One type of more meaningful motor act is hand-over-hand writing. For example, if the child is writing, the arms are not flailing. But what if the child doesn't speak and, therefore, doesn't read and doesn't write? Hand-over-hand writing assumes that the child does not have the ability to write her own language; that is why it is hand-over-hand. But the input of hand-over-hand movement does create meaning at a cognitive level, which punishing or reinforcing interpreted behaviors do not. Chapter 13 will discuss the spatial properties of writing being cognitive in development.

A good analyst of behavior can give a count of specific behaviors, under what conditions, and with what frequency (how often in a given time period), but a good analyst of behavior should also be able to see the conditions in terms of context. This means that behavior may need to be analyzed according to context.

Activity: What is meant by behavior analysis?

Ecological Approach to Behavior

Even in the strictest discrete trial of stimulus response, the trainer must consider the environment. Some researchers believe (e.g., U.S. Department of Health and Human Services, 1999) that the environment contributes greatly to psychosocial factors that influence whether or not a child is able to respond to specific stimuli. Unless the setting is very controlled by a strict stimulus-response pairing, such as a child sitting in a chair and pointing to pictures, the environment also provides input or stimuli. These outside stimuli could be the hum of the lights, the sounds of the feet of someone walking in another room, the tag on the neckline of the child's shirt, the smell of something cooking, and so on. So, understanding how behavior changes as the environment changes also gives support to understanding how to help a child with ASD. ***Examining how the behavior changes within a context or according to the environmental stimuli is part of an ecological approach to behavior analysis.***

Every time the input from the environment changes, the information the child receives through her learning system also changes. In a typical learning system, the ability to integrate these changing inputs allows the child to begin to conceptualize the environment. For example, a child hears a sound and recognizes the footsteps as his teacher's (conceptualization), so he doesn't need to jump up and run to the door trying to peer through the crack at the door's base "to see the sound." However, a child with ASD has difficulty conceptualizing sound, so he does jump up and goes to see what the sound is. A strict stimulus-response-controlled setting would not allow the child to jump up by keeping the child's chair within a confined space such as between the therapist's knees. In other words, if the child begins to move to stand up, the adult uses her knees to pull the chair toward her. The adult's knees around the chair keep the child from being able to stand up. The adult continues to "get smarter" because the adult is problem solving but the child's behavior kept under control does not make the child smarter. As a colleague once said to a group of students, "As long as I do the thinking and planning for our lessons, I will get smarter, but I thought you were here to 'get smarter.' If you want to 'get smarter,' you have to do the work." *Learning takes place in the learner's system, not in the teacher's learning system.*

From an ecological perspective, it is important to assign meaning to behavior in different contexts. So in the above example, when the child hears the person outside and begins to go to the door, the child is physically redirected and brought back to where information about what is heard is drawn and written about. If the child isn't ready to gain information from what he can't see, instead of drawing and writing about what the child hears, the adult adds meaning to what the present activity might be. For example, the child hears the sound and begins to stand. The adult physically assists the child into the chair and points to the food processor where the child is helping to fix lunch. The adult talks to the child as she puts her hand on the child's hand and tells the child to "mix up the food by pressing the button."

As the child acquires more meaning with each context, he is also able to move from situation to situation with enough meaning to override the outside input that was not originally integrated. Another way to say this: *Language assigns meaning to all input.* If input is meaningful, then concepts develop. Because the brain seeks out new information, not old information, the naming of concepts through language within each context makes the behavior meaningful. *Meaningful behavior replaces the undesired behavior.*

So, to make the ecological approach work well, the educator or parent must be able to see the individual movements of the child's body as acts (behaviorism) and then use the context to help assign meaning to random nonprocessed inputs (ecological). The child's learning system physically determines what the child can or cannot respond to (see Chapter 2).

Activity: How does the ecological approach to behavior provide replacement behaviors for undesired behaviors?

Physical Approach to Behavior

Chapter 2 described the learning system. The child's physical status includes the learning system and a set of biological structures that physically function according to the child's health status. Because this approach considers not only the status of the learning system but also the biological nature of the system, it is sometimes called the *biophysical approach to behavior.* The neurological system is central to receiving and processing input according to the homeostasis, or daily balance of the child's health.

In recent years, numerous studies (e.g., Aylward et al., 1999; Baron-Cohen et al., 1999; Courchesne et al., 2001; Osterhout & Holcomb, 1995; Piven, Arndt, Bailey, & Anderson, 1996; Piven, Saliva, Bailey, & Arndt, 1997) have attempted to determine differences in the body and brain of a child with ASD. As this research continues, more insight into physical differences will help educators and parents solve some of the mystery of working with children with ASD. In the meantime, specific differences in the brain such as enlargement in some areas may be a result of specific stimulation from use of the brain rather than biological differences. Researchers (e.g., Berard, 1993; Coch, 2002; McGuinness, 2005; McKay, 2001; Merzenich et al., 1993; Singh, 2004) continue to describe the way that processing in the brain may lead to better intervention practices. Many families and professionals try all sorts of health approaches in working with children with autism – some seem to work, at least for a while, others do not seem to work.

It is possible that we have a continuum of different physical bodies producing similar symptoms, which is why having a spectrum for diagnosis helps us understand some of the complex interaction between a child and his or her behavior. *One thing that educators and professionals have control over is how we assign meaning to differences in behavior that may be the result of biophysical differences in learning.*

Activity: How does the child's biophysical development affect behavior?

An 11-year-old child, significantly impacted by autism, scratched others as well as himself. As he grew bigger and older, he scratched deeper and harder. All sorts of behavior interventions using excellent behavior modification tools had not remedied the situation – reinforcers did not have long-lasting strength, and changing the schedule of reinforcement to increase his need for dependence on the reinforcer did not provide a safe way of dealing with scratching. He scratched whenever he could. Limiting access to his body by using gloves or restraints did not stop him from taking off the restraints or gloves and scratching himself or others who intervened.

When one of the authors was called in to consult, the paraprofessional aides (three of them), the two teachers, and the child looked like they had been dropped into a giant blackberry bush and had struggled to get out. The child did not talk, use sign language, gesture, read, write, type his ideas, or vocalize – he had no communication board or other form of expressing the input his learning system received except in nonverbal forms. Physically, his body kept bringing in sensory input but had no organized way of taking the input and forming concepts for organizing it.

The child's parent was in the health care field and had tried many different diets, creams, physical massage, and so on, to help the child's body not be so "irritated." With each new method and therapy, there was also some hope that the child would not be so aggressive. At home, the child did little scratching as he had a routine that he could follow where no new input would physically interfere. However, any time he was expected to respond to another person, he scratched.

As a consultant, the author saw the child's behavior as part of a context issue, as well as a physical issue. The child could walk, which means he could learn more than he could express since walking requires a lot of physical learning. And, because the child had no form of using his motor system to increase cognition (express the input as words, gestures, signs, typing, etc.), he had limited meaning for the background inputs of the contexts at school. The author began signing, drawing, writing, and even hand-over-hand drawing and writing. The author never was scratched. However, every time the author stepped back for the aides or teachers to try to assign meaning to the child's behavior or his context, he scratched them. He was using them as objects because they had been objectifying him. Another way of saying this: *If a child has no way to communicate what he sees, smells, hears, touches, or tastes, he has no way to appropriately respond to input.* Furthermore, the behavior of scratching was not the primary problem. Giving the child more assigned meaning so he can conceptualize his physical world was the solution to the scratching. Dealing with unwanted behaviors did not meet the child's internal physical learning needs. Assigning meaning to the child's world builds the child's brain for higher-order behaviors such as signing, gesturing, speaking, writing, drawing, and so on.

As long as this child's caregivers would assign conceptual meaning and use motor forms of assigned meaning such as hand-over-hand signing and pointing and writing, the child gazed at the adults, used spontaneous imitation to physically request needs, and changed behavior according to what they cartooned for him to do. His success was dependent on how the adults assigned meaning to his behavior. The adults had a choice: They could continue to work on his behavior or they could assign meaning to his behavior and give him the meaning of appropriate behaviors so that his physical body could make meaning out of the sensory input.

> **Activity: Why does assigning meaning to a child's unwanted behavior while adding new appropriate meaning help meet a child's biophysical needs?**

When an adult assigns meaning to a child's behavior so that the behavior is communicative and then gives appropriate ways to communicate other behaviors, a child's social as well as internal physical needs are met. Having an expectation of the child's behavior being communicative is the basis for a social contract approach. Social contract theory, as discussed below, provides the educator or parent with a way to balance assigning meaning and living with the behavior of a child with ASD. Social contract theory also suggests that the child's physical needs will result in behavior representative of the child's learning needs.

Social Contract Approach to Behavior

When the typical developmental expectation of a child is replaced with the diagnosis of ASD, parents and educators begin to look at intervention options. Living with aggressive or self-destructive behavior is not a viable option, so behavior therapy based on operant conditioning principles is often employed. But working on the behavior can only help change the behavior and build new behaviors. This type of deficit approach identifies the behaviors you want to change and then works on these deficit behaviors. In a deficit approach, the work is designed to eliminate the unwanted behavior, to "fix" the deficit, or eliminate the problem behavior. The deficit approach does not work on what the child needs to learn. It does not work on the child's strengths so that the child's physical and social needs begin to meet the child's learning language needs.

The child described in the previous section (we will call him Buddy) who scratched his caregivers had been in a program that used behavior modification principles to eliminate deficits. Specially trained adults had given him years of discrete trials of operant conditioning. He had had behaviors isolated as skills such as individual sounds for speech and then "remediated" through speech therapy. At one point in his development, he had been trained to respond with some signs (ASL) for basic needs. He had also been trained to point to identify pictures, he had been trained to imitate a list of sounds given to him by the speech therapist, and a special education teacher had provided him a communication board of pictures so that he could respond to discriminative stimuli. But the sum of all these parts of skills and behaviors did not add up to a child who socially interacted with others in an appropriate way. In fact, as Buddy became older and the individual parts did not become part of his repertoire, the parts were eliminated from his IEP. For example, he did not sign like others, so his hand movements were ignored. Staff no longer expected him to sign and didn't sign to him. He did not speak words, so speech therapists worked more on the movements of the mouth than the sounds. Eventually, he did not receive any speech therapy. He did not learn to read or write, so academics were dropped in favor of having him sort objects. He began to scratch, so his social goals were dropped and replaced by work on extinguishing aggressive behavior.

Social contract theory suggests that a child who demonstrates inappropriate behavior needs information about how to act as an agent, a person who does something. A baby who reaches for a bottle is treated like an agent by a parent who hands the bottle to the baby. The baby does something and the parent validates the child's power to make a request by handing her the bottle.

A child who scratches all the time is also an agent, who does a behavior that we don't like. For example, the paraprofessional reached for a picture of a pair of pants to put in front of Buddy and Buddy scratched her arm. Buddy had seen the picture many times before and had even carried out the act of putting on his pants in response to the picture at one time (matched behavior to pattern), but he lacked the language for the picture and, therefore, lacked conceptualization. His brain sought new information but the picture was old. As the para reached for the picture, Buddy's learning system saw the arm movements as new frames of input and since he could not tell her that he needed new input, could not sign or write his needs – the pictures in isolation did not express his needs – he acted on the arm by scratching it. The para grabbed his arms and held them while she physically wrestled to get his pants on him (forgetting the picture) and then quickly jumped back as she released his arms to avoid getting scratched again. Her words were isolated and punitive, "No, don't scratch." She provided no replacement behavior for what to do, and Buddy had no mental pictures for "no" or "don't."

Replacement behaviors include any behavior that takes the place of a wanted or unwanted behavior. For example, if a child scratches an adult and the adult teaches the child to hold a pencil to write, then the child cannot write and scratch at the same time. Writing is a replacement behavior for scratching. Or if a child is drumming on a desk with his hands and the teacher gives him a piece of paper and a pencil to draw with, then the child has a replacement behavior for drumming. The child cannot drum and draw at the same time. Replacement behaviors work best when they provide a more appropriate way to behave that is also giving the child more language and a more complex way to think.

In the aforementioned example, Buddy is being an agent in the only way he feels he can! He does something to the para, and she responds. He has her under stimulus control. She is responding to his stimulus, scratching. Likewise, the para (and others in Buddy's environment) acts on him (stimulus), and he responds by scratching more. His responses gain strength in intensity over time by scratching in more places on the body and deeper for more visible bleeding. The problem is that these scenarios increase scratching in a way that is replacing all of the caregivers' natural ways to communicate with Buddy. They are dealing with his behavior, not with Buddy. They treat his hands, not his mind. They are acting on his arms as objects. Buddy is literally being objectified. The irony is that a child with ASD has trouble with social development and, therefore, needs more opportunities to be treated as an agent and to become an agent. Buddy is getting older and bigger, and the more he is treated like an object with arms as instruments, the less he develops. Children like Buddy often show more regression in developmental behavior as they age.

Socially, for Buddy to become an agent and not just a set of arms that scratch, the caregivers must replace acting on him as a set of behaviors and begin to use his behavior to help him express his needs. Satisfying his needs then becomes *natural consequences.* Natural consequences are more sustaining and thus more powerful than any reinforcer, including primary reinforcers. ***A natural consequence occurs when there is a physical, internal change as a result of an act.*** For example, a child touches a hot stove and the child's hand pulls back as a reflex. The pairing of the reflex with what the child sees and hears (hot!) results in the child's learning system assigning conceptual meaning to the surface of the stove. Internally, when natural consequences occur, the child experiences permanent learning; that is, learning occurs within the cellular structures and among structures of the brain. Opportunities for a child to act as an agent in a variety of contexts allows him to develop the social concept of agency. The development of the concept of "agency" results in the development of more socially appropriate behavior.

Activity: Why is social contract theory a powerful approach to dealing with behavior?

Creating Opportunities for Learning

Learning is an active process. There must be a change in the cellular function in order for learning to occur. This change in cellular structure results in the memory of an event so that the child can recall and retrieve past acts (Agranoff, 1967, cited in Fields, 2005; Baylor College of Medicine, 2002; Fields, 2005; Hampson et al., 2004; Kotulak, 1997; Sprenger, 1999; West, 1997). A child's active learning system helps build concepts for language. Arwood's Language Learning Theory, which states that language is the product of the way a person receives sensory input and turns the sensory input into patterns that become systems of concepts (Chapters 1-5), explains how to use the various approaches for helping with the behavior of a child diagnosed with ASD.

For example, the child with ASD takes in the sensory input, which forms patterns, but the child is not able to use all of the sensory patterns for concept development. Specifically, as we have seen, most children with ASD use motor patterns to form visual concepts. Social concepts such as "agency" do not develop unless there are opportunities for the child to appropriately act as an agent with visual language meaning assigned to the child's motor acts. Since children with ASD use a lot of motor acts (movement) to create the shapes of patterns of ideas or concepts, agency can be developed by using hand-over-hand (motor set of patterns) drawing, writing, signing, typing, and so on, within the context.

An agent uses a variety of acts that represent typical learning behavior. For example, typical behaviors communicate a variety of needs such as requests for objects, requests for actions, assertions, denials, pretends, statements of information, and rule orders (Lucas, 1980). A child who scratches might be making requests, assertions, or even denials. The adult assigns oral meaning to the child's scratch, "Buddy, here you are sitting (as she talks, she is drawing a stick figure cartoon) with your bottom on the chair and you are looking at the paper where we are going to draw you thinking about putting on your pants" (see Figure 11.3).

Buddy is looking at the paper while I draw.

Here is the picture I drew of you putting on your pants.

Figure 11.3. Learning to Put on Pants.

As Buddy begins to reach for the para's arm, the pencil is put in his hand and the para hand-over-hand draws the picture again. By using his hand, Buddy is having the opportunity to act like an agent. Because the child can put on his pants and not scratch, the social contract between the adult and child is satisfied.

The social contract is met when the child acts in a way that is expected. When a child doesn't have the language to assign meaning to a behavior, the adult works the child physically and cognitively through a task. As the child completes the task with help, he is acting like an agent (putting on pants) and the action results in a natural consequence (wearing pants).

Pulling together what is known about behaviorism, learning theory, communicative needs or acts, contexts (ecological differences), and learning-language development helps establish a setting where the child works to meet the criteria of a social contract. For example, an adult expects a child to respond to pictures put in front of her with questions and behavioral compliance. But the child scratches the adult. There are now some intervention choices: (a) punish the behavior or (b) assign a different meaning to the behavior, such as "Oh, you want help with the pictures," and reach over, take the child's hand and have her draw, write, and/or sign what was expected so she knows what "asking for help" sounds like and looks like. This assignment of meaning may have to be accomplished hand-over-hand. Remember, the child may look like she is not attending but the hand-over-hand movement to create the shape of a help sign, or a written phrase such as

"I need some help," or what the picture of "asking for help" looks like, creates the shape of movements of ideas. Because the child is learning these concepts, her learning system is active, and the child is learning.

Learning is a socio-cognitive process, so assigning meaning to the child's behavior so the child is successful at completing a social contract increases the child's cognitive ability. More about how to assign meaning and complete these contracts using language will be offered in the next chapter.

Activity: How does a social contract help assign meaning to behavior?

Summary

An eclectic approach to behavior is the best developmental practice for children with ASD. Behaviorism provides training and tools for analyzing behavior. An ecological approach to eliminating unwanted behavior reminds us that the context affects the behavior as well. The child's physical status of health is also a reminder that the child's health represents how well the child's learning system functions. And finally, a social meaning needs to be assigned to the child's behavior, or the behavior will not be shaped into a form of agency. Agency means the child will be able to choose behaviors that affect learning. Learning is a permanent change in the cellular and neurological structures. Chapter 12 provides numerous examples of how to work a child through a social contract approach to learning how to behave appropriately while also discussing the social and cognitive needs of literacy.

Concepts for Chapter 12

What does pragmaticism mean with regard to behavior?

What are speech acts?

Why is studying language important for dealing with unwanted behavior?

How does language develop social behavior?

Behavior Support Through Language Strategies

I do what I see you tell me to do.

I behave as you show me how to behave.

I learn more when you use language with me.

I become socially competent with language-based behavior.

Learner Outcomes: As a result of reading this chapter, the reader should be able explain how to use various strategies for improving social and academic behavior through language-based intervention.

Chapter 11 provided an explanation for how unwanted behavior can be modified or assigned meaning. Modifying behavior and assigning meaning to the child's behavior are external ways of affecting the child's learning system. In essence, the previous chapter pulled together different philosophies about how to modify unwanted behavior into an eclectic approach that allows an interaction between learning and behavior. More succinctly stated, using behavior modification methods, any behavior can be modified, changed, or taught in a specified context. But whether or not a child *knows* when to use the behavior or *why* to use a behavior is a different challenge.

Cognitive choice about behavior is part of the process of becoming socially competent. Social competence is dependent on the child's level and use of language. This chapter will show the reader how to support behavior through language-based learning strategies using a social construct theoretical model coupled with pragmaticism (Arwood, 1983). The central premise behind this type of approach is that learning and behavior interact through the use of language for development of the whole child, and the development of the whole child is greater than the sum of the individual parts or skills.

Pragmaticism

Pragmaticism, a term coined in the 1800s by Charles S. Pierce, means that the "whole is greater than the parts." Current brain research (e.g., Bookheimer, 2004; Caine & Caine, 1994; Carruthers, 1996) supports the notion that the brain functions synergistically, or as a whole. Therefore, a brain-based approach to a child's behavior would involve understanding the synergy of a child's whole learning system. What is the synergy of the learning system with regard to how the brain functions?

Research on how a child acquires language suggests that the brain functions as a whole in the acquisition of language. Because language is the final product in the learning system, the child's use of language represents the way the child learns the underlying concepts (e.g., Diamond & Hopson, 1998; McQueen & Cutler, 2001) (see Chapters 2-5). As we have seen, learning a concept is a process of taking in sensory input that overlaps to create perceptual patterns that eventually overlap in the brain to form concepts. When the brain functions synergistically, it recognizes past input and inhibits the old input to allow new input to integrate with the old, for a higher function of the learning system. Every change in behavior shows how the underlying learning system works.

For example, an infant reaches out a hand and the parent puts a toy in the child's hand. The child takes the toy and puts it in his mouth. At this level of functioning, the infant does not know how to play with the toy but uses it for sensory stimulation. As the child acquires more information from physical and sensory experiences with this toy, other toys, others' actions, and so on, her brain begins to organize the perceptual patterns of experience into concepts. So, when the child reaches out and the adult hands her the toy, she takes it and sees that it is a concept, a truck, that she can push along the floor, put other toys in the back of the truck, and then pull the lever to dump the truck. Mom can even say, "Where is your dump truck?" and the child can go get the dump truck, not the logging truck.

With each level of input, the brain sorts old patterns from new patterns, layers the new patterns integrated with the old patterns, and creates a system of concepts that functions for higher-order behavior such as the ability to request, assert, inform, and so on. The child's behavior or play with the truck shows how much the child is learning about the objects, actions, and agents in her environment.

Activity: What does pragmaticism mean? How does this term relate to the way the learning system develops concepts?

The child's ability to learn is greater than the individual behaviors such as pointing to the objects, saying the names of the objects, imitating the functions of the objects, and so forth. *Learning is a cyclic process of inhibiting and integrating patterns to form concepts.* The concepts function for critical thinking and problem solving. The functioning of these concepts is greater than the sum of the individual skills or patterns such as naming objects, learning specific social rules, and so on (Arwood, 1983). Therefore, teaching the parts of a concept or teaching specific skills does not create a social way to choosing behavior. However, *learning the concepts allows the child to develop the language necessary to behave the way that society expects.*

Since behavior represents how the child's learning system is functioning, the more sophisticated the behavior, the better the learning. For example, a child who can make the choice to go home to do the expected chores rather than go with a friend to the mall, when the parents don't know about the latter, is learning a lot. The child's choice and subsequent behavior shows that his cognition and social behavior function at a level parallel to his development.

When the philosophy of pragmaticism is applied to children's language use, an evaluation of how well the child is using the language to learn can be made. And language, the mediator between behavior and learning, can be used to help the child make more conceptual choices about social behavior.

Activity: How do social choices represent cognitive changes in learning?

Behavior Representing Language

Language represents how well the child's learning system functions. Therefore, a child's behavior, which is a product of the learning system, represents how well the child understands concepts or is able to use language. When a child scratches, bites, or hits, she is communicating what she knows. She knows the relationship between what she does and the object she scratches. She does not know that she is scratching a person or agent and she does not have the language to tell you to assign a different meaning to this behavior. She does see the person pull back to keep from being scratched, and therefore realizes that she can act on the person like acting on an object. If the adult punishes the scratching, the child must use a different behavior to communicate. A different behavior may be hitting instead of scratching. Hitting isn't any better, so by behaving differently the child doesn't show any cognitive improvement for higher-order thinking or language.

Since behavior represents language, using the child's behavior for communicating concepts is important. For example, when the child's hand is held so that her scratching is replaced by pointing to what she wants, signing the words of a choice, or hand-over-hand writing what is occurring in the context, the child is producing (with assistance) a higher level of meaning or conceptualization that language represents.

The goal of changing behavior should always be to reach a higher level of communication that represents a higher level of language. As the child acquires more language through the motor overlap through physical assistance, his behavior also improves – the child will sign for help or write a request for help rather than scratch.

The authors have encountered several instances where children severely impacted by autism have begun to develop language through a visual-motor process such as writing and, therefore, dramatically changed their behavior. As a result of the dramatic improvement in behavior, diagnosticians questioned the original diagnosis. It should be noted that the diagnosis of autism is based on a lack of verbal ability coupled with stereotypical behaviors. Stereotypical behavior implies an understanding of patterns but not concepts. So, without concepts, the child lacks language. As soon as language begins to develop within a naturally functioning system (see Chapters 4 and 5), the natural language replaces the undesirable behaviors of scratching or hitting and the child no longer looks like a child severely impacted by autism. Furthermore, the natural behaviors replace the stereotypical behaviors.

When the stereotypical behaviors are eliminated by an increase of language, new meanings are assigned, and the child thinks differently because he is acquiring new concepts. For example, one child was always yawning, a simple need for oxygenation of the brain. In other words, the brain needs food! But the child's family and the child's psychiatrist along with the school's behavior specialist said that the boy suffered from fatigue and needed to arrive late to school (mid-morning) and limit most activities after school. When this 10-year-old came to an outside clinic for help, the educator explained through writing and drawing that his brain needed different input. (The educator labeled the different parts of the cortex and explained to him how he needed to use his temporal and parietal lobes along with his frontal lobes to do language tasks.) The educator explained to him that when he had to listen to learn, his brain was not getting enough stimulation. (The sensory input does not integrate, so it is a repetition of acoustic patterns that shuts down the brain activity.) She also pointed out that he had control over his brain. He could use a pencil and a piece of paper to keep his brain active by stimulating parts of the brain. His response was "Oh, I have control of my brain!" He told his family and others that he did not need to be tired, that he had control of his brain, and that he could use other strategies to learn. With knowledge about how he learns best, he was empowered to change his own behavior. His behavior represented his language.

> ### Activity: Why does explaining behavior in terms of the learning system help children change behavior?

Individuals diagnosed with ASD who have oral language may demonstrate a lack of specific types of concepts when they speak, read, or write. For example, an adolescent was seen taking a TV from a stranger's car. The author asked, "Did you steal the TV?" He emphatically said, "No!" So she asked, "Did you take the TV?" With less enthusiasm he said "No!" She then asked, "Did that hand (pointing to his right hand) pick up that TV (pointing to the TV)?" He solidly said, "Yes!"

The concept of "steal" requires that the adolescent has a language level high enough to understand others' perspectives. In other words, he has to realize that another person that he does not physically see bought the TV and put the TV in the car. This other person that he does not see has to be part of his cognitive picture. In other words, he has to be in the picture of the other person to understand the other person's perspective. Because he does not see the other person, he assumes the TV is there for him. Because he does not see himself but only his hands, the hands pick up the TV.

Furthermore, to understand the language concept of "steal," he would also have to understand that an interpretation of "wrongness" was implied. From his perspective he was not in the picture, only his hands were in the picture; therefore, he did not do anything wrong. He has heard that stealing is bad but he does not see himself as bad, so he could not steal. "Steal" is a language concept that involves implied and explicit semantic rules of a performative type of speech act. A performative act like steal is a concept that is bigger in meaning than the simple utterance of "steal." *Performatives represent multiple acts or behaviors with a single symbol.* Examples of other performatives include promise, vow, pledge, swear, lie, marry, or commit. When a person speaks these language symbols, he is creating an act greater than the spoken words perform. This young man's language level was not high enough to recognize the depth of the meaning of "steal." He knew that stealing was wrong, so he didn't steal, even though his hands took the TV.

He also did not see himself take the TV. In other words, he was not in his own mental picture of taking the TV so he did not take the TV. He only saw the lowest language level of the performative, the hands pick up the TV. His behavior shows how much he knows about the concept of "steal." He knows that to "steal" is bad and he is not bad. He knows that to steal is wrong and he didn't see himself steal so he didn't do anything wrong. He knows that the TV was not in someone else's hands and, therefore, no one else had the TV. His language and his behavior represent what he cognitively and socially learned. Behavior represents his language level of understanding a performative such as "steal." He understands a very low level of conceptual development.

In addition to performatives, other types of language concepts are difficult for individuals with ASD to understand, and therefore their behavior is often not well understood by others. For example, many individuals with high-end autism or AS lack an ability to use language for social development. On the other hand, if their behavior is separate from their language, they often become proficient at splinter skills such as reading, writing, and speaking but have major social issues. As their language development for social concepts is improved, so is their behavior.

For example, a 23-year-old male, Bill, with high academic skills was brought to one of the authors for help. He has tried to attend a couple of community colleges as well as some career or vocational classes, but is often asked to leave because he disrupts the class with his oral language, appears angry, and does not follow through with tasks or activities. When Bill talked, he had lots to say but his ideas were not connected. He would talk about the food court, about his family buying pizza, and the pizza he liked. As he moved his mouth, the motor acts changed his pictures, so his oral language jumped from one idea to the next.

When the author tried to have a conversation with Bill, he used a lot of advanced vocabulary and complete sentence structure but the author had to follow *his* flow of topics. His language sounded like this, "I like to go to the food court at Lloyd Center. My parents leave us sometimes and we get pizza. My sister and I don't like the same kind of pizza. She is a vegetarian and I, well, I like almost all meat combos, if you know what I mean." Upon questioning, the author found out that what he meant to say was that he likes to go to the food court so he can pick out a particular kind of food because at home his parents plan the meals. Sometimes when his parents leave Bill and his sister at home, they can order the type of pizza they want. In other words, the pizza had nothing to do with the food court. He could talk about the food court and he could talk about ordering pizza, but he could not compare the two situations. His language level of functioning referred to his "real-life" functioning and represented a socio-cognitive, preoperational level of language usage. At this level, everything he talks about is from his perspective. In order to compare the choices in a food court to the opportunity to choose a particular type of pizza when his parents were away from home, he needed to be able to use a higher function of language. Specifically, he needed to be able to talk about how the two situations were similar, a concrete task, not a preoperational task, as he was capable of.

Since Bill's language represents a preoperational socio-cognitive level of functioning, his other behavior would probably be at the same level. For example, when he was asked about why he gets angry in his classes, he said, "They are confusing." "What do you mean by confusing?" "Well, they don't tell me what I know." "Do you ask questions?" "I ask them to tell me what I know." "What if your teachers don't know what you know?" "What?" And then he went on to say, "They are just mean." "Bill, what is the meaning of the word 'confusing'?" "It means that I will have everything jumbled." "If your ideas are jumbled, then why are you angry at the teacher?" "'cuz' the teacher is the teacher." Bill could not take the teacher's perspective or realize that he is responsible for how he feels and how he acts. Because Bill, due to his AS, does not learn language from the acquisition of spoken concepts, his language level and, therefore, his socio-cognitive level, is not improving. He is involved in situations that require him to take more responsibility for his feelings and to problem solve the class assignments, but he cannot learn how to do this from oral language. His anger and the concomitant behaviors are getting worse.

To change Bill's understanding of the concepts so that his language and behavior improve, social rules were written with him. Figures 12.1-12.4 show a give-and-take, real conversation between Bill and his educator. Note that Bill is learning to "see" what others see in words that represent his behavior.

What are your plans for this weekend?

Mom
Dad +
sister? — Tonight I might go to Narnia with my
family. I'm going Christmas shopping for
cousins, aunts, uncles, and grandparents.

Tonight is Thursday... not part of the weekend...

When are you shopping... what day?

Saturday and if there's a midnight
showing of Narnia tonight then we'll
probably go to it that time.

Have fun!!!!!
I'm going to change topics now...

How does a person feel when they are
yelled at?

They feel bad or sad, maybe depressed.

Is that how your dad felt last night
when he came home after 6:30 and you
yelled at him for being late?

I have mainly no idea.

I do think you know. You wrote that people
feel bad or sad when they get yelled at and
you yell at your dad.

Maybe he felt bad or sad, but I think he
just got mad.

Figures 12.1-12.4 Learning Social Language Concepts Through Writing.

What made your dad mad?

I yelled at him because, he lied.

Oops... Thomas you are the son, the child, of your father. It is **not** your place to yell at him.

He always says like 6:30 and in his time that is 7:30 or 8:00.

Well, since you KNOW that 6:30 means 7:30 or 8:00 then plan for him to be home then. But you **don't** yell at him... any time for any reason.

When he says 6:30 he isn't sure how long his last project will take. He is a dedicated worker — that means he is responsible for doing all his work before he leaves. Sometimes **we**, workers, can't tell how long a project is going to take until we **do** the project. So we guess.

His trip home might run into problems too... If the traffic is slow, if there are lots of red lights, if he stops and does an errand, if there are too many people in line in front of him, if his car needs gas... he will be late getting home.

Do you know what a lie is? It is when someone gives false information to keep something a secret so they don't get into trouble.

Your dad is not telling lies. He is having trouble estimating time. That is not a lie.

He mostly always makes up lame excuses why he doesn't have to do something. When he wants popcorn when he watches television he demands someone else should get it and he whines about the lights being on when he's right next to the light switch.

Let's go through your ideas one by one... You think his reasons are lame excuses. His excuses are his reasons. It is his house you live in. He (and mom) worked hard, saved money, bought - repaired - keep up the house. You are a guest. You do not work, you do not pay bills, you do not have a right to live there. They allow you, a 23 year old, to be a guest in their house.

After he works hard all day to make money to pay the bills, to buy groceries, to take you to movies, to pay for your clothes, you can make him one bowl of popcorn a day. You leave on the lights — You can turn them off.

Your yelling at your dad is disrespectful. You are not his parent — you are not his boss — he is not the guest in the house. You are.

I don't like it when he procrastinates doing things he said he was going to do and then never does.

I understand but... it is his house and there fore he makes the rules. He can procrastinate in his own house.

As a guest, ~~====~~, you can move out if you don't like the rules.

The main reason right now is my trailer is over flowing and I'm ripping up old tiles so we can put down new lenoilium.

Then this is the rule. As long as you live in your parents home, you will have to follow their rules. They are the boss, not you. You never would tell your "boss" what to do, so ~~you~~ the rule is don't correct your parents,

If your mom has a problem with Dad she will deal with it. Not you.

After just three hours of using writing as a way to assign meaning to pictures and to "relate" concrete to formal concepts such as "respect," Bill's whole demeanor changed. At the end of the third one-hour session, he sat up taller and appeared to be part of the process. At the end, he looked at the author, shook her hand, and said, "Thank you for helping me. See you next time." This type of social behavior was *not* taught as splinter skills, but he had begun to take another person's perspective, so his behavior began to change to show the language development. *Behavior represents language.*

> *Activity: How does learning concepts about social development through the way a person learns best change other behaviors that may not be worked on directly?*

Language Concepts, Not Patterns, as the Goal

Language concepts are meaningful ideas that connect social and cognitive behavior. For example, a student reads out loud the print on a page. Reading out loud is a behavior. Moving the mouth in the shapes of the acoustic patterns of the visual words on the page is a set of behaviors that represent the patterns of print. Word calling requires recognition of visual patterns and the production of acoustic-motor patterns. But pattern repetition can be stereotypical and routine-like, something that individuals with ASD are quite capable of. Explaining the content of the material requires language. *Language positively influences social and cognitive development. Therefore, increasing language concepts, not patterns, should be the goal for educating individuals with ASD. Social development will parallel cognitive development when the emphasis is on language.*

> ## Activity: Why is language important in developing academic or cognitive behaviors?

An 11-year-old female, Keesha, diagnosed with high-functioning autism sought help with academic skills, specifically reading comprehension. Her oral reading was quite good, but she did not understand what she read for content. Furthermore, it was apparent from meeting with Keesha that she did not understand social relationships. She did not greet the educator, ask appropriate questions, or engage in behavior that showed that she was aware of someone else being in the room. For example, she might pick at a scab, wipe the pencils around inside her mouth, or play with her hair. Figure 12.5 shows her writing. She writes many ideas, but they are not specific to the story she read, a passage about a boy skiing.

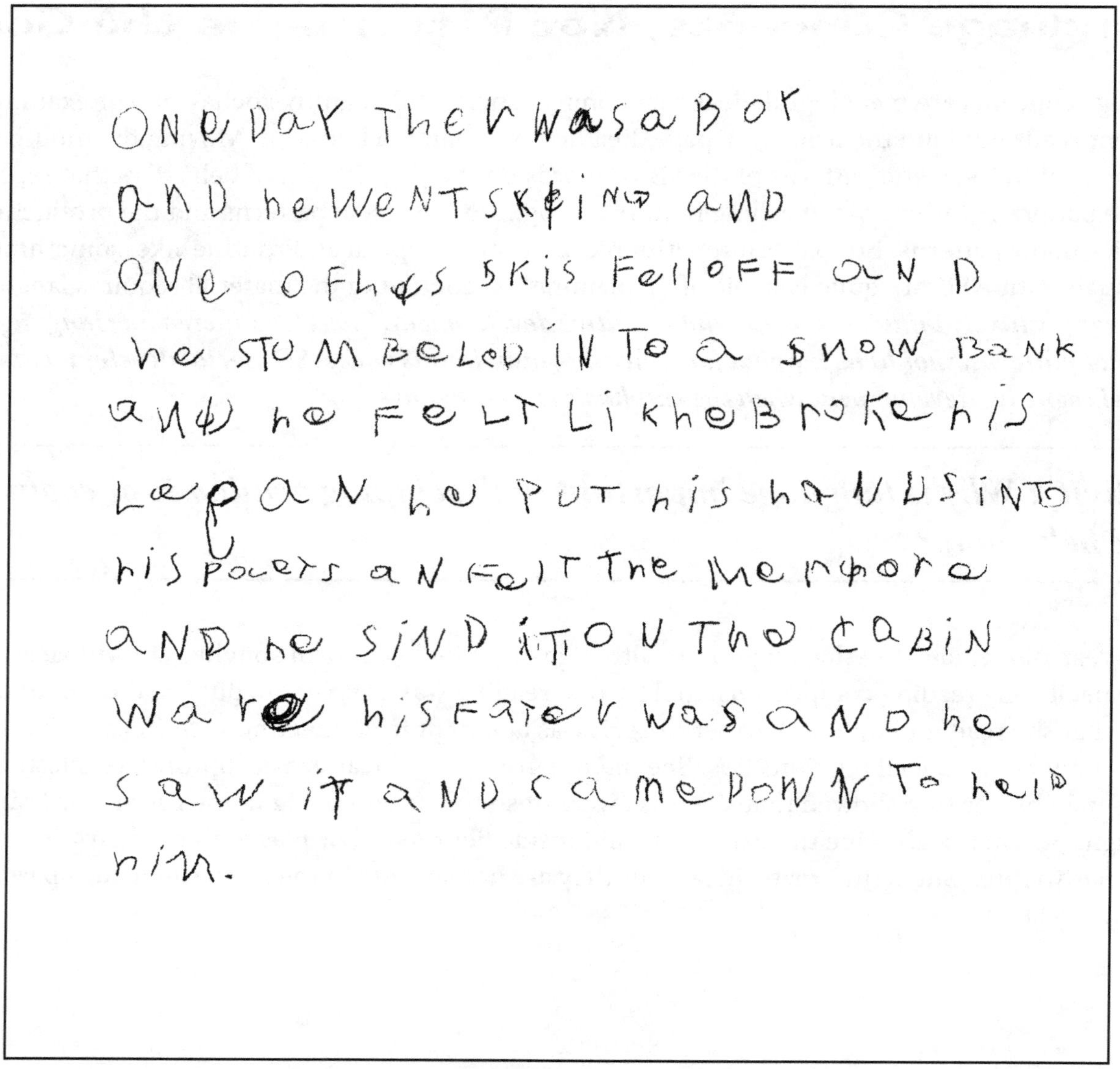

> ONE DAY THER WAS A BOY
> AND he WENT SKEING AND
> ONE OF Hes SKIS FellOFF AND
> he STUMBELeD INTO a SNOW Bank
> AND he FELT LiKheBroKe his
> Leg AN he PUT his hANDS INTO
> his Pocers aN FelT The Mepora
> AND he SiND iT ON The CABIN
> WARe his FATer was AND he
> SAW iT AND CAME DOWN To helP
> him.

Figure 12.5. Writing About the Reading.

Her writing showed that Keesha could read the passage but had no idea of what the passage was about. So, the educator asked her to draw her ideas and then write out the meaning of her drawings. Figure 12.6 shows her writing to her drawing.

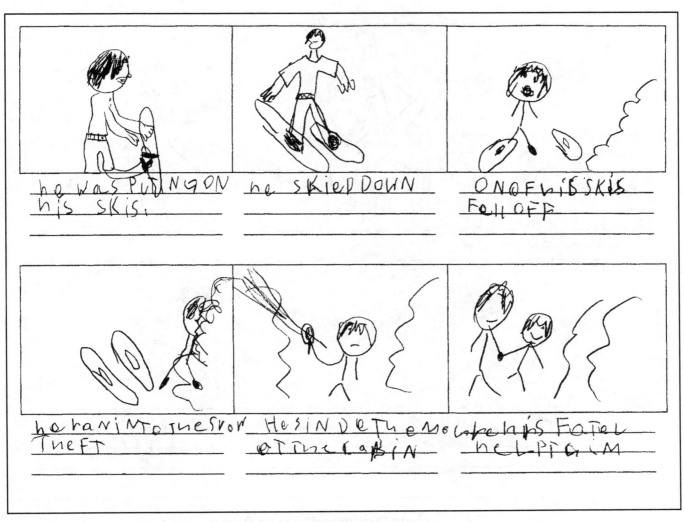

he was puttingon his skis.

he skied down

one of his skis fell off

he ran into the snow theft

He sinde theno of the cabin

(perhaps) fatel helpfigim

Figure 12.6. Writing to the Pictures.

The drawings are concepts. The patterns of writing do not match well with the drawings, which suggests the student does not know what the patterns of words mean when she reads. Figure 12.7 shows Keesha's first drawing after therapy began and her educator helped her match the drawing or concepts to the patterns or writing. Notice the refinement in drawing and how the language in the first frame is refined.

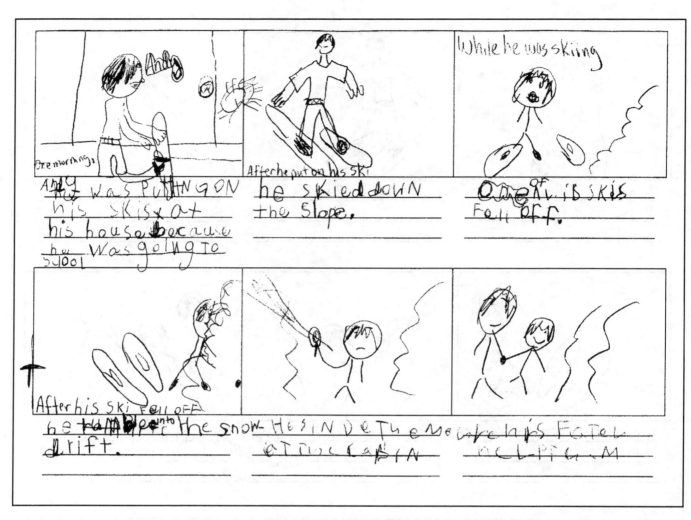

Figure 12.7a. Matching Writing Patterns to Drawn Concepts.

Keesha does not spell well (an auditory task consisting of acoustic and visual patterns) and her understanding is very simplistic. Figure 12.7b shows work on a picture dictionary to increase the meaning of the concepts while refining which patterns go with the concepts.

Figure 12.7b. Picture Dictionary Work to Increase Concept Development.

Since learning is a synergistic process, combining all the products into the goal of increasing language should improve the way Keesha behaves, as well as increase her language for academic skills. She has to be given the rules for using her learning system in order to have the cognitive tools to change her behavior. The rules for her work were written out so she could see the meaning of the spoken words. Figure 12.8 shows the written rules for her academic work.

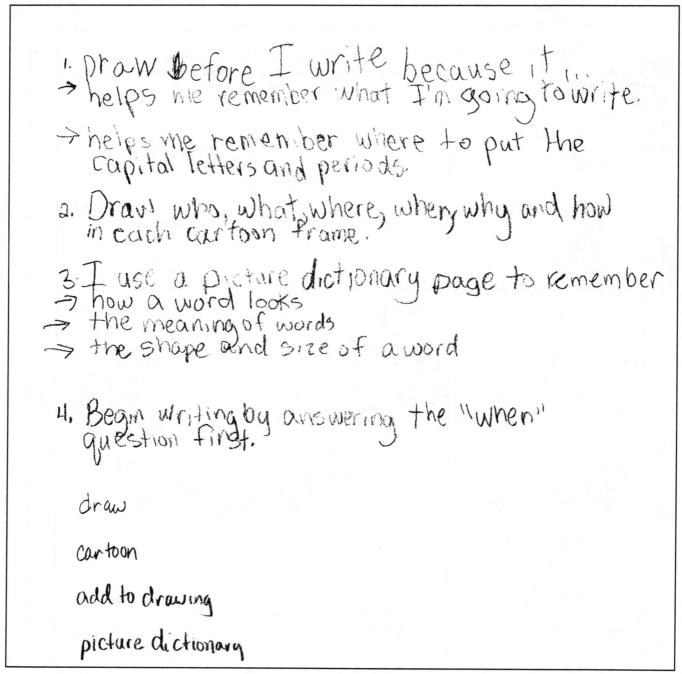

1. Draw before I write because it...
→ helps me remember what I'm going to write.

→ helps me remember where to put the capital letters and periods.

2. Draw who, what, where, when, why and how in each cartoon frame.

3. I use a picture dictionary page to remember
→ how a word looks
→ the meaning of words
→ the shape and size of a word

4. Begin writing by answering the "when" question first.

draw

cartoon

add to drawing

picture dictionary

Figure 12.8. Rules for Work.

These rules are strategies delivered in the way Keesha learns; in other words, in the way that she processes sensory patterns (overlapped motor patterns form visual mental concepts) so that she can develop the language for her academic behavior. This same type of emphasis on how she learns language concepts for teaching her reading, writing, math, and social products continues. Figures 12.9-12.12 show that she is also learning about the social aspect of behavior, not just academic behavior, and that there are social rules that she has missed because social rules are usually taught in a spoken auditory way. Note that most of this work was generated as a written (overlap motor patterns) conversation. It also should be noted that this educator is very honest and very assertive in her communication. This type of communication is the most healthy form of communication (Adler & Towne, 2002). Educators often shy away from being confrontational or exact in their language. This results in not being direct and, therefore, giving mixed messages. For example, the educator tells Keesha that when she does not come to school, the teacher "has to waste her time later teaching [her] what the others came to school to learn." This may seem a harsh statement, but it is in a context of why Keesha has a responsibility for going to school and it is honest ... the teacher will use time that she could have spent on something else, which is a waste of the teacher's time. She does not say that Keesha is a waste of her time, nor does she say that teaching is a waste of time, she simply lets Keesha know that her staying home affects other people and why staying at home affects others.

It is amazing how much more bonding individuals like Keesha do with people who are honest. As one adult told one of the authors, "I do so much better with people who are not clouded." Arwood asked her, "What do you mean by 'clouded'?" She explained, "Well, people smile, but their words don't. They use words that aren't honest. I would rather have someone be honest than have someone smile." As you read Keesha's interaction with the adult, keep in mind that the tone is one of honesty and caring about what Keesha really understands and how to help her function better in the real world where smiles don't always say what needs to be said.

①

When you put your fingers in your mouth
what are you ALSO putting in your mouth?

germs

What do germs do after they get in your mouth?

They s̶l̶i̶f̶f̶e̶d̶ (spread) ... where?

inTo your Blood and your Mouth

You put your fingers (and germs) in to your mouth
and the germs spread in to my blood and mouth?

I see what?

I MenT (see)   Write what you understood
meant

inTo MY Blood and into my mouth
       d

So t̶h̶e̶ what do the germs do inside your body?

They Make me yet sick

You must like to be sick a lot,

Kin̶d̶ of

You like hot fevers, runny noses that make your nose
sore from wiping the snot off, stuffy noses so you can't
sleep at night and are tired all day, sore throats so you can't

swallow good food or drink ... you like that??!!

Figure 12.9-12.12. Learning to Behave Through Written Language.

I Dont Know — it is a yes or no question. ②

Pick yes I want to feel bad or pick no I don't wish to feel bad.

no But I KinD OF Lik, ~~r~~ when~~want~~ Don't have to
go   school
~~Go~~To SCooL

When you are sick and stay home who takes care of you?

if   I'm   with
MY MOM or iF ~~I~~M Wits ~~v~~ey DaD, him
usually   does
~~Likely~~ MeyMoM Dose

Did you Know that when your mom (or dad) stay home with you, that they miss work ,,, when they miss work they let their students (clients) down ,,, when they miss work people are disappointed they are not there ,,, when they miss work they get behind in their job ,, they have to work extra time and much harder to catch up ,,, they have to do these things ; miss work, let down other people, work harder BECAUSE you choose to put germs in your mouth, That is a little bit selfish on your part.

about   I can stay by myself
~~oBout~~ Paragraph 2 ; that I ~~I can stay By my self~~
at my Dad's because he's only upstairs ,,,
                                        stairs
       at   work
he Lives ar~~this~~ ~~we~~ wK

③

What about mom? What about school?

You let down your classmates when you are not at school.

Why DOTheY neeJ Me: you are not suppose
To help jnClass because Becas You will give Me answers

array AND GET IN TROUBLE.

You raise your hand and partipate in discussions, you share your wisdom, you help when there are groups, you follow rules which helps others learn the rules by watching you.

You let the <u>teacher</u> down too. The teacher and class mates get up, get dressed and make the effort to go to school because that is a teacher and student <u>job.</u>

You can't learn what the teacher tells the class when you are not at school. Then she has to waste her time later teaching you what the others came to school to learn.

When you make yourself sick that means you don't care about your body. A person who chooses to not take care of their body is showing <u>bad character.</u> Someone who takes care of their body, by staying well, by not putting germs in their mouth, by not putting fingers in their mouth is showing g<u>ood</u> character and good <u>discipline</u>... <u>self</u>-discipline... and is taking care of their body.

I Know But

④

What if the teacher send you home?

Then you go home... but what came first?

healthy → touch germs on things → put germs into mouth → 7 days later → you're sick go home

What if you just catch a cold or something like that?

Is it still your fault?

1. What causes a cold?
   BY BEING OUTSIDE and
   AN INTLE rain
   Nope... not true.

A cold is caused by germs — all colds, every type of cold is caused by germs. Cold germs are <u>viruses</u>!

<u>All</u> sicknesses; vomiting, diarrhea, cold, strep, fever, cough, influenza, etc. come from germs.

Some germs are viruses, some are bacteria, some are fungi and protozoa.

What about me? At the beginning, you wrote that you have germs in your mouth. So you put your fingers in your mouth, then you put your wet fingers on my pencils, my table, my books, my chairs my door knob... then I touch where you touched and get your mouth germs on my hands. You are exposing me and others to your germs.

In order for language concepts to develop, the language for the concepts must be presented in the way the person learns. This sixth-grader learned best with a motor access to her visual mental pictures. Therefore, she began to develop language for what she did in the academic areas. To learn the language rules, she was given assistance with writing along with the cognitive rules for learning. Her academic products such as spelling began to change as did her reading for comprehension and her writing. Most noticeable were changes in her social behavior. She did not play with her hair or suck on pencils. She walked tall and attended to what people said. She is developing appropriate social behavior. The next section discusses the way meaningful concepts develop in a language-based therapy.

Activity: Why does work on language in the way a person learns concepts affect all areas of behavior?

Therapy for Meaningful Concepts

Language-based therapy always considers the concepts underlying the behavior. For example, if a child pulls at the teacher's neck, the teacher leans into the child and says "I like to give hugs too." As the child lets go because of the hug, the teacher redirects the child's hands into a hand-over-hand hug. All behavior can be redirected into something meaningful. When the adolescent said he did not steal the TV, the language was changed to a lower level so that it became meaningful for him. When Keesha could word call print but could not understand the print, the spoken (acoustic) pattern was changed into a visual-motor pattern of writing that would have meaning for her. *All behavior can be assigned meaning that is conceptual. All conceptual meaning must be learned in the way the person acquires concepts. Most individuals with ASD learn best by motor acts that represent their visual mental concepts.*

For therapy to be meaningful, it must be based on the way the person acquires concepts for language, typically a motor way for individuals with ASD. Language must be visual in nature (Chapter 5), so there must be context for their language acts. The authors have set up contexts for individuals with ASD to use their language as a way to learn socially and cognitively since 1971 (e.g., Lucas, 1976, 1977, 1980; Lucas & Hoag, 1976). The principles for maximum effectiveness are as follows.

- **Language functions in the way the person learns.** Since individuals with ASD use motor patterns for visual concepts, a motor system of expression (ASL, typing, H/H writing, H/H drawing, etc.) must be accessible for language to develop to represent behavior.

- **Language mediates the academic behavior (reading, writing, speaking, etc.) as well as the social behavior.** Therefore, drawing and writing about social, academic, and cognitive or learning behavior increases all areas of development (synergy of the brain and mind; Arwood, 1983).

- **Visual language is very contextual or relational.** As a result, language used to assign meaning must overlap orally (Chapters 10 and 14), in writing (Chapter 8), or in drawings (Arwood & Brown, 1999).

This section addresses some of the ways that a language emphasis in therapy through visual-motor ways of learning can help individuals with ASD to develop more appropriate social and academic behavior.

Drawing Behavior

In previous chapters, examples of drawing behavior of social events were shown. Figure 12.13 is a drawing of a child learning the social need to raise his hand in class.

Figure 12.13. Child Learns to Be Social in the Classroom.

From Arwood, F., Brown, M., & Robb, B. (2005). *Make it visual in the classroom,* p. 55. Portland, OR: APRICOT, Inc. Reprinted with permission.

The language of the thought bubble represents the desired behavior. The child can match his own thinking with the expected behavior. Drawing the thought bubbles in context with the language of the event helps represent the desired behavior. Behavior is *always* in context if it is language based on visual conceptualization. Therefore, pictures or drawings are always in real time and part of a bigger picture or event. Drawings of a person doing something are event-based and in two dimensions, which is easier for the brain to interpret than the use of photographs. Symbolic pictures use a picture or pictures of an object to represent an idea. For example, a bell might represent that the country supports the concept of liberty for all. Or a simple picture of a hamburger might be used to represent that the child wants something to eat. These symbolic pictures look easy to the adult but, in reality, they require a high level of language. That is, the child must have enough language to think, "That is a picture of a hamburger. When I point to it, they will get me something to eat even though I don't want a hamburger." If the child who is pointing does not have this level of language, he will only point to the picture for a limited amount of time without quitting unless the pictures and responses change with different meanings. Photographs, like symbolic pictures, are also more difficult for the brain to understand because language must fill in the missing or incomplete objects. For example, a photograph will only show part of a person who is sitting down, or only the one arm in front of the body, so the child must use language to know that there are other parts of the body or arms or that he is seeing a person. However, cartoon types of line-drawn, 2-D pictures (Arwood & Brown, 1999) are easier to understand and match the use of functional language for social development and academic success.

As the child looks at one frame of the picture and the educator or parent tells about the picture, the language overlaps or creates meaning that relates what the child sees and the language that goes with what the child sees so that the child can mentally see the visual concepts of the behavior. The language sounds like this: "When you see the teacher's mouth move, words spill out of her mouth. These words fill the room so you can see what she says. Because the teacher is filling the room with her words, you must keep your mouth shut so your words do not also spill out. If your words spill out at the same time the teacher's words spill out, the words are on top of each other and there are too many words in the room. And because there are too many words in the room, the teacher's mental pictures go away and the teacher doesn't know what she was saying or thinking. Because there are too many words in the room, the other students don't know what the teacher's words are saying, so their thought bubbles go away. To keep the teacher's pictures from going away and to keep the other students' pictures from going away, you must keep your mouth closed while the teacher is moving her mouth." This language relates one frame of the picture the child sees as his reality to another frame, to another frame, and so forth. The words take the child through the cartoon of what happens in the classroom when he is talking while the teacher is also talking.

A replacement behavior such as writing down or drawing an idea is also offered so that the student can remember his ideas and also wait for the teacher to stop talking before he offers a contribution by raising his hand, for example. The language in the oral story is relational, and therefore contextual. It is relational language that overlaps to create sufficient meaning for the mental pictures to develop a whole context or big picture. Some students do okay with less language, but others only learn pieces of the context without using a lot of the relational type of language.

Activity: What is relational, contextual language? What are some different ways to use this type of language?

Using "Sabotage"

Lucas and Hoag (1976) used a form of "sabotage" (see Chapter 10) to set up an event for students to learn the value of language so that their behaviors would have meaning. For example, a 9-year-old female took off her clothes when she needed something. Stripping always got someone's attention but did not change her behavior. Until she quit stripping, she could not attend a general education classroom. By setting up situations for her to use appropriate language requests for help, she learned to use words instead of stripping.

Lucas and Hoag might turn off the water at the sink when they knew she was going to get a drink of water. At first when she started to strip, one adult would prompt her to say, "I need help" while doing hand-over-hand signing, and the other adult immediately gave her the water. This type of situation might be solved with the water being turned on, a paper cup filled with water, a prompt for her to go ask someone to turn on the water, and so on. It was always important to provide different solutions to the same problem and to give her the language to solve the problem. *Concepts of language represent behavior when the same behavior can be expressed in a variety of ways. Intervention must use language in a variety of ways for concepts to develop. Doing the same task or saying the same words over and over shuts down the development of social and cognitive concepts.*

Activity: Why does using different words with the same types of actions or different actions in response to the same problem help develop cognition as well as language?

By sabotaging the environment, the child is helped to engage in language that problem solves and, therefore, develops concepts for learning how to act socially and cognitively in more appropriate ways. Lucas and Hoag were able to take their students on field trips that others did not permit because their students learned appropriate ways to act or behave within context. These students were soon able to function in general education classrooms without paras meeting their social needs.

Using Speech Acts

Setting up situations for individuals with ASD to use speech acts to perform conceptual meanings also improves cognitive development. For example, drawing out the relationship between a person's face looking angry and the concept of being disappointed helps the child to see the difference in cognitive meaning between anger and disappointment. The child can now use a speech act about disappointment instead of anger. Figure 12.14 shows the relationship between the behavior of drawing on a desk and what another person thinks when someone destroys property.

Figure 12.14. Relational Language for Contextual Stories.

This type of social language provides the metacognitive meaning necessary to increase cognition to change social behavior. *Language is the mediator for all learning. The medium, whether it is pictures, words, stories, and so on, does not provide the meaning. The meaning comes from the language. The language is provided by the adult in the way the child learns best.*

Activity: Why is the language level of all methods and materials an important consideration in learning?

Language functions to mediate concepts of social behavior such as when a person uses a performative type of speech act: "I promise I won't destroy property." To make a promise is different from just telling. Figure 12.15 illustrates the difference between a performative such as "promise" and the simple utterance or choice act such as just telling.

Figure 12.15. Promise Is a Performative Speech Act.

Figure 12.16 shows how writing along with the pictures helped to get a student, Sarah, to comply. Implied additional language-based speech acts are necessary for Sarah to understand that other people expect to use the same objects that she uses. These implied meanings are drawn and written so that Sarah can see the meaning of her social behavior.

Sarah and the other students like to listen to CDs during break.

So that Sarah and the other students can find the CDs, all CDs are kept in the red bin.

So Sarah, after you listen to CDs, put the CDs back into the red bin so that other students can find the CDs when they want to listen to CDs.

Figure 12.16. Other People Use the Same Objects.

Computer technology can be used to generate picture signs to represent behavior. Figure 12.17 shows an example of a behavioral event created with computer signs.

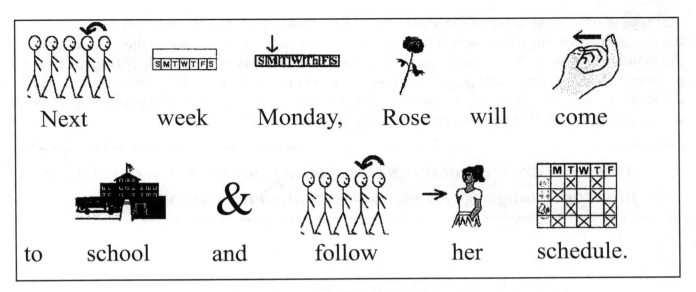

Figure 12.17. Use of Technology to Draw a Picture.

Reproduced with permission from Heather Carvalho, co-parent. Made with Picture It ©1994-2007 from Slater Software, Inc.

Some of the words have different meanings but use the same picture. For example, Rose is a person, not a flower. The concept of "will come" is difficult to see. While this type of pictographing provides a level of structural language that allows for compliance for some students, the symbols do not provide functional language. Functional language is based on understanding differences in symbols that represent semantic meanings. In other words, the visual symbol for Rose, the girl, must be different from the visual symbol for the flower, rose. The same concept can be drawn in real time and written with language types of relationships for better use of language. When these relationships are shown, the language is more relational. Relational language is functional language, which in turn improves cognitive and social development. Figure 12.18a shows how language influences the meaning of the behavior.

At 8:45, Rose leaves home so that she can walk to school and begin her school day.

At 9:00, Rose sees her schedule, sits down at her desk and begins writing to a pictured event.

At 10:15, break time, Rose goes to the corner to drink a hot chocolate before going back to her desk to look at a book.

At 12:00, Rose puts her book in her desk so that she can walk to the lunchroom and buy a hot chocolate.

Figure 12.18a. Functional Language Is Relational and Improves Cognition.

This type of functional language can show visual relationships with drawing in real time. In this way, the process of acquiring the concepts through the movement of the hand and/or the movement of the mouth can be seen. Note that in Figure 12.18b the educator has used technology to generate the pictures, which are refined and produced in real time to improve the student's cognition – not just the student's behavior. Figure 12.18b shows how the language connects the ideas or thoughts through the language in a way that the pictures and words match in meaning.

> *Activity: Why are the semantics of speech acts important in developing the function of language for social and behavioral purposes?*

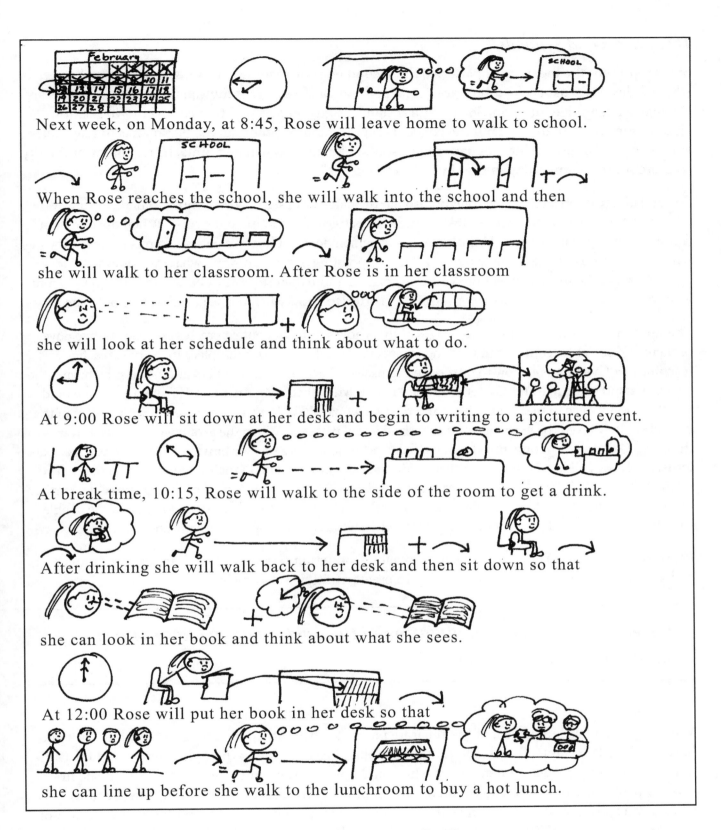

Next week, on Monday, at 8:45, Rose will leave home to walk to school.

When Rose reaches the school, she will walk into the school and then

she will walk to her classroom. After Rose is in her classroom

she will look at her schedule and think about what to do.

At 9:00 Rose will sit down at her desk and begin to writing to a pictured event.

At break time, 10:15, Rose will walk to the side of the room to get a drink.

After drinking she will walk back to her desk and then sit down so that

she can look in her book and think about what she sees.

At 12:00 Rose will put her book in her desk so that

she can line up before she walk to the lunchroom to buy a hot lunch.

Figure 12.18b. Matching the Meanings of Words with Pictures.

Using Signs and Symbols

Signs represent the meaning of patterns, the second level of acquired meaning or perceptual patterns (the first level is sensory). Symbols are language-based and represent multiple concepts. Symbols are the highest cognitive function. So, a gestural sign (g-sign) such as pointing connects two relationships of meaning. To understand the concepts represented by pointing, the person has to have fairly sophisticated language. The language might sound like this: "When he points, he is looking at the sky so there must be something in the sky I need to look at."

Social skills are often a set of rules taught through the patterns of signs. For example, a child who always talks might be taught to take turns. Taking turns is a patterned response to the rule: "When the other person stops talking, you can talk." Unfortunately, if a person does not hear his own spoken language, knowing when to take a turn is like learning a gesture such as pointing but not knowing what the pointing refers to. To understand the social conventions of a conversation, more than rules must be learned. The person must learn the content of how to have a conversation in order to know when to speak and when not to speak.

Therapy that works to develop the messages of the whole setting or context creates better cognitive development and social outcomes than working on specific social skills. For example, a first-grade teacher was teaching all of her students how to introduce themselves. Each day, she would begin the class by having the students stand in a circle and say, for example, "I am Ellyn. What is your name?" The other person would say, "I am John. Nice to meet you, Ellyn," and the two would shake hands. The one child with autism in the class absolutely loved the exchange of memorized social patterns. When the group would move towards the circle to do these routine introductions, their movement was a *sign* for him to get ready to practice patterns. All of the children sounded mechanical in their use of voice and in their introductions. For an introduction like this to be symbolized, other ideas, words, and ways to greet would have to be possible. Furthermore, a real context would be required since all of the children knew each other, a violation of the simple rule that we don't usually reintroduce ourselves when we greet someone we already know.

Learning to symbolize an event such as a social introduction requires a lot of language, not memorization of rules. The language must overlap to create multiple relationships.

Activity: Why does symbolization of the parts of an act help improve cognitive and social learning?

When a person has knowledge of the separate pieces of an auditory act like "greeting" but does not have the visual concepts, the person might not apply the right rule to the right context. Figure 12.19 is an example of a college student, Katy, who could not read the signs of what to say when she first saw her professors or peers. She would often run into a person and say something like, "You weren't in your office today." More than once, the person receiving the message was put off by Katy's lack of social interest. Since Katy thinks in pictures, she needs the visual contexts to give her the language meaning to symbolize how to greet someone. Figure 12.19 shows a lot of language used in a written way (it was written and drawn together) to show Katy some of the many social rules that have to be symbolized conceptually to use appropriate language behavior.

Katy, I see you walking on campus so that you can go to your classes. Sometimes while you are on your way to a class you see someone you know who is also walking to a class and you decide to stop and say "Hello." When you see someone who is also a student, you can stop and talk to the student and call the student by their first name such as saying, "Hello Mary, how are you today?" Then you wait for the student, in this case Mary, to respond back to your question. Watch Mary's lips move as she talks to you and picture what she is talking about. When Mary's lips stop moving, it is your turn to talk to Mary about something that she said to you … something that you pictured Mary saying as she talked to you. This is called turn taking, and it is an important part of having a conversation.

Sometimes while you are walking on campus, you see a person walking who is a professor. When you see a professor walking on campus, you will also want to greet, but the way you greet a professor is different from the way you greet a student or friend, like Mary. When you see a student or friend you call them by their first name, but when you see a professor, you will need to greet differently. The different way you greet a professor is by using the professor's title and last name. I know that one of your professors is Dr. Johnson, so when you see Dr. Johnson what you would say is "Hello, Dr. Johnson." Sometimes when you see Dr. Johnson, you might remember that you have a question to ask about your class. You might think that it is a good time to ask Dr. Johnson a question, but it might not be a good time for Dr. Johnson to be asked a question. What if Dr. Johnson is on her way to teach a class? What if Dr. Johnson does not have her appointment calendar with her to see what time is a good time for you to make an appointment with her? What if Dr. Johnson is busy thinking about what she will be presenting at the class or meeting that she is walking to?

We also need to think about how you learn best. You are walking; you do not have a pencil and paper in your hands to write down the answer that Dr. Johnson might give you. When Dr. Johnson talks to you and answers your questions, you will try to remember what Dr. Johnson said, but as soon as you see and talk to someone else, you will no longer remember Dr. Johnson's words. Now you will need to find Dr. Johnson again and ask her the same question, and when you ask the same question two times, because you were not prepared to write down the answer the first time you asked the question, because you did not have a pencil and paper in your hands, you will have wasted Dr. Johnson's time as well as wasting your time too.

So, when you see Dr. Johnson as you pass on campus, greet her and keep walking. Then later, you can call Dr. Johnson and make an appointment to go to her during office hours to talk. Dr. Johnson will be prepared to work with you and answer your questions. You will need to prepare to work with Dr. Johnson. Being prepared to work with Dr. Johnson means that you will write down your questions before going to your appointment so you can focus on listening and understanding her answers. Being prepared for your appointment also means that you will bring your pencil and paper with you to the appointment so that you can write down what Dr. Johnson says as she answers your questions.

Figure 12.19. Greet Others with Symbolic Language.

Role play, videos, pictures, signs, and stories are all ways to show what the meaning of an event might be (linguistic marking), but for a person with ASD to symbolize the ideas within these role plays, videos, pictures, stories, and so on, there must be a symbolization of the multiple ways that concepts connect. Symbolization means that the person can draw, write, talk, listen, view, and so on, about the concepts. In this way, the person becomes more than a responder to the signs or patterns of the structured environment and learns to use symbols to initiate and maintain relationships. When a person has the language to initiate and maintain social relationships, he is considered socially competent. The socially competent person can flexibly move from one setting to another, organize and plan an event, prioritize an activity, or engage in multiple tasks. In other words, a socially competent person exhibits multiple ways to put himself into the event with language. Chapters 13 and 14 discuss how to create the space or time of events.

Activity: Why is the use of symbolic language more important to social competence than the response to social rules with skilled behavior?

Using Language to Develop Social Behavior

Language is a set of conventional symbols that assigns shared meaning to concepts. Social concepts develop as a result of learning the language that represents the concepts. Unless pictures, words, and signs are used relationally and contextually in the way language functions, only the skills, not the concepts, are acquired. Without relationships and contexts, the child learns to say his name and shake hands even when he has already met the other person before. Without relationships and contexts, the child greets everyone with the same "I am here and ready to work" even when it is not a work event. Without relationships and context of language, the child does not know why picking his nose when alone in the bathroom is okay but not okay in the classroom, and so forth.

Language is the explanation or story of "who, what, where, when, and why" social behavior occurs in the events of specific contexts. When the contexts connect, multiple events provide the development of improved social and cognitive behavior. *The child learns not only why a behavior is okay but when to use it, who expects what of the behavior, and so on.* The language for these expectations is always relational and contextual. The language meets the following criteria of linguistic function:

1. **The language must tell the learner how the concepts relate to one another.** To create relational language use oral cartooning (Mabel Mini-Lectures; see page 248) or draw the overlapped language to connect one picture to another. Writing can also connect these types of overlapped ideas. Figure 12.20 shows how the thought bubbles of the past, present, and future overlap so the language can represent the concepts. The cognition overlaps with the written words to create more symbolic language than a simple set of rules might express.

This past summer, Cindy and Kathy were my teachers during summer school. Cindy and Kathy helped me write and draw my ideas.

As this new school year begins, Cindy is leaving my school to work with a different student at a new school.

I will miss Cindy and sometimes I will feel sad that she is gone, but I can also remember Cindy working with me and feel happy that she worked with me for an entire summer!

I can also think about how my teacher, Kathy, will still be here to work with me just like she did last summer. I will feel good knowing that teacher Kathy will still be here to work with me.

Next week, a new teacher, Jodie, is coming to my school to work with teacher Kathy and me.

Teacher Jodie and teacher Kathy will help me with my writing and drawing this school year.

Figure 12.20. Thoughts Overlap with Language.

2. **The pictures and words must overlap for maximum language function.** Figure 12.21 shows the symbolized language that goes with the cartoon.

This past summer, Cindy and Kathy were my teachers during summer school. Cindy and Kathy helped me write and draw my ideas. As this new school year begins, Cindy is leaving my school to work with a different student at a new school. I will miss Cindy and sometimes I will feel sad that she is gone, but I can also remember Cindy working with me and feel happy that at she worked with me for an entire summer! I can also think about how my teacher, Kathy, will still be here to work with me just like she did last summer. I will feel good knowing that teacher Kathy will still be here to work with me. Next week, a new teacher, Jodie, is coming to my school to work with teacher Kathy and me. Teacher Jodie and teacher Kathy will help me with my writing and drawing this school year.

Figure 12.21. Symbolized Written Language Shows Relationships.

3. **Relational language must represent the way ideas overlap to show connections among the people (who), what they do, where, when, how, and why.** If the writing or oral language does not identify these constituent elements (who, what, where, when, why, or how), the concepts will not interrelate to create the depth of concepts needed for better cognitive and social behavior.

4. **Oral language must follow the same overlap of pictures contextually to create a mini-visual movie.** The mini-movie occurs when the words create mental pictures that cartoon the overlapped meaning. The authors call this type of language telling a "contextual story." Figures 12.20 and 12.21 showed how pictures and the written language overlap to create a contextual story that increases social and cognitive development. This type of language overlap increases the academic ability of writing, speaking, reading, and so on, as well as develops the concepts of the content of the pictures for better social development.

5. **Language, whether written or oral, must create the meaning of how other people view the situation.** The authors call these types of language usages Mabel Mini-Lectures, named after the illustrator who wonderfully advances children's social and cognitive development in all types of settings. An example of a Mabel Mini-Lectures might go like this.

Robin, an 8-year-old male, begins yelling "whoop, whoop, whoop" as he runs through the hall, opens and then slams the door into the clinic. "Robin, do you know I could hear you before I could see you today. Do you know how I could hear you? I could hear you because your mouth was making sounds that were so big they came into my office and covered me up so I could not do my work. Since your words were so big that they came into my office and I could hear you before you were in my office, it means that your words also went into the office of the man next door who makes special shoes for people. If your words went into his office, then he was not able to make the shoes. If he was not able to make shoes, then the people who buy his shoes won't have any shoes to buy and the man who makes the shoes won't be able to make any money for his family because he won't have any shoes to sell. Since your words went into my office and into the man's office next door, then the words also went into the doctor's office that is next to the office of the man who makes the shoes. When your words went into the doctor's office, the doctor was listening to a patient's heart but your words made it so he could not hear the patient's heart so the doctor does not know if the person's heart is okay. And if your words came into my office and upset the man next door who makes the shoes, and the doctor who was listening to the heart, then your words also went into the office at the end of the hall where the new mothers are taking their babies to see if their babies are okay. When your words go into the office where the mothers take their babies, then your words wake the babies up. When your words wake the babies up, then the mothers are not able to get any rest and the mothers of the babies need rest so they can take care of their babies."

This Mabel Mini-Lecture continued for a couple of more minutes as Robin's eyes got bigger and bigger. Robin worked for an hour without any loud words. At the end of the hour-long session, Robin's mother, who was in hurry to get to a meeting, grabbed Robin's hand and said, "let's hurry." Robin looked at his mother and said, "SHHHHHH, you will wake the babies up." Robin had learned the concept of what happens when there is noise in the hallway. Because Mabel used such rich, overlapping visual language to share meaning with him about what others are thinking when there is noise,

Robin was able to create a movie in his head of what he was supposed to be like when he was in the hallway. Mom was making noise, so Robin told her one of the many reasons Mabel had given to him to help her understand that she could not make noise either. Robin never made noise in the hallway again! That was six years ago.

Activity: What is a Mabel Mini-Lecture?

Summary

Language-based therapy improves concepts that represent social, academic, and behavioral skills. Because language represents concept development, improving language also improves social and cognitive functioning. Social and cognitive development is conceptual in nature and supports the entire learning system. As the learning system develops more concepts and more language, the child has more opportunities to choose higher-order socially appropriate behaviors. With adequate language the child can use the social development to increase cognition as well. In other words, the child with more language can make more choices of socially appropriate behavior that is conceptually developed, and not just skill-based.

Concepts for Chapter 13

How are concepts of space learned?

Why does a person who uses clock time think in spatial concepts?

Why do symbols for time have to be overlapped or
cross-referenced to be learned?

What is meant by the term "space of movement"?

CHAPTER 13
Strategies for Creating and Organizing Space

I am in a box without right or left direction.

I can feel the pressure of the shape I am in.

I know you are nearby, but how far away?

You are the shape of my space, and my space is as far as I can see!

Learner Outcomes: As a result of reading this chapter, the reader should be able to explain the importance of *social space* for understanding *clock time* and show how to teach the formal level of conceptualization of events.

Individuals with ASD cannot use sounds and sights in combination to form words for reading, writing, or speaking. That is, they do not use an auditory form of metacognition – the meaningful sound of one's own voice, in one's own words, and with one's own form of self-talk. Since they can generally hear, they use an acoustic or phonographic way to reuse what others say, or in repeating sound combinations like phrases or sentences. However, acoustic information is not auditory. As discussed in Chapter 8, acoustic patterns do not form concepts or metacognitive language. Therefore, for students with ASD language art forms such as reading, writing, and speaking must be taught in ways that do not depend on sound. Furthermore, individuals use sound on a continuum of ability to process visual patterns into concepts. The children with ASD on the low end of functioning cannot connect sound to visual patterns to form visual concepts or pictures, limiting all forms of language in our auditory culture. On the opposite end of the autism spectrum are children with AS, who are able to overlap visual patterns, especially when generated from motor movements, and are able to attach acoustic patterns to their visual concepts. The result is that they engage in a lot of motor acts such as speaking, writing, completing worksheets, and so on. This acoustic (not auditory) ability is often thought to be sound-based but is really visually based. For all individuals with ASD, the best way to facilitate the development of academic skills and the acquisition of concepts is to use the shape of movement to create a visual concept that is in space (see Chapter 8). The purpose of this chapter is to discuss intervention strategies that depend on the shape of various spaces to help a person with ASD to learn.

The Shape of Space

The eyes record the pinpoints of light on the surface of a plane. These points of light create the shape of the edges of planes that the eyes look at. Since planes are flat spaces, all objects develop the shape we perceive from movement of the eyes or head through multiple planes. Each time the eyes or head moves, numerous planes intersect to form a shape. Figure 13.1 shows the shape of an object.

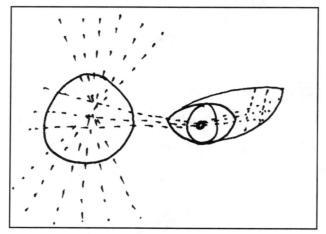

Figure 13.1. The Shape of an Object.

The eyes record the multiple points of the planes as they intersect. The eyes are curved internally so that they record the intersections of multiple planes to create the dimension or depth of a shape (Figure 13.1). So seeing the depth and shape of an object depends on two factors: (a) the light streaming photons reflecting off the object and (b) the eyes reflecting or angling the input to help create multiple dimensions of planes. This is important to intervention because being able to see all of this detail of light and movement is a major strength of the child with ASD. And if a person's learning strengths are known, they can be used to compensate for any deficit.

A person with ASD can see the many planes of a shape of an object. Written words are similar in that they consist of a shape of a plane when bubbled and held visually constant (Chapter 8). Figure 13.2 shows a bubble shape of a sentence.

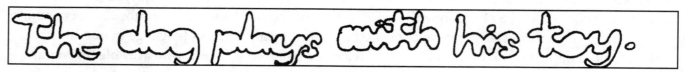

Figure 13.2. The Shape of a Sentence.

The shapes of ideas have no letters. The shapes are not words but patterns of movement. The movement is the shape of the hand creating the sentence. And the sentence is a whole idea, not a series of words.

Knowledge about space and visual concepts helps create intervention options for people with ASD. There are many applications of the knowledge of how space is the product of visual shapes. One application is to understand the shape of an event. Events are people (agents) who do (actions) something in a shared context. The whole picture of an event is a shape. Understanding how events are shapes or social spaces helps create social and cognitive intervention strategies for individuals with ASD.

> **Activity: How does light along with movement of the eye form concepts of object shapes? What is meant by the shape of an event?**

Events as Social Spaces

When a person with ASD walks into a room, she is physically in the space that she sees. Every person and object is in her space. She is part of the space of everything she can physically see. When she can put her body against any of the people or objects within the space, she feels comfortable or "grounded." For example, a low-functioning individual might slide along the wall to stay physically part of the shape of the room or might roll along the floor while other children sit up to "listen" to a story in kindergarten. This type of spatial grounding is like being in the bubble of an idea. Figure 13.3 shows a child in the shape of a room or bubbled idea.

Figure 13.3. A Child Grounded in the Shape of an Idea.

Over the years, many educators have reported effective ways of "comforting" children or adults with ASD by methods that have one common principle – the child or adult is in the space they are in; therefore, physical grounding to the space makes them feel safe. Some of these methods include programs of massage, holding a child in a fetal position against the adult's body, putting a child into a restricted area with pillows and other soft covers and mattresses, putting a child into a timeout that is in a restricted area, pressure holding, facilitating of the position of the arm, tight clothing, and visually reducing the variety of items in the space. The bottom line is that *the child or adult with ASD is in the space he or she sees.* When the child's or adult's body is against the space of the shape, such as against the wall, he or she feels grounded. Figure 13.4 shows this relationship between feeling uncomfortable and grounding to the corner of a room.

Figure 13.4. The Child Is Uncomfortable and Grounds to the Corner.

As a person gains knowledge about the space he is in, he can begin to ground to that knowledge. For example, an adult with ASD, Miguel, who has good language, feels ungrounded in a new setting such as an oral interview. He doesn't know the questions that will be asked and doesn't have a mental picture of what the room will look like. He feels "unsafe" in the process. As a result of this unsettling feeling, he may prefer to use the computer for the interview. Seeing the typed questions and seeing his answers helps Miguel ground to the sight of the printed words. And physically, he can rest his wrists against the keyboard to ground to the computer. But after many interviews, Miguel knows what the questions and answers will look like and, therefore, feels safer in the oral interview. It is still not a really comfortable setting as sound is not the best way for a person with ASD to learn, but the experienced interviewee can sit still or ground to the chair and watch the shape of the interviewer's mouth. The shapes of the mouth create mental visual concepts for some people. Others prefer to look away and allow the mental visual concepts to be brought up by the acoustic patterns of the speaker. Unlike the shapes of the written words, the shapes of the mouth continue to move so the interviewee looks away or watches the mouth and sits very still. Because the speaker's mouth moves, the interviewee sits very still so that there are no additional movements to change the mental pictures. With the experience of what a situation looks like and what people say, a person with ASD can learn to move away from the wall and into a more conversational type of environment.

Knowing what another person looks like, what the room looks like, and what the spoken words look like, creates the shape of the event for the person with ASD to become a part of the event. For example, a young child, Lorna, diagnosed later in life with AS, was an accomplished musician (acoustic or phonographic ability) by the time she was 9 years old. However, her mother always provided Lorna with a routine before each public recital. The mother dressed Lorna up with the exact outfit she was to wear for the recital and then they went to the recital hall and played the entire piece she was to play during the recital. The mother did not know why she did this, but she knew if she didn't, Lorna would not feel safe and would not be able to perform.

By the time Lorna was 9, she was performing at a national level, which meant traveling and not always having access to the recital hall before the performance. Suddenly Lorna would not perform. Lorna's behavior consisted of tantrums, meltdowns, and noncompliance. Yet, she did not want to drop her piano recitals. Mom was told to draw out all of the steps of what Lorna would look like and what the hall would look like, where the piano would be, and so on. This type of cartooning provided

Lorna with what her space looked like. More specifically, the cartooned event allowed her to see herself in the picture and, therefore, *be mentally* in the event. Once Lorna could see herself as part of the event, she could travel to new places and perform because she had the pictures of the event in her head. Lorna could "ground" herself to the space she was in by seeing the pictures. The pictures were her space or grounding.

Events are in space; therefore, moving from one space to another expands the space. Multiple spaces are events that represent the space on a clock or "clock time." The next section shows how understanding the development of space helps create clock time for individuals with ASD.

Activity: What does grounding to the physical space mean? Can a person ground to mental pictures?

The Space of Clock Time

Because individuals with ASD do not use sound to create meaning, sound does not form auditory time concepts. Auditory time concepts use the acoustic part of hearing called "duration" to produce an internal form of time. People who do not use an auditory form of conceptualization do not use auditory time. But events can be sequenced to match the changes of the shape of the clock. Figure 13.5 shows how the shape of the clock corresponds to different events.

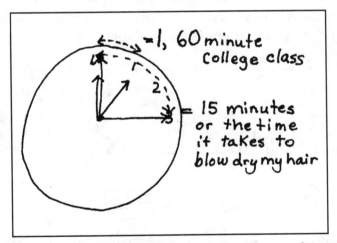

Figure 13.5. Clock Time Measures the Shape of Events.

Notice there are two ways to change the matching of events to the changes of the clock hands: (a) external to the clock is the measure of an event such as a college class takes 60 minutes; and (b) internal to the clock is the event that takes a certain amount of space on the clock such as blow drying one's hair takes 15 minutes.

In an auditory culture, time is important. People work a certain amount of time (internal) in order to be paid (external) a certain amount of money. In such an auditory culture, most activities are based on the economic principle that time is money. Even though persons with ASD do not "feel" this auditory principle as a part of their visual learning system, they are expected to follow auditory ways of dealing with time if they are to fit in the mainstream of the auditory culture. Using the space of the clock to measure how much space an activity takes (external) and how much space (time) a person takes to do an activity (internal) helps develop the concept of clock time. There is also a third dimension of the concept of space: the external and internal clock times overlap to create the relationship between what the person does, what she did, and what she will do. These overlapping spatial or event-based activities are another way to provide past, present, and future. Future is created from the way past activities looked.

To explain clock time a bit further, let's look at a case study. Arlene was a 23-year-old female diagnosed with autism and functioning with high levels of skills. She went to high school, graduated, and got a job at a fast-food place. She lived at her parents' home. Her high school friends moved away, went to college, and got jobs. The structure of high school had provided Arlene with an external way for her to "ground" to the social events of high school, for her to know what she was to do and what she did do. When she no longer had school to provide the social events, the work events, and the calendar of events, Arlene began to battle depression and other symptoms of mental illness. Living in an auditory world with a visual brain did not make sense to her. For example, she did not understand why her friends from high school were no longer in her picture and she could not do some of the simplest tasks such as being on time for an appointment. When she was late and people got angry with her, she did not understand their anger.

Arlene was referred to a speech and language pathologist, Kitty Mulkey, who was asked to help her deal with her social skills. Arlene was always 15-20 minutes late, so after working with her for a while Kitty decided that Arlene needed to learn about time. Figure 13.6 shows the cartoon Kitty drew to show Arlene what the clock (external) looks like as Kitty prepares for Arlene to arrive at 5:30. But Arlene is late so Kitty waits for Arlene to arrive for therapy (internal). In other words, this cartoon is about Kitty and what Kitty does while Arlene is doing something else.

Figure 13.6. A Cartoon for Clock Time.

Kitty showed Arlene that she is sitting at the table and ready for her by 5:20 and that she is ready for Arlene to walk in the door and sit down for therapy when the clock shows 5:30. Kitty also showed Arlene that she was arriving when the clock says 5:45 or so. Kitty pointed out to Arlene that she (Kitty) is sitting and waiting for Arlene when Arlene is not there to see Kitty. This is an important point: *Individuals with ASD are in the space they see, so if you are not in their space, they don't infer what you are doing.* For example, when children are taken out of a classroom for therapy, they expect the room to look the same and the people to be doing the same thing when they return, just the way they saw the space when they left. People with ASD cannot take another person's perspective very well because they cannot see the other person. The other person is not in their space when they are not where they can see each other.

Kitty drew a clock for Arlene to show her how a clock measures the space of an activity. Arlene was surprised at the activity. She expressed that she never knew what the little marks on the clock meant. She did not know how to use the clock except to "word call" the name of the time words that went with the position of the hands on the clock. In other words, you could ask Arlene what time it was and she could read the clock – she could tell you the minutes and hours based on what the clock looked like – but she did not know the concepts that went with her vocal patterns. Figure 13.7 shows the drawing of the clock.

> **Remember that all of these drawings are done with the person or in "real time;" otherwise, the pictures may not be very meaningful as the person drawing is putting in the exact information that the specific learner needs. Also, once all of the information is in the picture, the picture looks messy. In real time, on the other hand, the learner is following the meaning of the motor movements of the hand drawing and writing and, therefore, acquires meaning that cannot be gathered in a still picture that has already been drawn.**

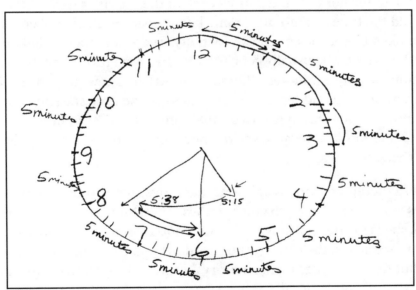

Figure 13.7. Clock Time.

Activity: Why are drawings done in real time when a new concept is being learned?

Kitty asked Arlene for a list of what she does after work and before therapy (see Figure 13.8).

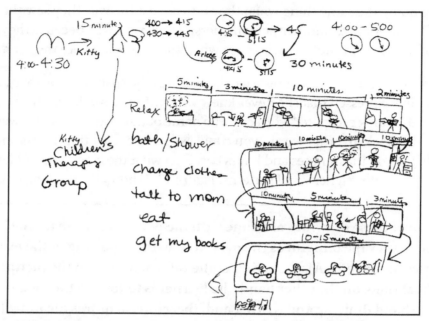

Figure 13.8. A List of Events to Measure the Space of Time.

Kitty also asked Arlene to tell her how much time each of the activities took. Kitty cartooned (see Figure 13.8) as Arlene told the times (external). Arlene knew what the clock looked like for each activity and what the clock looked like at the end of each activity. These activities added up to about 78 minutes or 1 hour and 18 minutes. She usually gets home at 4:15 p.m. Kitty expects to see her at 5:30 p.m., which is about 75 minutes, only 3 minutes difference. So Arlene knew the time for each event (external). Her before-therapy activities added up to being close to the time she had to spend before she was to work with Kitty, about 78 minutes of external time, compared to 75 minutes. So why was she always 15 to 20 minutes late? She was late because she did not account for one activity that was not an external time activity – driving to therapy.

When Arlene drives to therapy, driving is an event that moves her through space. She is not staying in place like she does when she rests or changes clothes. Therefore, for Arlene there are no external markers of the space she is in. The car moves, she does not; therefore, she moves through multiple spaces while sitting in one space, the car. In other words, the space of an event provides a typical one dimension of time. But for time usage in an auditory culture to be effective, time must be at least two-dimensional – external and internal. External markers are the things that a person sees to tell her what the event of the space is. For example, when Arlene takes a nap, she sees her room. So lying on the bed in her room is the space of the event of taking a nap. When she lies down the first time, someone like her mom probably gets her up. Arlene sees the way the clock looks when she lies down and again when she gets up, so resting becomes an event in the space of her bed in her room. Arlene is the person who lies down and gets up, so the clock time is external to her in that she sees it before she lies down and again when she gets up. The routine of resting involves the same sights before and after each rest. In this way, Arlene can tell you how much time the event of lying down to rest takes. She can measure the time according to the way the clock looks, which is external to her movement. She measures the clock movement for the event, lying down, in the space of her bedroom that she is in.

But driving the car is different. She sits still and the car moves. There are no external markers to the movement of the car. She is in the space of the car and she does not move, so the clock does not move. When she climbs into the car, she sees herself going into therapy because that is where she is driving to. The space she is in is the car and then the therapy room. There are no events and no additional spaces between the car and the therapy room, so there is also no transition time. Arlene was late 15-20 minutes each day because she did not allow for the time passing as she drove the car to therapy.

Because space is time for Arlene, Kitty showed her that she only had 60 minutes of activities to complete at home before she left at 5:15 to get to therapy by 5:30 to be on time. If Arlene wanted to rest, bathe or shower, and change clothes, she would have only 30 minutes of "other" activities. Kitty told Arlene that she would have to cut out space so that Kitty would see Arlene walk through the door by 5:30. So Kitty pulled out another piece of paper for Arlene to write out this new schedule, and Arlene took over the task (Figure 13.9).

Figure 13.9. Measuring the Space of the Events.

Arlene left out the part about talking to her mom and getting the books ready. She decided that she would not talk to her mom (10 minutes) and she would have her books ready the night before (5 minutes), which would give her the space of another 15 minutes. In this way, Arlene would be in the space of Kitty at 5:30 p.m.

This case study shows how being able to tell the numbers on a clock does not mean a person understands the internal meaning of time. By Kitty showing Arlene how to see the events in multiple ways,

Arlene was able to put herself in the event of therapy. The external markers were cross-referenced in three ways: (a) cartoon of Kitty in one space and Arlene in the cartoon of her space; (b) the way the clock looks for Kitty's space and the way the clock looks for Arlene's space; and (c) matching Kitty's clock to Arlene's space of her events. Arlene was never late again. The language of time for being late had become symbolized.

For a set of relationships such as the space of a series of events to become symbolized or language-based, they must be cross-referenced in at least three ways. Symbols of language represent the underlying concepts. Learning concepts is a permanent way to change behavior.

Activity: Why does the language of time have to be cross-referenced to be symbolized?

Behavior such as changing clothes occurs in the space of an event, and movement occurs as a series of events. A series of events changes the mental concepts that one sees. For example, as a child with ASD walks down the hall, each step changes his position in relation to the hallway so walking down the hall becomes a series of events, not just one event. Space becomes time when the external events become internalized symbols related to the space of the clock. The next section discusses how movement changes mental concepts.

The Space of Movement

As mentioned in Chapter 3, movement creates the space of an idea. Ideas record the information in the visual cortex of the cerebrum, which means that a person who records space from the shape of movements uses a visual form of mental conceptualization. As the person moves, the movements create new shapes, which record new concepts in the brain. There is a developmental hierarchy of movements that leads to a hierarchy of visual-conceptual development.

Initial primitive reflexes of the newborn record the sensory input, but no real space at the brain level is involved. But as the child begins to move more intentionally through space, the child's movement is the extension of the space the child is in. For example, very young children or children with little language prefer to be as close to the physical space (walls, arms, floor, bed, etc.) as possible. If they are moved away from the external space of the event they are in, they look like they are falling as they lean forward and hurry to the next space. This tip-toe type of "bolting" is really their bodies falling through space. They may also twirl as they move around in their space to record where they are. Developmentally, they should be able to be grounded in a cartoon to show them the space they are in. This level of spatial development is preoperational. To bring the person up to the concrete level of spatial development, cartoons for academic, social, or behavioral language (Arwood & Brown, 1999) are drawn to help her see herself in space in relationship to others.

The structure of events such as school or work or the routine of home provides these individuals with the structure of their space in relationship to others in their space (concrete). Events are comfortable because the person with ASD literally moves into the space of an event (preoperational to concrete spatial development), and the events in these concrete situations are secure by their familiar visual structures.

By seeing recognizable points of reference such as people and their activities, the person with ASD is able to move from one activity or event to another (concrete). For example, Arlene saw the same people she did activities with when she went to school so she saw these people as her friends. When these people no longer did the same activities as she did, they weren't in her picture and she could not understand why they were not her friends any more. Arlene must be able to see herself in a separate space different from the space others are in. And she must be able to see that other people can be friends even if she cannot see them, and even if they are doing different things than Arlene is doing.

To visually show Arlene how people can do the same thing in different places and still be friends, a visual language flowchart (Arwood, 2001) was drawn. In Figure 13.10, Arlene and her friend are put together in the same space (see middle of page) and then what they did together was drawn in different bubbles or events on the left side of the page. These ideas are connected by their relationship to space.

Figure 13.10. Learning How Friends Can Be in Other Spaces.

One of the events was graduating from high school, which is shown with a high school diploma and a year. Jenny, Arlene's friend, goes away to college (KU). Multiple structures of events are drawn for Jenny: What she does for school, what she does for work, what she does to get good grades, and so on. The space of Jenny is drawn for Arlene so she can see Jenny's space. On the same page, Arlene is drawn in her space going to work and going home. In this way, Arlene is put into the space she is in that is a different space from the one that Jenny is in.

Because Arlene creates meaning through movement and because she no longer moves within the space that Jenny is in, she does not understand the social relationship of Jenny to Arlene. For example, Arlene wanted to know why Jenny does not call. But she does not see that she can call Jenny. She does not see that Jenny has new friends, a new job, new school responsibilities, and new job responsibilities. When these concepts are drawn in relationship to each other, Arlene can begin to increase her conceptualization of what it means to be in "other spaces" but, more important, she can see what movement in other spaces looks like and what friendship means at a formal level. Instead of friendship being structured by the space of the events shared, it becomes a concept that relates people to people.

This type of flowchart creates a series of cartoon types of ideas in language relationship to a bigger picture. When a person with ASD can see many viewpoints to the same idea, the formal concept of the idea begins to emerge. ***Formal concepts such as friendship, liberty, freedom, and respect are developed through the movement of the person away from the referent.*** In this case the referent is Jenny, but how she functions as a friend requires multiple concepts shown in relationship to one another. This type of language-based flowchart is similar to multiple language-based cartoons that show how ideas are interrelated conceptually.

Since individuals with ASD must acquire these formal concepts through movement, and since movement is in space, the only way to acquire some of these concepts is to draw their meanings in space as a language-based flowchart. For many people, these concepts can also be written with relational language (see Chapter 12).

Arlene had trouble with all academic, social, and behavioral concepts that were formal unless she acquired the meaning through the movement of drawing and writing. When she knew the concepts, she was extremely "bright" in her ability to demonstrate the ideas. For example, she read a paper and thought that two men died because of a tornado (see Figure 13.11) but, in reality, the article was nothing about people dying from a tornado.

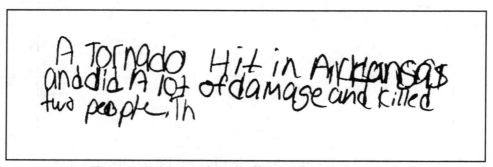

Figure 13.11. Understanding Formal Material.

Kitty took Arlene through each of the ideas in the article. For each idea, Arlene was to draw and write. See Figure 13.12.

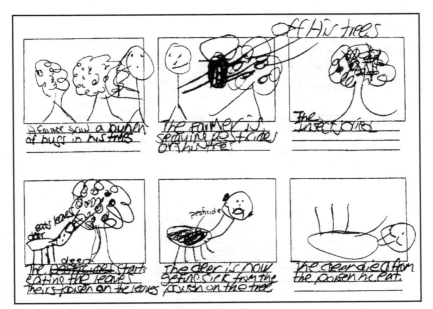

Figure 13.12. Draw and Write About Formal Ideas.

Note that when Arlene goes to the second page of ideas shown in Figure 13.13a, she does not show the relationship between what the farmer does and what happens, so Kitty draws the farmer into the picture and she helps her with some of the space-time relationships such as "so now." (All of these writing samples and flowcharts were originally drawn and written on 8-1/2 X 11 inch paper.)

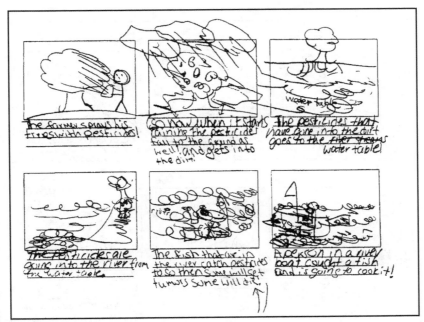

Figure 13.13a. Connecting Formal Ideas.

Arlene has difficulty with the time elements such as tenses (she sees ideas, which is space, not time). In Figure 13.13b, Kitty helps Arlene see the interaction of relationships by drawing arrows for her. Kitty has to draw out the spatial time relationships of "because" (cause and effect) and formal concepts such as "threatened" and "extinct."

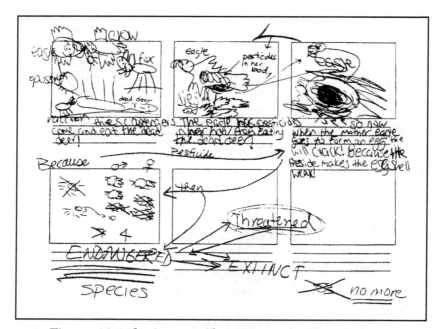

Figure 13.13b. Arrows Show Formal Relationships.

In Figure 13.14, Kitty helps Arlene understand more formal relationships that explain how the pesticides "contaminate" the water, and so on. Again, Kitty has to draw the people relationships as shown in the fifth box, but Arlene can draw the picture of a single person because she in the space of the person in the picture.

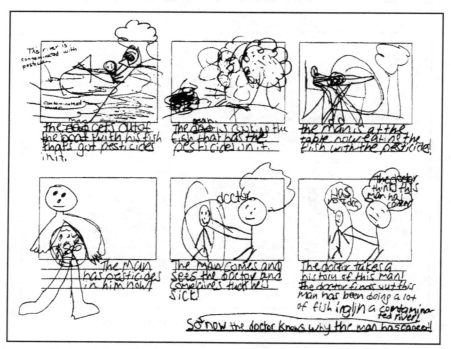

Figure 13.14. People in Formal Concepts.

Drawing these multiple pictures in a series creates the movement of space for Arlene. She is literally "walking" through the space of the cartoons and understands the formal concepts from what "she

Learning with a Visual Brain in an Auditory World

sees" in each box. Because she is mentally in each box (preoperational conceptualization), she can move through the boxes and begin to overlap the meanings so that she begins to see the farmer in relationship to the animals and the animals in relationship to the farmer (concrete). When she can explain the relationships among all of the people and their actions within these events, she is at a formal level of conceptual understanding.

Because Arlene thinks best in the movement of space, it is best to allow her to use the pictures and the matching words (writing is still in space) to write (not tell) about the event. Arlene would be able to tell what she heard (acoustic) but later not show the conceptualization of what she said. Instead, when she writes, she sees what she says and the ideas record in the space of the event as semantic memory or long-term memory of visual concepts. Then she shows changes in meaning or better conceptualization. To help Arlene write, the words are put into a dictionary with arrows showing the relationships for her to use as she writes (see Figure 13.15).

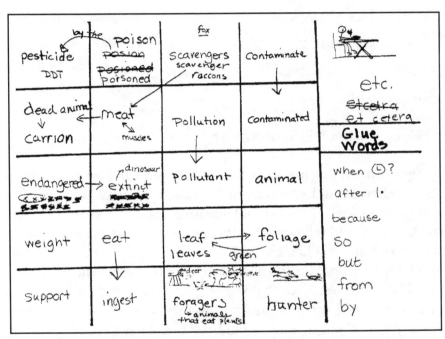

Figure 13.15. Using Picture Dictionaries for Vocabulary.

Arlene then uses the pictures, the written ideas, and the written words to write her essay about the article. She shows much more understanding and conceptualization (see Figure 13.16a & b).

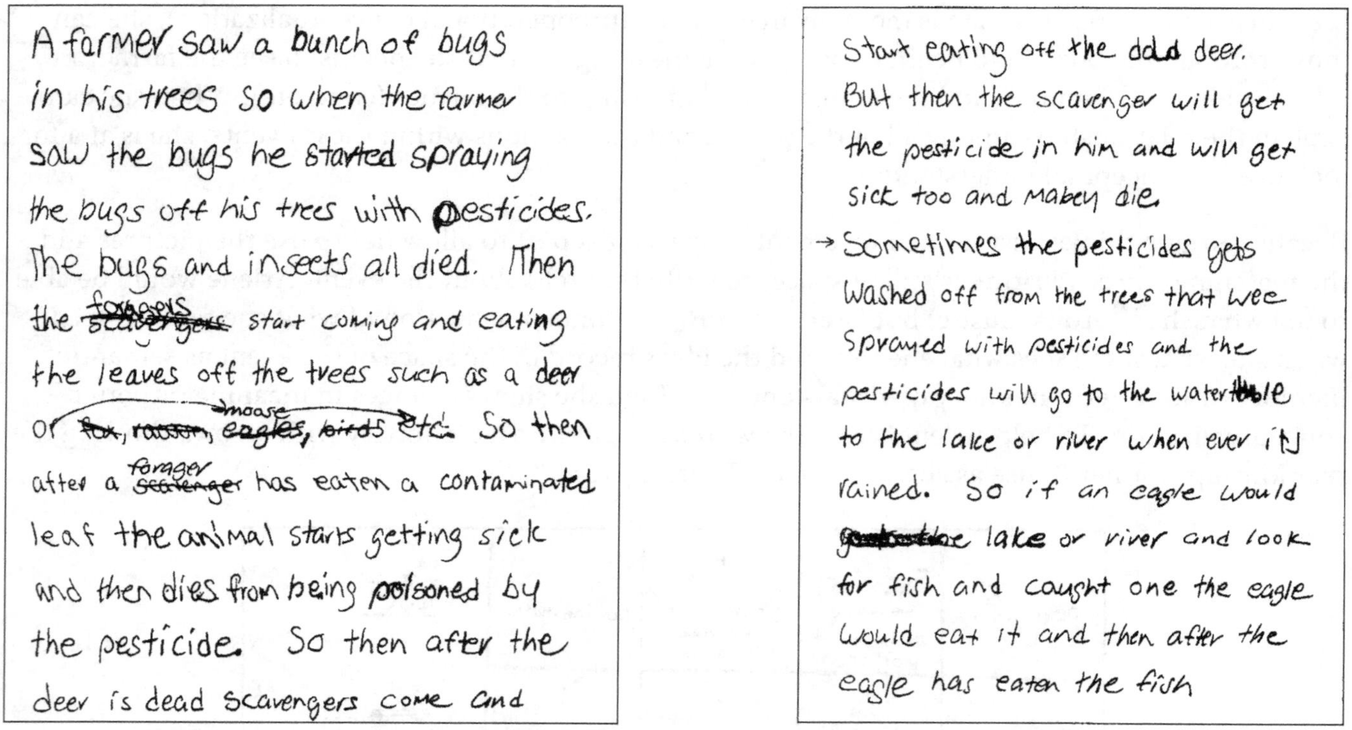

A farmer saw a bunch of bugs
in his trees so when the farmer
saw the bugs he started spraying
the bugs off his trees with pesticides.
The bugs and insects all died. Then
the ~~scavengers~~ start coming and eating
the leaves off the trees such as a deer
or ~~fox, raccoon,~~ eagles, ~~birds~~ etc. So then
after a ~~scavenger~~ forager has eaten a contaminated
leaf the animal starts getting sick
and then dies from being poisoned by
the pesticide. So then after the
deer is dead scavengers come and

start eating off the dead deer.
But then the scavenger will get
the pesticide in him and will get
sick too and mabey die.
→ Sometimes the pesticides gets
washed off from the trees that wee
sprayed with pesticides and the
pesticides will go to the water~~table~~
to the lake or river when ever it
rained. So if an eagle would
~~go to the~~ lake or river and look
for fish and caught one the eagle
would eat it and then after the
eagle has eaten the fish

Figure 13.16a & b. Writing with Formal Conceptualization.

Because Arlene had high-functioning skills, she often repeated what others said or asked, and she learned lots and lots of patterns, but her conceptualization had been limited in many ways because she had not been able to make formal conceptual meaning out of the space of events or ideas. For example, in the past, Arlene would follow what others told her to do for homework, to connect with other people at school, to complete a job, and so forth. Without the structure of school, school activities, and parents helping with school tasks, she had to learn that different people do different things in different spaces at different times. With that information, she could understand why her former friend was still her friend even though she did different things and lived elsewhere. Arlene could feel comfortable to call Jenny even though Jenny did not call her. Arlene could begin to understand why other people were irritated with her for her tardiness, and so forth.

Activity: How does a person with visual conceptualization develop a formal sense of time by overlapping multiple events?

Summary

Persons with ASD walk through their own space seeing other people and their activities as belonging to the space they share. To increase their cognition of space, they must see how movement through events creates relationships that change the meaning of space. Chapter 14 discusses additional interventions to help develop the space of social development.

Concepts for Chapter 14

What is an event-based story?

What is oral cartooning?

What is a Mabel Mini-Lecture?

What is meant by using relational language for social development?

CHAPTER 14
Social Intervention Strategies

I see you see me.

I move and I see you move.

I know your name,

But I don't know our relationship.

Learner Outcomes: As a result of reading this chapter, the reader should be able to explain how language provides learners the opportunity to develop socially through different stages of cognition. Additionally, the reader should be able to suggest several ways that language can provide social boundaries and limits.

As defined in Chapter 1, people with ASD have difficulty with social development (for additional understanding, see Attwood, 1998; Grandin & Barron, 2005; Wiley, 1999; Winner, 2000). Throughout this book, strategies for improving learning have been mentioned. Since learning is a socio-cognitive process, any strategy designed to improve learning can also be used to improve social development. The purpose of this chapter is to summarize the many ways to improve social development.

Social Development

The lowest level of human social development is to "be an extension" of the environment, as described in Chapter 6. To begin to separate from the physical properties of the world around him so as to increase social development, the child who acts as a physical extension of the environment must begin to be in his own mental picture. To be in the picture, the adult helps a child draw hand-over-hand and write hand-over-hand to put the child into the picture. Figures 14.1-14.5 show a sequence of work by a 7-year-old female, Niki, who does not speak, read, or write. These figures show the sequence of steps used in therapy to set up opportunities for Niki to learn to speak through the motor movements of typing patterns to develop visual concepts.

Niki types "box" and points to the box on the floor.

Teacher says, "Yes, the box is on the floor."

Niki looks frustrated so the teacher says, "Oh, you mean that you want to look in the box."

Niki types, " I want look in box."

Figure 14.1. Assigning Meaning to Niki's Typing of Patterns.

Later, Niki types "tangrams" and points to the box on the floor.

Teacher says, "I don't see any tangrams ... I don't know what you mean."

Niki then types, "tangrams plus."

Teacher says, "Tangrams are pictures that are made from shapes."

Figure 14.2. Teacher Assigns Different Meanings to the Typed Patterns.

Again, Niki types "tangrams plus" and points to the box.

Teacher says, "I like to play with tangrams. Niki, do you like to play with tangrams?"

Niki types, "play with tangrams."

Teacher takes the tangrams out of the box for Niki to use.

Figure 14.3. Different Meanings Are Assigned to Form Concepts.

Later Niki types "puzzle" and points to the box on the floor.

Teacher says, "Puzzles <u>are</u> fun!" What do you want to do?"

Niki types, "I want puzzle board." Teacher opens the box and hands Niki the butterfly puzzle.

Niki looks frustrated.

Figure 14.4. New Meanings for Old Patterns Create Concepts.

Niki types "puzzle board box."

Teacher says, "I know ... you want me to hand you the shapes puzzle that is in the box."

Teacher instructs Niki to type ... "Please take the shape puzzle out of the box."

Teacher says, "Now I understand what you want ... let me hand you the shape puzzle from the box."

Figure 14.5. Meanings Overlap and Become Concepts for Language.

A typewriter was first used to move Niki from acting on objects to begin to socially act as an agent in using the typewriter to communicate with others. As mentioned in Chapter 8, the reason an old-fashioned typewriter is often chosen in situations like this is that the student needs to see the motor movement of the key strike. With most modern forms of technology, the letter, speech sound, or word comes up and there is no motor connection between the child's behavior and the response. With the typewriter, the child sees the different strikes of the keys match the behaviors of the hand to create overlapped motor patterns. These figures show how typing the patterns can begin to form labels to pictures and create concepts. Even though this child prefers to respond to patterns with patterns, it is important to continue to have her act on the environment so that she acts as an agent. By doing hand-over-hand with her (manual signs), she is an agent and the adults respond to her hand-facilitated movements.

No matter how old or how big a nonverbal person like Niki becomes, it is important that the adults around assign meaning to the nonverbals. The assigned meaning must change to stretch the child's understanding. For example, Niki likes to do patterns – stacking cups, putting puzzle pieces in the same nonlanguage-based puzzles, pointing to the same pictures over and over, reading the same books, jumping up and down, and so forth. As long as the same meaning is assigned to what she does, she complies. Niki is good at patterns! But patterns do not automatically form concepts. For a person to develop concepts, the patterns must be in the same sensory form as the person acquires concepts.

Niki's learning system, like that of most children diagnosed with autism, works best when given motor patterns to form concepts. Niki uses many different kinds of motor patterns such as typing letters, pointing, and stacking. But her motor patterns must overlap and integrate for concepts to form. She types (motor) patterns or words. This typing overlaps with the signing (motor) of words, which overlaps with the visual-motor activity of the event (motor acts). Niki types "girl," which is one motor act, but when the educator says, "Yes, you are a girl," there is sound but no motor overlap. Niki watches the mouth move. The movement of the mouth could be a second motor movement to overlap with the typed word. Niki tends to watch the educator's hands. Hand movements are also motor tasks. But the educator attempts to add meaning. "Here is another girl in this picture. Her name is Betty." Niki begins to hit the educator. Why? Because the additional meaning affects the way Niki "sees" girl and she does not use the sound of the mouth for meaning. She hits to get the words written down so she can watch the adult's motor movements of the hand write. The overlapped motor patterns of the written word with the typed word help Niki form cognitive ideas (concepts), but the spoken words are getting in the way of Niki developing concepts. Niki needs to learn the concepts through overlapping the motor patterns.

Learning is both cognitive and social in nature. Socially, Niki does not want the educator to talk about the girl because the girl is not Niki. "Girl" does not just refer to Niki but to others who look different than Niki. The educator works on writing with Niki not only for the cognitive development but also to impose a higher level of agency, to create the concept of others (the girl) being in Niki's mental picture. Trying to keep the motor acts overlapped and the social development increasing is difficult. Niki whines and hits whenever the meaning doesn't match with her past learning. In other words, as the educator creates new patterns for Niki to learn concepts, she is likely to fuss and hit because the new meanings don't fit past patterns. Sometimes educators and her parents think that Niki "doesn't like" learning but, in fact, the change in Niki's behavior suggests that she is learning and soon the hitting is replaced by language, "Girl not me."

Niki wants the safety of repeating patterns. But as long as people do her patterns with her, she will not develop socially. If she does not develop socially, she will also not develop cognitively. If Niki only does patterns, the number of patterns or tasks increases but *not* in cognitive depth or social function. In order for Niki to develop as an agent in relationship to other agents, she must be able to see others in relationship to her, to what she does, and to what she knows.

One solution to Niki's hitting is to go back to working on patterns. When she does familiar patterns, she looks good. She sits and points at the pictures and appears to be compliant. But as she grows older without conceptual development, her frustration and subsequent aggressive behaviors become worse. Patterns occur at a sensory-motor level with little cognition or conceptualization. At the next cognitive level, the child is in her own picture. So, as long as the adult does what Niki does and Niki leads, she looks compliant. This level of conceptualization shows Niki in her own picture, or functioning at a preoperational level. The world revolves around her. But to be a part of other people's lives, Niki must fit into their world through shared rules. She must be able to see the concepts of how others behave in relationship to her, not just repeat patterns given to her or act with patterns that others assign meaning to. As Niki is put into pictures that are drawn and written about, she is challenged to grow more meaning neurologically, which makes her want to physically act on the discomfort of the added meaning. This discomfort results in hitting or some other unwanted behavior to show that she has some control. Going ahead with the meaning being assigned by drawing and writing about different people and how they relate to her will help Niki develop concepts.

Once she begins to see herself in pictures, cartooning and writing to the cartoons helps move her socially from the world revolving around her to her being a part of others' lives. The content of the relationships among people in the events she shares becomes part of relational language, which forms context for functioning in a variety of events. Figures 14.6-14.10 show a series of motor acts used to help Niki go into the next level of becoming an agent.

Figure 14.6. Niki Is Typing Patterns.

Figure 14.7. Hand-over-Hand Drawing and Writing of Patterns.

Figure 14.8. Hand-over-Hand Development of Patterns to Concepts in Picture Dictionary.

Figure 14.9. Hand-over-Hand Writing and Drawing to Develop Concepts from Patterns.

Figure 14.10. Develop Pictographs to Assign Language to Concepts.

Activity: Why does adding new meaning for higher conceptualization result in cognitive discomfort and possibly short-lived unwanted behavior? How does working on the conceptual meanings for patterns improve cognitive development?

Social Contexts for Event-Based Learning

To increase cognitive development, social assignment of meaning must also occur. The use of social contexts with relational language increases cognitive development for better social development. As we have seen, there are three levels of cognitive development: (a) The *preoperational learner* is in his own picture. The picture tells a story about the learner even if other people and other names are given to people in the picture. A single picture of a stick-figure child doing something describes the event of the child in the child's own story. Multiple pictures in sequence of relational language such as cartoons (Arwood & Brown, 1999) of a child put the child in multiple single pictures as if the child is walking through the depicted event; (b) The *concrete thinker* is able to relate to rules and others' actions and to learn from watching the pictures or cartoons of others or the oral cartoon stories about others; and (c) The *formal learner* does not need a story for new material but learns formal concepts such as "liberty" best when these concepts are presented in the context of relational language (concrete to preoperational).

All materials (e.g., Dunn, 2003; Dunn et al., 2004; Gagnon, 2001; Gray 2000a, 2000b; Hagiwara & Myles, 1999; Myles, Trautman, & Schelvan, 2001; Savner & Myles, 2000; Selsor, 2004; Simmons, 2002; Sobotka, 2000a, 2000b), including the use of pictures (e.g., Arwood, 1985; Arwood & Beveridge-Wavering, 1989), have a language level of conceptual meaning (e.g., Arwood, 1983, 1991). Using a variety of ways to represent conceptual meaning helps a variety of children (Corso, 2002). All people who use a visual way of thinking such as individuals diagnosed with ASD use context to relate one idea or concept to another. Visual cultures, or people who think in visual metacognition, use a lot of context, which is why these cultures are often referred to as storytelling cultures.

Activity: Why do materials have a developmental level?

Preoperational Context

A child who sees himself as part of a picture is always part of a story because he thinks at a preoperational level. Once a child is able to talk about himself in a picture or write or manually sign about himself doing an activity or participating in an event, he is ready to move from being alone in the picture to relating to others and their actions. To move the child into another picture, the parent or educator must draw him into a picture and then label or write the words that go with the meaning of the picture. Figure 14.11 shows how a child might be drawn into her own picture.

Figure 14.11. Preoperational Context.

The pictures can be expanded into any sequence of behavior or social skills. Figure 14.12 shows a behavior sequence where a child is expected to sit on a carpet square in the classroom.

Figure 14.12. Preoperational Social Behavior.

Even though the child is at a preoperational level of thinking, multiple pictures to help her see herself in an event. Once the child sees herself in an event, this helps her move to the next level of socio-cognitive learning. This cartoon strip is best drawn hand-over-hand with the child or with the child watching the movement of the adult's hand drawing the cartoon strip. Some children need to feel (hand-over-hand) the shapes of the hand to create the motor patterns for conceptualization. Other children need to watch the movement of the hand to create a visual hand shape to go with the motor movement of writing an idea. The lower the child's level of language, the more the child will need hand-over-hand patterns to increase cognitive development of social behavior. Some students close their eyes as their hands are moved so seeing the patterns does not get in the way of their feeling the shapes of the hand movements.

The use of a cartoon, either drawn for the child or drawn hand-over-hand, is a way to move a child from preoperational social development to a concrete level (Arwood & Brown, 1999). Each picture holds some of the context (other people, objects, actions) "still" while the child in the picture moves through each frame. In a literal way, the child is in a picture, and with each different picture frame, the child walks into the next picture as if walking through the pictures of an event. As a child moves through the story depicted with cartoon frames, the child is an agent, a social actor. By linking the cartoons, the child can be drawn into an entire day of activities so she can see herself function throughout the day. Figure 14.13 shows part of a day for an older student who was functioning without verbal skills but could use the single picture paired with cartoon strips in each area along with written words to structure her day and help her learn to socially behave, academically develop writing skills, and begin to communicate verbally.

| At home on the cupboard. | On the desk. | On the wall. | On the seat of the bus. |

Figure 14.13 Contextual Concrete Day.

Until contextual pictures, oral cartooning, and event-based relational language stories were used with this student, her behavior was abusive. When the visual-motor context was created, she had close to 30 symbolized pictures showing her day. The day's activities became a series of events. Each activity had a cartoon story. Then the cartoon became one symbolic picture representative of a series of activities. Each symbolized picture represented the relational language of a cartoon type of story that provided social context. With these types of cartoons symbolized as single pictures from the event of cartooned ideas, she began to function throughout the day in a more social way as a person in relationship to other people, at a concrete level. Multiple cartoon strips help establish a concrete way of thinking and acting.

Activity: How can relational language used for drawing a student into social events such as "fixing lunch" raise a child's social and cognitive development?

Concrete Event-Based Learning

Being able to see how others' actions relate to one's own actions helps establish the context of events and the rules of actions within events. Being able to relate to others is a concrete level of cognition. At the concrete level of socio-cognitive learning, most children with ASD have lots of language. Even children who have high-functioning language need to see themselves put into the events of a day in order to better organize their activities, to better problem solve, or to better multitask. Figure 14.14 shows a set of overlapping pictures used to show a student how to organize the different parts of his day (going to school, schoolwork, homework, and job) so that he remembers to turn in his work on time, makes it to his job on time, and is able to balance homework with other activities.

Figure 14.14. Organizing the Events of a Day.

From Arwood, E., & Brown, M. (2001). *A guide to visual strategies for young adults.* Portland, OR: APRICOT, Inc, p. 36. Reprinted by permission.

Learning the concepts of a context is relational and is also concrete, since one activity of an event relates to another activity of the event (Arwood & Unruh, 2000). Event-based learning allows cognition to improve while increasing social development.

When children can begin to see what others do, they are moving out of being the central character of their pictures (preoperational) and are beginning to see others in their pictures (concrete). They can then begin to see social relationships as part of a bigger picture of rules and beliefs. With or without pictures, oral language must maintain its visual form of referring and marking ideas through the addition of visual cues. Visual cues include signs, gestures (g-signs), cartoons, drawings, and written words accompanying the oral language of an event. Since the person is central to an event, higher forms of event-based learning increase a child's social development of agency. APRICOT II pictures developed by Arwood and Beveridge-Wavering (1989) are black-and-white complex social scenarios for working with students at this higher level. Figures 14.15-14.16 show an APRICOT II social picture for creating stories with written relational language as part of an event to go with the picture.

It is lunchtime at the Meyer house and John and Bob are busy making themselves sandwiches while also warming up some soup on the stovetop. Jake, their youngest brother, is also hungry. John and Bob are not being respectful of Jake's need to also eat; they did not ask Jake if he was hungry and they did not offer to make him a sandwich. The older brothers are not respectful of Jake's young age and high level of curiosity, as they have left the pot handle turned so that Jake can reach up and grab it, thus spilling hot soup on his body and seriously injuring himself. By being older, John and Bob can take care of themselves, but they have a responsibility to respect their younger brother by taking care of his needs and his safety.

Figure 14.15. The Language of the Story Shows the Social Relationships of the Event.

Figure 14.16. APRICOT II Picture of a Social Event.
From Arwood, E., & Beveridge-Wavering, A. (1989). *APRICOT II Kit.* Portland, OR: APRICOT, Inc. Picture #2 "Fixing Lunch." Reprinted by permission.

Learning with a Visual Brain in an Auditory World

Event-based learning coupled with relational language provides tremendous overlap of patterns for better conceptualization. This event-based story has significant overlap of content so that formal concepts such as "respect" can begin to develop.

Figure 14.17 shows how this event can be drawn and written to create a concrete level of cognition that puts both the boy and his brother into the picture. Notice that the words that go with the picture are written with the picture. Most children with ASD will attend to the words first. By writing the words below the picture, the words are closer to the child's body than the picture. Therefore, the child sees the words first, and relates to the meaning of the words. The words are patterns that match the meaning of the writing to the picture.

John and Bob decide to make soup and sandwiches for lunch.

While the soup is heating on the stove, John and Bob begin to make their sandwiches

Their little brother, Jake, smells the soup cooking, which makes him hungry, so he reaches up to help himself to some soup.

Figure 14.17. Event-Based Social Contexts for Concrete Language Development of Formal Concepts.

Formal Event-Based Learning

Context by itself sets the scene. An event with context includes the people with a backdrop. At the preoperational level of cognition, the people revolve around the child. At the concrete level, the people relate to each other within the context, and multiple activities across different contexts create multiple events. Multiple sets of events help develop social skills in relationship to what others expect. The best learning of even formal concepts such as respect occurs when the individual can relate his or her own experience (preoperational cognition) to what others do over multiple activities and events.

So, what does "respect" look like? To understand how people use this formal concept, a person needs multiple sequences of events in which the actions could be viewed as "respectful." Examples might include how somebody helps another person to show respect for actions, how somebody shares kind words to show respect of the other person, how somebody talks to another person to show respect of ideas or beliefs or authority, how somebody uses other people's property to show respect for them and their property, how somebody takes care of property to show respect for the property and the people who bought it, how somebody washes her clothes to show respect for her hygiene and for the clothes, and so on. These language concepts are about how others view a person's actions within the context of an event. Figures 14.5-14.7 showed the beginning development of one meaning of the formal concept respect.

The only way to learn a formal concept such as "respect" is to take the concept through multiple pre-operational to concrete sequences to show the relational language that would represent the formal idea or concept. All concepts that cannot be seen, touched, or felt such as "respect" are related to other formal concepts such as "trust," "consideration," "worth," and "kindness." Therefore, to really understand a formal concept, a person must learn how to use these concepts in multiple ways over time and in relationship to other formal concepts.

Notice how the words in Figure 14.5 overlap in meaning. Oral language also connects the relationships of activities within a context. Using the culture of visual language, these events with relational language tell a story that creates visual mental cognition.

Activity: What is event-based learning? Why does event-based learning have to use relational language? How do multiple events create formal concepts such as "respect?"

Social Language

Language that works best for a person to learn adequate boundaries and limits must take the person orally through the same types of visualized relationships. For example, Roland is an 11-year-old male who regularly blurts out in class, lacks friends, and has difficulty being appropriate in certain situations. He was recently diagnosed with AS. His parents have home-schooled him off and on as a result of his lack of academic achievement even though he tests as having above-average cognitive ability. Roland's new teacher uses a lot of "social language," emphasizing giving credit to individuals for who they are (Arwood & Young, 2000), recognizing individual classmates for what they can do, and supporting each student as part of the whole class.

Within the first hour of class on the first day in this new teacher's classroom, Roland blurted out a math fact. The teacher, Mr. Jackson, had not asked for an answer as he had merely said they would work together on some math as he approached the board. Roland's blurting out met with some giggles from the class. Mr. Jackson quickly used social language with the group. "Excuse me, I didn't hear this fine young scholar's words. Mr. Sinclair (Roland), would you please repeat your contribution, I am not sure everyone heard it?" Roland said, "12 X 12 is 144." Mr. Jackson said, "Mr. Sinclair, where did you learn this mathematical concept?" Roland said, "I learned my multiplication tables for 12 this summer." "That's very good work. I appreciate students who work hard to share their knowledge. We always need plenty of help learning." Mr. Jackson then checked with others in the class to find out what they had learned. He was planning to review some mathematical concepts, and eventually they did review, but Roland was never seen quite in the same light as he had been seen by his peers in previous years. Mr. Jackson's respectful use of social language to bring Roland into the positive light of other students continued throughout the year. He grew tremendously and went on to junior high where his grades were an A- average.

Mr. Jackson used language that was inviting, that explained how people fit with others and how to feel supported, nurtured, and protected. This type of social language established boundaries while setting limits. The limits of behavior for Roland became known to him as he learned how to fit. Soon he raised his hand to contribute and he learned strategies to use motor skills such as writing to maintain his focus while others talked. He developed many social skills by being part of Mr. Jackson's social language (Arwood & Young, 2000).

Boundaries define the social nature of a person's self. In the example above, Roland did not understand that his actions were pushing into the boundaries of others' limits. In other words, his voice was in the space of the other students and the teacher and, therefore, within their boundaries. Roland did not understand the limits of his actions and, therefore, did not understand how his behavior affected someone else's actions, thoughts, or behaviors. *To develop good boundaries so as to understand others' actions and to function appropriately as established by the implied rules of the dominant society's expectations, oral language must establish boundaries through setting limits.* The reason why oral language must define the boundaries and set the limits is that the dominant society uses an auditory language, English, for doing business, academically and socially.

Activity: *What is social language?*

The following list from the *Language of RESPECT* (Arwood & Young, 2002) provides some tips for fostering oral social language function.

- **Use "because" language.** For example, "Jeff, I want to see you put your bottom in your chair. When you sit on your bottom on the chair, your feet can reach the metal bars on the bottom of the table. Your feet on the bars help ground you so you can make better visual pictures when you work because your eyes will be able to see the words on the page better." Neurologically, by sitting still, the child's physical body does not move the mental pictures, and the child can free up his hands so he can write and move the shapes of ideas mentally.

  Another example of "because" language might sound like this: "Marie, ask Aaron to help you pick up your desk. By picking up the desk, you won't scratch the floor. The janitor likes the floor without scratches because it takes less time to clean the floor. If there are scratches, the janitor has to stay late and if he stays late he cannot be with his family for dinner. He likes to eat dinner with his family so by picking up the desk you are helping the janitor."

  "Because" language does not have to be long and drawn out. For example, the child asks, "Why do I have to go to swimming?" "Because you signed up for lessons, the swim instructor expects to see you for eight lessons." As one of the author's students said, "Because language is like mini-supports." Because language can overlap into a type of oral cartooning or Mabel Mini-Lecture (Chapter 12). Figure 14.18 is an expanded example of an earlier Mabel Mini-Lecture (Chapter 12) that is detailed.

Robin, I knew that you were here before I saw you at my door. Do you know how I knew you were here? I was sitting at my desk thinking and writing and suddenly the sound of a voice going whoop, whoop, whoop out in the hallway came through my office wall and into my head, which made the picture in my head go away so I couldn't work.

When I heard this noise, I stood up and walked to the door and opened the door to see who was making that loud whoop whoop noise with his voice in the hallway, and I saw that it was you. And if your voice was loud enough to go through the walls of my office and into my head, making my pictures in my head go away so that I couldn't think to get my work done, then your voice was also loud enough to go through the walls of the doctor's office next door. The doctor next door is trying to use his stethoscope to listen to his patient's heartbeat. Because your voice was loud enough to go through the walls of my office and into the doctor's office, then your voice was loud enough to get into the doctor's head, so that the doctor couldn't hear his patient's heartbeat. And if the doctor can't hear his patient's heartbeat, then he can't get his work done, and his patient will be angry with him and then they both will be angry with you for making the loud whoop whoop noise that made the doctor's pictures go away so that he couldn't get his work done.

And if your voice was loud enough to go into my office and the doctor's office and get into our heads so that we couldn't get our work done, then your voice was loud enough to go into Scott's office next door and make his pictures go away so that he can't get his work done either. Scott makes shoes for patients who can't walk because their feet hurt. Scott was busy in his office making special shoes for these patients, but if your voice was loud enough to go into my office and the doctor's office and make our pictures go away, then your voice was also loud enough to go into Scott's office and make his pictures go away so that he couldn't think, which means that he probably ruined the pair of shoes that he was making. So, when Scott's patient with the sore feet stops by Scott's office later this afternoon to pick up the special shoes to wear to make his feet stop hurting, the shoes won't be ready. Scott and his patient will be angry with you for using such a loud voice in the hallway that it made Scott's pictures in his head go away so that he ruined the patient's pair of shoes so that he won't be able to help the patient's feet from hurting.

And if your voice was loud enough to go through my wall, the doctor's wall, and Scott's wall and make our pictures in our heads go away so that we couldn't do our work, then your voice was loud enough to go into the doctor's office at the end of the hall. That doctor sees the new mommies and their babies. The mommies in that office are tired because having a new baby takes a lot of time and work. The mommies want their babies to sleep so that the mommies can get some rest, but when you made your voice too loud in the hallway saying whoop, whoop, whoop, then your voice also went into the doctor's office where the tired mommies and the new babies were resting. And when your voice went into that office, it was loud enough to wake up all the babies. Now all of the babies are crying instead of sleeping and the mommies who were resting are now up trying to quiet down the crying babies who woke up when your voice was so loud that it went through the walls and into the heads of the mommies and babies.

This is the rule … When you come to my office to work with me, you will need to use a soft, quiet voice in the hallway, an indoor voice, so that your voice will not make people's head pictures go away by being so loud that your voice goes through the walls and into the heads of the people who are tying to work.

Figure 14.18. Mabel Mini-Lecture.

- **Use specific referents.** Children with ASD often pick up empty patterns such as "stuff," "whoa," "well, you know," "sort of hate those things," or "once-in-awhile maybe." If a person uses a particular phrase such as "Get it on!" many children with ASD will pick up that pattern and repeat it in too many situations. To prevent this borrowing of unwanted stereotype patterns, use language that has specific meanings or referents. For example, instead of saying, "Let's get crackin,'" say the actual meaning, "It is time to walk to the cafeteria so we can eat lunch." In this way, the child hears the actual sound patterns to go with actions. Or instead of rewarding a child with saying "high five" and doing the hand slap, say, "I really like how you sat and did all seven math problems" or "thank you for sitting and doing all seven math problems."

- **Use rich language.** Rich language refers to saying more, not less. Many support specialists, parents, and special educators have been taught to simplify their language, but the use of lots of ideas overlapped with pictures creates more meaning (see Chapter 4 on language development) and helps create social meaning. For example, "Sarah threw mud in your face. I know you are angry that she threw the mud. You can tell her that you don't like mud thrown in your face." Then it is fine to reduce all of the language to what you want the child to socially perform, "Isaac, say 'I don't like the mud in my face.'" Then it is great to prompt Isaac to look at Sarah (at least face her direction) and give him the exact words, one by one, if necessary, such as "Don't throw mud." By building up and then breaking down and building back up the language, the child experiences how the language functions to socially develop limits for himself as well as for what to accept or not accept from others and, more important, how to communicate those social expectations to others. Rich language is relational, contextual, and highly meaningful.

- **Use measurement words of space, time, quantity, and quality.** Spatial (related to space) words include *above, over, under, in, between, in front of, before, after, next, on, beside, along,* and so on. Temporal (related to time) words include some of the space words plus words that define time, including *during, while, again, tomorrow, morning, Sunday, week, afternoon, so, also, hurriedly, slowly,* and tense changes. Quantifiers (related to quantity) include *more, another, some, many, few, thirty, lots, first,* and so on. Qualifiers (related to quality) include adjectives such as *soft, gigantic, cold, red, furry, tall, deep,* and so on.

All of these measurement words set limits. For example, all words in these categories (semantic fields) come in pairs or cognates. If there is a word for "in front of," then there is a word for "in back of." If something is "slow," then something is "fast." If something is red, then something is not red. By using a lot of these types of words, children and adults learn the limits of what they see, do, and act. For example, "Corey, when you walk on the seat, then your shoes that you use outdoors and that have dirt on them get dirt on the seat. When the seat is dirty and someone with white pants comes to sit down, she will get dirt on her pants. She will not be happy because her pants will not be white but will look dirty and she will have to go home and wash the pants." The language provides concepts related to space and time. Another example might be, "When will I see you at my house so I know when to expect you?" "How about June 1st?" "June 1st will work for me. Will I see you with the finished cabinet at my house on June 1st?" "Yes, I think I can finish the cabinet by then!" "Okay, so what is the next step that we have to do to be sure that you are at my house with the finished cabinet on June 1st?" This conversation actually took place. The cabinet builder was worked through all of the steps until he had mentally created a time line with all of the activities of the events in his mental pictures that would lead to having the cabinet finished on time.

- **Use possibility language.** People who think visually do not see into the future but expect future events to happen because of past experiences. Possibility language gives the words that go with what future events might bring. For example, "Martin (a fifth-grader), when you did all of your math problems, you showed that you know what you will do when you get to sixth grade." Possibility language also helps set the limits to social behavior such as, "Marty likes you to tell him how to throw the ball so you can catch it. When you can catch the ball, he likes to play ball with you. Because he likes to play ball with you, he thinks about you coming to his house so that you can play ball together." This type of language gives "because" consequences but sets the stage for future happenings. In this way, the language builds event-based thinking.

- **Walk in the student's shoes.** Use language that shows that you understand a situation from the student's perspective so that he can begin to recognize the relationships among people. For example, "When your words fill my space, then my pictures in my head go away." This is said so that the student can understand the meaning of "Don't interrupt." "Don't interrupt" does not make any pictures, so say the meaning of the words in a way the student understands. The more a student understands, the more confident and capable he feels. "Make your lips so they don't move" is a visual language way of saying "Be quiet." Or "When I see your lips move, I know that there are words that are coming out that will fill my space."

Many children with ASD, even very high-functioning ones, do not realize that they are talking, and talking, and talking. The motor movements of the mouth keep the shape of pictures moving but they do not realize that there is also sound. One of the authors said to a 7-year-old male, "I see your mouth move, and when your mouth moves, words come out." He said, "There are?" "Yes, I hear the words come out and then the words fill my space and make my pictures go away." The child said, "Can you hear the words?" "Yes." To the child, the author said, "Can you hear the words?" "No." For the rest of the morning, the author watched the boy try to move his mouth smaller so that fewer words would come out, but the level of sound never changed. Once in a while he would ask the author or other students, "Now what am I saying?" The author would tell him the words and the boy would say, "Can you hear my words?" This continued until the author showed him how he could write words, move his hand, and draw his ideas instead of moving his mouth and how the moving of his hand would let him think. He put his lips shut tight and then drew a picture to write about. He asked, "Do you hear my words fall out of my mouth?" "No, your mouth is shut."

- **Use consistent language.** Consistent language does not mean saying the same thing to the same behavior or the same picture or the same event. Consistent language means that you respond in a similar way to a behavior or event but that you may use different words or say the same thing in a different way to increase conceptualization. For example, the child "digs at his skin" and you say, "Jerald, when you use your fingers to tear off the scabs, the skin is broken and the cut bleeds open." Jerald digs again, so you draw out the relationship between what he does with his fingers and what he sees happen with the cut. He digs again! You now put written words to the pictures of what you draw. Remember to write complete sentences to provide the maximum level of meaning. He digs again! Cartoon out what happens when skin is torn and his arm bleeds and how germs infect the wound, and so on. This may become a flowchart. See Figure 14.19 as an example of what was drawn for a child.

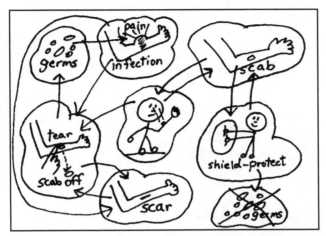

Figure 14.19. Drawing to Understand Social Language.

The consistent language comes from always letting Jerald know that digging was not okay. Giving different language to each time he dug at his arm provided layers of meaning for more patterns to become concepts. *Consistency means the child does something and you know what the limits are and therefore you respond each and every time!*

Activity: What are some different ways to provide social language for a child or adult?

Summary

All children learn to behave based on the way the auditory world sets limits and boundaries through spoken words and auditory ways of communicating expectations. Children with ASD learn to behave socially by being given the nuances of social expectations in the way they learn best, by visual-motor shapes of movement patterns matched to the meaning of visual-motor concepts. Parents and caregivers must provide this information or they cannot expect their children to grow up with appropriate social development. Chapter 15 discusses the role of the extended family in providing social limits and boundaries for children with ASD.

Concepts for Chapter 15

Why do families struggle with expectations?

How can parents support a child's social development?

How can parents assign positive meaning to "uncomfortable changes" in learning?

Why are separate identities important in development?

Family Intervention and Support

I see my child,

I hear my child,

I love my child.

I don't always understand my child.

Learner Outcomes: As a result of reading this chapter, the reader should be able to describe what makes family members healthy supporters of children with autism spectrum disorders.

Family support for persons with ASD is usually outstanding (e.g., Attwood, 1998). Families of children with ASD have founded a number of organizations to help develop knowledge about the disorder as well as how to best serve individuals with autism. This form of advocacy has boosted the assistance for children with ASD. For example, family advocacy has been able to maintain and often increase the funding for classroom support in the form of one-on-one paraprofessionals, therapeutic services, and enhanced intervention programs. Many parents of children with ASD understand the differences in their children's learning systems. Parents who understand their child's differences in learning, coupled with higher levels of parental education, often lend support to advocacy. However, there are still areas where families need support. This chapter addresses several of these areas. Three areas of need that parents often talk about include dreams and disappointments; progress and failures; and social developments and success. Actual family examples will be used. Just like the individuals with ASD, families are very different and have different needs. Therefore, not all families will identify with all of the areas to be discussed.

Dreams and Disappointments

It is normal for parents to dream of what their children will be like before their babies are born. In this U.S. culture, these dreams are often about what the parents believe their child will be able to accomplish – maybe their child will play football. Maybe their child will be a great student of science or math. Maybe their child will be a friend to all and a lover of everything fun and pleasant. Parents dream of their child being healthy, happy, running through fields of grass and flowers, enjoying the sights, sounds, smells, touches, and tastes of everything at the playground. Sometimes these dreams are further developed as their child is born, appears to be healthy, and begins to grow. Then the parents see those little milestones begin to develop such as taking the first step or beginning to talk. And, with each milestone, the dreams seem more likely and more real.

At some point, most parents of children with ASD ask "why?" Why is my baby fussy but doesn't really cry? Why did he stop talking? Why doesn't he talk? Why does she not eat well? Why does my child push me away when I try to feed him? Why does she spit out her food? Why does she hide under the table? Why does he hit his head on the wall when I put him down for a nap? Sometimes these "why" questions come early, in the first few months of development, and sometimes they come later after some of the development appears to have been lost or changed, maybe at 18 to 30 months of age. These questions are the beginning of a search – a quest to make the dreams and disappointments match. To resolve the conflict of the dreams not matching the reality of experience, many parents begin a process of grieving.

Grieving is a cyclic process. A person has a dream but discovers reality is different than the expectation. So the parent must lose the original dream and replace it with a different one. The dream can be as simple as expecting a child to develop "normally." The reality can be as simple as the child does not begin to talk when expected. The difference between the dream, talking, and the reality, not talking, results in cognitive dissonance. *The difference between the dream and the reality means that the person must resolve the conflict in thinking between what is and what will be.*

To resolve the cognitive conflict, the griever usually gains as much information as possible. Knowledge helps the griever work through some stages that he or she may cycle through many times. For example, the child with ASD may not feel comfortable when Mom tries to cuddle her. The child's body reflexes, and Mom interprets this behavior as "rejection." At first she feels hurt and then anger at being rejected. But support systems such as family members or the doctor tells her to keep trying and that the child will "outgrow" this. Mom keeps trying and finds that if she holds her child in a fetal type of position very tightly up against her body, the child relaxes. She interprets "this resolution" as the baby enjoying being held a certain way. Mom has had a disappointment and a dream. Her disappointment was that the baby did not respond as she expected to her holding and her dream is that she thinks she has figured out something the child likes.

Mom's holding of the child is one small victory. This little bit of success provides her a little bit of knowledge to work through the grief. The grief is from being disappointed that the child did not like her touch. Her stages of grief went from being shocked that her baby would reject her, to anger that the baby had to be held and didn't "like" being held, to gaining some knowledge about what worked with her baby. Cognitively, Mom is also reworking her dream list. She may have dreamed that being a parent would be a positive experience where she held a happy baby cuddled into her arms. Now she rethinks that concept and how she has to work to help meet the baby's needs. This cognitive resolution is both a gain and a loss: She gains information about how to hold the baby and she loses her original thought about what holding the baby would be like.

The more a parent can offset gains with losses, the easier it is to move through the grieving process. Figure 15.1 shows this process as a learning spiral where each level of conflict is met with more knowledge and a greater understanding.

Figure 15.1. The Grieving Cycle.

Every success brings the parent or family members closer to accepting the child for who the child is – not for what the child can or cannot do.

For many families of children with ASD, learning "what is wrong" is the beginning of finding what works to help the child. In other words, having a diagnosis allows the parents to feel relieved as they now have knowledge or access to knowledge about the child's disabilities and about what people recommend to do for the child. This type of "help" moves the parents along the grieving process from the initial anger of "Why do I have a child like this?" to more knowledge about the disorder and new dreams about what can be done to help their child.

With knowledge about ASD resulting from trying to resolve the difference between gains and losses, the parents begin to adjust their expectations and begin to resolve the cognitive conflict. The resolution is made by letting go of past dreams and replacing them with future dreams. Replacing past dreams with new dreams helps the parents and family members "feel" better. The parents have replaced a set of what the child could do with another set of dreams about what the child will be able to do. Replacing one set of what the child can do or might do with another set of dreams about what the child might do is a temporary "feeling of relief," but the replacement of "whats" does not help the parent accept the child for "who" the child is. Dreams about what a child can do is *not* who the child is ... the child's who is about the child's interests, passions, desires, personality, and so on.

The U.S. dominant culture tends to be authoritarian and, therefore, tends to view children in terms of what they can perform or successfully do (Arwood & Young, 2000). When children perform differently from their parental expectations, their parents and families look to find a way to "fix" their children's "whats." So parents with children who perform differently than expected seek the best ways to help "fix" the child's "whats." Replacing one set of whats with another set of whats reduces the parent's cognitive dissonance. For example, a mom who figures out how to hold her child so the child doesn't scream and push away feels more successful as a mom. Therefore, she replaces her expectation of the child not screaming and pushing to another "what," how she holds the child. Finding ways to help their children act more "appropriately" helps parents feel better. In the dominant U.S. culture, parents work hard to provide the best for their children and in turn to feel the best about their parenting.

Unfortunately, parents do not always have as many successes as they hope for. Many children diagnosed with ASD who function at the lower end of the spectrum often do not provide parents with enough balance between dreams and disappointments. When this happens, some parents work until they are physically exhausted, the family unit breaks (e.g., divorce is high among these parents), or they resolve to the "fact" that their child is not the child they expected or even wanted.

Remember Jackie? (Chapter 4) A videotape exists that documents the tremendous change in her behavior in a few weeks even after 12 years with few gains. But even when her parents saw the tape, they did not see the changes that everyone else saw. They have accepted their daughter for what she cannot do. They see her as someone who is nonverbal and can't make choices. She can be ignored while at home and will not cause a problem, and they see her as someone whom they have to take care of. They see Jackie as a set of products or unfulfilled dreams to the point that they have replaced those positive dreams with negative expectations. They see her for what they expect her *not* to do – their expectations are deficits and that is who their daughter is. After experiencing too many disappointments and unfulfilled dreams, these parents resolved their cognitive dissonance by accepting the deficits as their child.

Dreams or expectations, fulfilled or unfulfilled, is not "who" a child is. A child is a person. A person has a personality, specific desires, and personal needs. Whether a child talks or walks is different from "who" the child is as a person. ***Parents who can find their child's personhood can see their child's personality and needs outside their own dreams and expectations for the child.*** When the child has a success, the parents can see the joy of the child and when the child has a setback, they can see the child's struggles. In this way, the parents can separate the child's behavior from who the child is. When parents can see the child as a person separate from the behavior, they work with the child's needs but are not driven to "fix" the child. Likewise, such parents are able to share in the joy of unexpected successes. Finally, when parents can separate the child from the needs of the child, they can also separate who they are from their need to help the child. By accepting a child for who the child is, the parents are more open to changes that the child might show and at the same time are able to enjoy their child whether or not he makes huge changes.

Perhaps another example might help make clear the difference between accepting children for who they are, separate from seeing children's behavior as their identities. An educated mom in her twenties gave birth to a baby of her dreams. The family had education, wealth, and the support of extended family, including four devoted grandparents. The child was a very fussy baby who didn't eat "right" and did not vocalize "right," so Mom sought doctors' opinions, therapies, diets, and whatever she could find. Mom gave "who she was" to trying to provide everything the child needed. Dad divorced Mom when the child was 3 years old. Even with all the family and professional help, the child did not talk or walk unassisted, and was not toilet trained at age 6, when one of the authors first met this mom. Mom carried the child everywhere. Mom developed huge biceps, but otherwise was frail and exhausted. The child's day was filled with equestrian therapy, play therapy, speech therapy, physical therapy, hydrotherapy, visits to nutritionists, behavior therapy, and more. Mom had not worked since the child was 3 years old. The grandparents helped pay the long list of alternative care and therapy bills, and the state and local schools helped with many of the resources for the more conventional therapies. Mom dreamed of "help" with each type of therapy but soon felt the disappointment of little gain, if any, in her child's development and, so, read and looked for another way to "fix" her daughter.

As the author assigned meaning in a variety of visual-motor ways to this child, the child began to develop across most of the domains – cognitively, socially, motor, physically, and language (communication). The child, age 6-1/2, began to pull herself up and tried to walk with assistance. She began to sign basic needs and would visually gaze and point for her needs, the beginning of social development. She soon was beginning to be toilet trained and show specific desires for dress, grooming (how she wanted her hair combed), and so on. After a year of great progress, Mom had to take a vacation. When the author asked where they were going and for how long, Mom said, "I need to find myself. I lost myself when Annie was born and I don't know who I am. I have been chasing all sorts of therapy to help her but she has been here all the time. It is me who has not been here! I see her changing, so I don't have a role any more. My role was who I have been for the last three to four years. Ever since I knew Annie had special needs, I went after anything that could help. I am worn out! We are going to a cabin in the mountains where there isn't any therapy, just the love of family and the generous support of my parents. I don't know when we will be back."

About three to four months later, Mom called up. She was back in town and ready to resume services. When she came in, she was relaxed, ready to be a part of Annie's development, however fast or slow. When asked how she was doing, she replied, "I am here now. I know who I am. I have gone back to school to finish my degree. I have hired a person to support me in the home, and we have pared down the therapy to what I can see actually helps. There are no cures and no fixes, just me and Annie and we both have needs."

It should be noted that Annie did not regress during her time away from services. In fact, the communication system of ASL coupled with gestures, along with drawings in real time by Mom, continued while they were away, and Annie made comparable quantitative developmental growth during this time as she had been making with all of the therapies. This parent learned some lessons about families:

- All family members are equally important – Dad, Mom, and other siblings – not just the child with ASD.

- All family members have needs – emotional, psychosocial, physical – and these needs must be met for them to be "whole."

- A child with special needs may require more time while seeking support, but the support is best when the other family members balance their lives.

- Support services should provide help, not demand time, and enrolling in more services does not mean automatic solutions. Quantity does not equate to quality.

- If some approach or method is not working, maybe letting go of an expectation or spending more time on what works is better than just filling the day with everything possible.

- Grieving the loss of dreams or expectations for a child requires replacing those dreams with more realistic options.

- Accepting a child for who he or she is means living with the child and seeing the child separate from the child's behavior.

- Assigning meaning to what the child does means accepting the child for what he or she can do. As the child does more, then more is accepted, and so on.

- Accepting a child for who he or she is means accepting changes in what the child can or cannot do, separate from the parent's own needs.

- Dreams are okay when balanced by disappointments.

- Dreams are about the whats, not the who. Dreams and disappointments can change but the child is always a person.

Activity: Why must family members balance dreams and disappointments?

Progress and Failure

From the previous section it is evident that family members often measure their own success in how much progress or failure their child makes. If the child acquires a new skill, the parents feel they have made progress. All parents feel the positive effects of progress of their children, but recognizing that the child's progress or lack of progress belongs to the child, not the parent, is healthy. *The parent is separate from the child. The child has his or her own life and own personhood.* The parent can work and work and work and still not meet her own expectations for progress and then feel like a failure. These expectations for progress and the parent's feelings belong to the parent, not the child.

Understanding that a healthy relationship is one that accepts the people in the relationship for who they are establishes boundaries for members of the family unit. A boundary defines the separate individuals, their separate needs, and their shared experiences. Figure 15.2 shows the healthy boundary of a child and a parent.

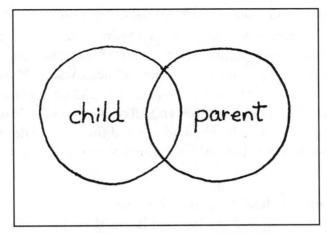

Figure 15.2. A Healthy Parent-Child Relationship.

Each oval represents a person, and where the ovals overlap is where they share their time, their interests, and their desires, their "who." The child is not the parent. The parent is not the child. Each line around is a boundary. Where the boundaries overlap is where the limits overlap. Each person shares a piece of another family member's "who."

As long as each person in the family shares in the working of the family but remains separate in needs, desires, interests, personalities, and so on, the family unit is supported by the individuals within the unit. The goal of all parents is to nurture, support, and protect the child to help the child develop his or her own identity. Children with ASD have difficulty developing these social identities, which is why it is even more crucial for parents to know who they are as separate individuals in relationship to their children's identities. To have separate identities with separate needs and desires, parents must assign meaning to family members' actions so that there is a common overlap of shared meaning. The following example is from a family with a young adult, Charlene, for whom the parents have sought help since she was an infant.

As an infant, the parents sought help for their daughter from their pediatrician. Later a multidisciplinary team served Charlene when she was 3 years old. The primary diagnostic labels were autism with developmental delay across cognition and language. When Charlene reached school age, the labels shifted slightly, and her parents were told that she was probably a child with high-functioning autism. By age 9, the parents sought help for Charlene's mood swings, anger, and frustration. The medical team said she was probably bipolar and ADHD but also had AS.

The parents, both professionals, focused on increasing their daughter's academic skills. Charlene developed more ways to perform academically. Her best tool was talking and letting others do the inferring from her oral language. She would talk and the teacher would give her high marks for anything she said. In fact, teachers often said that Charlene was so bright that others, including the teacher, didn't understand her. Charlene's language sounded like this: "Well, this germ, it wasn't bacteria or protozoa but a virus, so antibiotics wouldn't do any help but they could do harm The bacteria, the good bacteria, could become resistant, well, resistant to the antibiotics and then the antibiotics, well the drugs like penicillin, doesn't work on the bacteria, well, not all bacteria, just the resistant ones … the ones that don't die when you use an antibiotic, but not all bacteria need antibiotics … some are good bacteria and help you digest, well digest your food with good bacteria and so good bacteria don't need antibiotics … just the bad, and so on."

Parents and teachers did not assign meaning to Charlene's "run-on" verbal behavior, her rolling of the eyes or shoulder shrugs. Charlene was not always on topic, and she often talked more than her share, taking up time and lacking consideration for others' ideas or needs. She continued to acquire skills and knowledge but as she became older and "bigger," her social skills seemed even more inappropriate. For example, she would talk to someone while she picked her nose, twisted her hair, or had her fingers in her mouth. Charlene could tell you all of the rules for "rude behavior" while she engaged in the behavior she said was rude. She had learned the social rules but not the concepts. The parents realized that she was different but did not know how to assign meaning to Charlene's inappropriate behaviors.

When the parents sought help for their daughter when she was a young adult, the educator began working on her behavior by drawing and writing. But it was the educator's, not Charlene's, drawing and writing and, therefore, the results were limited. The educator then used writing as a system of communication. Writing involves motor movements like the mouth but without the sound. Figure 15.3 shows an example of a writing exchange between the educator and Charlene. The actual exchange is several pages long and includes very specific limits of what is okay and not okay behavior and what other people think about specific behaviors. The educator also sets boundaries between Charlene and herself, thus helping to model a healthy relationship for Charlene. This is just one issue.

When you drink the last drop of a drink using a straw, what sound does the straw make?

The sound of a straw sucking up something.

Who hears that sucky noise?

I do

But today there were other people in the room with you when the straw made the sucky sound.

Do you think others like that sound?

I don't know. they never say any thing about it.

Today I am saying something about it, because everytime I am here when you suck the last drop out of your glass, you make that awful sounding noise. The noise that straws can make is considered impolite and rude when you are in any room where there are other people

When you use a straw around other people →

Figure 15.3. Communication Through Writing.

Once Charlene understood how her behavior would affect someone else, she began to make changes that were greater than the individual skills that had been practiced. Charlene came into therapy standing taller, sitting straighter, with hair combed, clothes clean – without the educator or the parent talking to her about these types of changes. These changes were the result of Charlene being able to see in writing what she was doing and could do, thus empowering her. As Charlene became empowered she began to show the posture of a person with a higher self-esteem (achievement), positive self-concept (who she was), and better self-image (how others saw her). Charlene's progress in developing her ability to problem solve, to make appropriate choices, and to see how she affects others, made a difference in how she felt about herself. She could choose to be successful and, therefore, she began to look like she was more socially competent. From this example, we can draw some important lessons with regard to individuals with ASD.

- Being able to choose how to behave develops the person's social skills better than working on the individual skills because choice helps empower a person.

- Choices of behavior come from language. For example, a psychiatrist and parent said a child would not touch paper; he had a phobia about paper. The educator explained to the child that when he touched the desk, the desk was smooth but when he touched the paper, the paper would feel like little fibers – like the strings he pulled on his sweater. These strings in the paper are from the tree. The tree has fibers that are pressed to form paper. She then had the child feel the fibers in the paper. They never again had trouble working on paper.

- Writing is better for older students than watching someone else draw and write because the students do the writing or motor patterns and the learning becomes part of their own system.

- Using one's own learning system is part of learning how to learn. Learning strategies for how to learn is better than learning a specific skill.

- Developing functional language as an agent results in changes in other areas of development such as social and cognitive development because learning the role of an agent is both social and cognitive in nature.

- How a person sees himself is also how others have assigned meaning. So a student who can see himself doing a task is more likely to perform the expected task. Being unique or eccentric is not an excuse for inappropriate behavior or antisocial acts.

- If a person receives no feedback within the context of how he or she looks or acts, then there is no reason to change behavior. Without feedback the student may not know what others see or hear.

- Seeing how others behave does not provide sufficient feedback to make personal changes for matching one's self to what others look like. Modeling behavior does not show the child or adult what he or she looks like doing a particular task.

- Progress in learning facilitates the developmental changes better than working on the individual products. Learning is dynamic and crosses all developmental levels of growth.

- Success is a measure of how well meaning is assigned to what a person does. Failure is the absence of meaning being assigned to what a person does. Success results in better self-esteem, and assigning positive meaning to acts of improved self-esteem enhances self-concept.

Activity: What are some principles about progress and failure?

Successes are greater than the work on the individual pieces. If a parent perceives a child's growth as important, whatever progress the child is making will seem like enough. As the child grows, the child needs more and more feedback so he learns how to fit into society and how to be successful as a person, not just with academic products or social skills. Conversations of what "appropriate behavior" looks like, even if it is in writing, increases the way the child perceives his own contributions and helps him feel like a success, not look or act like a failure.

Activity: Why is working on the process of learning better than working on products?

Social Developments and Cognitive Successes

Social competence is the ability to initiate and maintain healthy relationships. In a previous section of this chapter, healthy relationships were defined in terms of separate identities and separate needs. Relationships share the needs that overlap. For example, two family members may both have the need to feel successful as musicians, so each develops his and her own musical talents, which are occasionally shared by them playing together at a family get-together. Each plays an instrument. Each has musical talent. Each has a psychosocial need for being a good musician. And they overlap their musical interests on occasion. They can share their separate musical gifts with one another in a healthy relationship. Socially, they are both competent as they initiate relationships with other musicians with whom they can share other social aspects such as a good meal together. How well a person develops socially is also how well the person can identify successes related to social competence. The following example is from a family who saw their son's accomplishments as part of "who" he was, and as a result continues to give him feedback so as to refine his social development as part of his successes.

One of the authors (Arwood) first met Jason when he was in junior high school. When he was asked to work with her, Jason began yelling and screaming while sliding down the front of the waiting-room chair into a heap on the floor. The author reminded him that in order to do his work he would need to stand up and walk into the therapy room, look at the paper, and then read, write, draw, and talk about the paper. As he stood up and began to walk with Dr. Arwood toward the other room where he was to sit and work at the table, he began to "jabber" (not real speech) as he moved through space. (This probably indicates that he uses the motor access [mouth moving] of his learning system to visually keep the room constant as he moves through space.) Jason's mother explained that he got agitated by the lights and sounds of the room. She raced to his side and said, "It's okay, you don't need to do this if you don't want to." She then turned to Dr. Arwood and said, "Children with autism don't like new places. Jason is very sensitive to lights and sounds. Your voice is too loud and he doesn't like the fluorescent lights."

Jason immediately began to flap his hands and stand in one place rocking back and forth. He had been given two messages: (a) You are expected to walk into the other room, sit at the table, and read, write, draw, and talk; and (b) You can socially act any way you want. Dr. Arwood said, "Mrs. Smith, I planned on spending my time working with Jason. But it sounds like you would like to work with me instead?" Mrs. Smith looked puzzled and said, "Well, I brought Jason for an evaluation." The author replied, "Then I need to ask Jason to do some tasks and I will help him be successful. But Jason and I have to work while you watch or you can choose to do something else during the time that Jason and I work."

Parents want so much for their children to be successful that they sometimes give "mixed messages" about social competence. Social competence is the ability to initiate and maintain healthy relationships. Jason needs to initiate and be able to maintain a relationship with the author that is appropriate for the context. Screaming, lying on the floor, flapping, rocking, and so on, are not appropriate behaviors for any situation where a person is expected to interact with another person. Furthermore, Mrs. Smith is doing all of the initiation. She talks for her son, she brings him for an evaluation, and she interprets his behavior for others. Yes, she has had lots of dreams and disappointments, but she has also seen progress. Unfortunately, she has adjusted her dreams to more easily accept the failures than the expected success of performance. She expects Jason to be upset and to show behaviors that express how upset he is. Mrs. Smith is socializing Jason into *unhealthy* patterns of behavior, and Jason does not have the meaning or conceptualization to know how to break out of these unhealthy patterns.

After explaining the limits and boundaries to the mother, Dr. Arwood gave Jason the language one more time about how it was time for him to walk to the table, sit at the table, and read, write, and draw with the author. Jason actually looked at Mom for approval this time. She said, "Do what you feel is comfortable. Dr. Arwood wants to see you work." Unfortunately, being comfortable and working are not always the same. So Jason started walking back to the chair where he slid down to the floor, again screaming. While his mother watched, Dr. Arwood took a piece of paper and drew him sitting up and then standing and then walking. He stopped screaming, took the paper, and stood up and walked to the table. As soon as Dr. Arwood drew him writing and drawing in the pictures, his Mom immediately said, "Jason can't read and write." Jason then began punching holes in the paper and tearing it up. Dr. Arwood asked Mom to step outside where she could watch through a two-way mirror but would not be heard. In other words, Dr. Arwood asked Jason's mom, Mrs. Smith, to not talk. In about 30 minutes, Jason was looking appropriate socially as he wrote hand-over-hand and refined drawings and interacted with Dr. Arwood. Mrs. Smith saw all of this interaction.

When Mrs. Smith was called back into the therapy room, she immediately said, "Well, I guess I was right. I didn't think he would work for you. He only works for me." Dr. Arwood was amazed, "But he worked so well. Let me show you what he wrote and drew and what we read." She said, "Oh, well he doesn't really want to be here. The lights and noises bother him."

That was about six years ago. The authors have heard that Jason still lives at home and does not venture out, hold a job, or function independently. Mrs. Smith socialized Jason into dependency by not allowing his learning system to be *uncomfortable* by the conflict between past and new information, which is how learning occurs. Jason needed to use motor acts such as writing to show learning. He needed to learn how to be socially appropriate as part of the process of improving cognition to be independent. Because he had so much motor movement, he needed to produce more motor acts (written or speech-like) to help him retain the pictures of what he was to do. These appropriate behaviors would take the place of the screaming, flapping, rocking, and so on. For Jason to develop socially, he needed to have academic or cognitive types of successes. Likewise, to be academically successful, he needed to see himself do appropriate behaviors that are deemed socially successful.

For some children and young adults with ASD, the only way to break through the lack of cognitive development is with social success. But social success for a person with ASD may not look like it does for other developing children, adolescents, or young adults. For example, social success for an adolescent by the name of Mike was the ability to interact and maintain with people through written conversation. Mike was a self-destructive, low-functioning child with autism. He spent his first nine years with people trying to develop his compliance behavior and splinter speech and literacy skills. None of these attempts was successful in the long run because Mike just got bigger and was compliant only under specific stimuli as the skills did not generalize into thinking with concepts and language (skills typically don't; see Chapters 3 and 4). At about age 9, Mike's parents were able to connect with a speech and language pathologist who would draw with him, which helped his overall behavior because Mike understood the drawings better than spoken words and, therefore, began developing concepts. But writing was not used to develop Mike's way of interacting until he was about 13. The schools tried isolated pictures and pointing, and signing types of outputs but none of these worked to increase Mike's overall functioning because these activities had no contextual language (see Chapter 5) value. Without context, the language is also not relational and does not create the concepts within events. So his cognition didn't grow.

When Mike was 13, the same speech and language pathologist along with the parents began writing with Mike. Mike learned to be compliant, make basic choices and decisions, and willingly attend school through shared writing among participants. He would write, and the teachers, parents, aides would write. Different types of technology such as machines that would speak when words were typed, computer adaptations of the keyboard, the use of a regular keyboard, and electronic communication boards were tried, but the actual holding of the pencil and writing the words (hand-over-hand motor shapes became independent motor shapes) seemed to work the best.

When Mike turned 15, he was ready to attend high school. He went to school, but no one would write. Mike did not have the oral motor ability to speak unless he was writing. Without writing he had no verbal form of communication. As a result, his inappropriate behavior escalated and the school personnel wanted him out of the special education "mainstream" model and on a one-to-one for behavior. Mike refused to go to school. Mike's mom called Dr. Arwood early one morning for advice about Mike's IEP and how to help the school work with him.

While Dr. Arwood and Mike's mom were talking, Mike woke up and came to his mom. He wrote to her, "Is this a school day?" She excused herself from talking and wrote back, "Yes, but we do not go to school until 10:00." He wrote back, "Why 10:00?" She wrote back, "We have a meeting with the teachers at 10:00." He wrote, "Can I watch a video?" She said, "Yes." He did not understand, so she wrote, "Yes, you may watch a video until 9:30." He left, selected a video, and turned it on while Mom returned to the phone call. Having been to their home when Mike could not initiate or maintain a social interaction of his liking was a painful experience and this interaction was so opposite; it was socially successful for everyone. Social competence can be developed in different ways. Without a form of personal expression to say what Mike wants to say and when he wants to say it, Mike's social development was arrested. When he was given the opportunity to be an agent, he could initiate and maintain relationships. With the ability to use symbols, his cognition could also grow.

Some social development and success principles include the following:

- Social success means being able to express one's own ideas. For example, a person has to be able to "talk" or write for him or herself. All people need a voice even if it is expressed with paper and pencil.

- The goal of social development is social competence. Social competence is the ability to initiate and maintain healthy relationships. Healthy relationships result from the sharing of power through likes, dislikes, and so on.

- Social development is part of learning. Learning is a socio-cognitive process. This means that if social development increases, so does cognition. But an increase in cognition does not necessarily mean a person will be socially successful. Only if the cognitive increase is also about how a person looks, behaves, and so on, does the person increase in both social and cognitive learning.

- Social development has to be within the person's own learning system of conceptual development. For example, Mike was able to socially initiate and maintain when he could use writing, not signing, or speaking, or a computerized form of technology.

Activity: *What are some principles about social developments and successes?*

Social competence is the ability to initiate and maintain healthy relationships. Therefore, a child who does not initiate or is not able to maintain a healthy relationship is at risk for antisocial behavior. Antisocial behavior does not help a child become a healthy citizen. Healthy citizens maintain relationships necessary for functioning in the dominant society. Figure 15.4 is part of a written conversation between a young adult diagnosed with ASD who academically should be independent but is not because of his lack of social competence. This conversation lets the young adult know that his persistent excuses are not helpful ways to deal with the challenges he has. Although his perception is valid, he needs information about how to interact with others that is not based on the excuses.

People expect you to look right at their faces as you say, "Hello,"

I have some trouble with that but very rarely.

Today you did not look at me... you looked at my books on my desk while saying, "Hello."

One problem was I was awake until 2:00 AM.

What you wrote is an "excuse" but excuses are not OK for explaining anti social behavior.

I'm in pain and I think a little stress and I might just be kind of tired

Tired... pain... stress ... are not reasons for rudeness.

We all have problems... I could list out for you all of my problems I feel today, too. But adults have rules of conduct, rules for behaving appropriately around others.

Figure 15.4. Becoming Socially Competent.

As this young man began to rid himself of excuses for how he behaved, he began to take on additional responsibility and look the part of a young adult who was ready to accept a job (he really wanted a job). He was becoming socially competent.

Summary

Families consist of several members who share dreams and disappointments, progress and failures, social developments, and cognitive successes. Each family member requires his or her share of support in order to have the energy and stamina to work with any special needs a family member may experience. Dreams for all family members can be balanced by accepting disappointments and failures as part of the moving-forward process. Each "real" step forward requires letting go of something in the past as part of an active and healthy grieving process.

Parents "know" their children whereas experts have knowledge. Applying the knowledge to a specific child requires a marriage between the parents and/or family members and the experts. Experts need to learn to actively listen. When a parent says, "My child can write," the expert needs to see what is meant by "can write." When a parent says, "Phonics does not work for my child," experts need to look at how the child learns to see how he might learn to decode using a different input (see Chapter 8). Likewise, parents need to learn to actively listen. When a professional says, "Your child has made a lot of progress. For example, he can now ask for help and tell you what he needs," parents need to grieve the loss of what they thought the child could not do and begin to see what the child can do. The process of actively listening to children and their parents requires the same reciprocity of parents or family members actively listening to professionals.

Working together to hear what each other says gives our children the best support and models a form of community respect. Community respect results in support for everyone who works together. Working together to assign appropriate social meaning to all behavior results in children growing up to be socially competent citizens. Within this community, your child is my child and my child is your child. Together we are a community of respectful citizens who each has needs and the support necessary to personally grow to our maximum potential.

EPILOGUE
Autism: Where Do We Go from Here?

We know the words.
Not everyone says the same thing with the same words.
These same words have different meanings.
How do we make sense of the words?

This book started 15 chapters ago with a reminder to the reader that emphasis would be on Arwood's Language Learning Theory. In this theory, the learning system is seen as more than just sensory input forming patterns. These patterns must also form concepts for language development. For typical learners, the process of developing concepts from the patterns seems effortless. However, for children diagnosed with ASD, this learning process can be frustrating. The patterns keep coming into the child's learning system but the system can only process certain types of patterns. The result may affect any or all of the conceptual areas of development, including language, social, academic, and behavioral.

Many different areas of development are affected in a child with ASD, and representatives from many different disciplines are involved in determining the knowledge base for how to define ASD, how to develop methods of assessment, and how to find and implement the most effective remediation. Each discipline has its own "jargon" for explaining the learner's strengths and weaknesses. This book has used the words used by neuroscientists and experts in languages. We have been very careful not to talk about learning styles or preferences. We also have been careful not to talk about the modality or the method of instruction.

Children with ASD do not have a learning style or preference that keeps them from learning like other children. They have a learning system! And their learning system is different. This learning system is specific to the way that sensory information comes in and becomes recognizable patterns. Recognizable patterns are meaningful and, therefore, can become concepts when given conceptual meaning through the way concepts form for language purposes. Children with ASD have strengths and weaknesses based on how their learning system processes sensory perceptual patterns.

However, the reader may have seen some of the words used in this text to define the learning system used in other contexts. In other contexts, some of these words have different meanings. The authors wish to emphasize that words such as "visual" and "auditory" can be used to describe the sensory input, the perceptual processing level of the learning system, the conceptual form or mental ideas (metacognition), as well as the linguistic function (language characteristics). For example, if a person is given a test for visual perception, the tester is examining the way the patterns form concepts. How well a child does on the test is dependent on how well the child's language interprets the concepts of the test. Therefore, the child will have both strengths and weaknesses in vision perception. However, these results do not talk about how the child learns new concepts in the best way.

Similarly, in many disciplines, the term "auditory" is often used to describe any function of the ear, including sensory input (discrimination), perceptual processing (perceptual patterns), comprehension, and language function (memory, recall, and retrieval). In this book, the authors were careful to use the word "acoustic" to define the sound input and patterning at the ear level, with "auditory" used to describe the meaning of specific types of patterns (acoustic plus visual) that form auditory concepts represented by auditory types of language. The term "auditory" is used because learning beyond the ear travels along the auditory pathways to the brain.

All sensory patterns that form concepts need a way to rehearse and track the recognizable patterns for long-term or semantic memory. So permanent learning of concepts is always affected by language. The ability to remember and to retrieve ideas is very dependent on the way that information in the brain is connected among the physical systems, meaning that memory is a function of language. So if an evaluator tests a child on acoustic patterns and calls it auditory memory, the child may be said to have good auditory language concepts. The child doesn't really have auditory concepts or auditory memory but can do acoustic pattern matching, which does not require language. Again, these test results do not explain how the child learns best.

We recommend that, as you make your way through standardized tests, formalized testing, and IEP meetings, you keep the learning system in mind. If you use your knowledge of the learning system to interpret the testing, you will be able to determine where in the system there is a breakdown. *Everything that a child learns is a product of the child's learning system.*

We hope you found the material in this text helpful. We would like to offer one more table that might help you navigate through the terminology used by the different professionals. This table shows Arwood's Theory of Language Learning and the way learning may be interpreted by different professionals for the four different levels of language learning.

ARWOOD'S LANGUAGE LEARNING THEORY			
	Neurological Function	*Physical Structures*	*Interpretation*
Learning Level I	Sensory input	Receptor organs: eyes, ears, nose, mouth, skin	Acuity Discrimination Recognition Reflexive responses
Learning Level II	Perceptual patterns	Brain stem structures: Cortex of cerebrum • acoustic patterns • visual patterns • motor patterns • auditory patterns	Attention Pattern recognition Pattern completion Perception Psychological processing Copying Matching Short-term memory Episodic memory Memory Digits +/-7 Pattern organization Word call Imitation Closure Focus
Learning Level III	Conceptual organization	All previous structures plus inhibition of recognizable patterns by cortex • acoustic + visual patterns = auditory concepts • visual + visual patterns = visual concepts • motor + motor patterns = visual concepts	Signal-to-noise ratio Figure-to-ground ratio Cognition Comprehension Retrieval Recall Motivation Thoughtful, conscientious classification Categorization Synthesis
Learning Level IV	Language	Maximum cortical synergy of different conceptual systems • auditory language characteristics • visual language characteristics	All of these tasks are dependent on language: Long-term memory or semantic memory Oral natural conversation Reading synthesis Analysis Using math to solve daily problems Planning an event Organizing one's day Following through Writing an essay with natural language Independent living Active listening Taking another person's perspective Multitasking Problem solving Being socially competent Being communicatively competent

Based on Arwood's model of Language Learning, we propose the following principles regarding intervention:

1. Work at the sensory level of input does not develop language.

2. Intervention at the perceptual level of learning increases the quantity of patterns or skills but does not improve conceptualization (cognition) or language unless the patterns are in the form of the person's linguistic function (the way the person learns concepts).

3. Language intervention is based on how well the educator uses the child's or adult's best way of learning concepts. Only language learning as a process results in natural language function.

4. Work at the conceptual level of learning in the way the person integrates patterns to see progress in conceptualization or cognition.

5. Intervene at the client's language level of learning so he or she learns concepts.

6. Intervention that uses the learning system to develop concepts will assist in perceptual processing for improved functioning in memory, recall, retrieval, focus, attention, and all processes leading to functional independence.

REFERENCES

Adler, R. B., & Towne, N. (2002). *Looking out/looking in: Interpersonal communication* (10th ed.). New York: Harcourt & Brace.

American Psychiatric Association. (2000). *Diagnostic and statistical manual of mental disorders* (4th ed., revised). Washington, DC: Author.

Arwood, E. L. (1983). *Pragmaticism: Theory and application.* Gaithersberg, MD: Aspen Publishers. Available through APRICOT, Inc.

Arwood, E. (1985). *APRICOT I Kit.* Portland, OR: APRICOT, Inc.

Arwood, E. (1991). *Semantic and pragmatic language disorders* (2nd ed.). Gaithersberg, MD: Aspen Publishers. Available through APRICOT, Inc.

Arwood, E., & Beggs, M.A. (1992). *Temporal analysis of propositions (TEMPRO): A tool for analyzing language functioning.* Portland, OR: APRICOT, Inc.

Arwood, E., & Beveridge-Wavering, A. (1989). *APRICOT II Kit.* Portland, OR: APRICOT, Inc.

Arwood, E., & Brown, M. (1999). *A guide to cartooning and flowcharting.* Portland, OR: APRICOT, Inc.

Arwood, E., & Brown, M. (2001). *A guide to visual strategies for young adults.* Portland, OR: APRICOT, Inc.

Arwood, E., & Brown, M. (2002). *Balanced literacy: Phonics, viconics, kinesics.* Portland, OR: APRICOT, Inc.

Arwood, E., Brown, M., & Robb, B. (2005). *Make it visual in the classroom.* Portland, OR: APRICOT, Inc.

Arwood, E., Kaakinen, J., & Wynne, A. (2002). *Nurse educators: Using visual language.* Portland, OR: APRICOT, Inc.

Arwood, E., & McInroy, J. (1994). *Reading: It's so easy to see (RISES I).* Portland, OR: APRICOT, Inc.

Arwood, E. L., & Unruh, I. (1997). *Reading/writing: It's so easy to see (RISES II): A way for all levels of students to develop literacy skills.* Portland, OR: APRICOT, Inc.

Arwood, E. L., & Unruh, I. (2000). *Event-based learning handbook.* Portland, OR: APRICOT, Inc.

Arwood, E. L., & Young, E. (2000). *The language of RESPECT: The right of each student to participate in an environment of communicative thoughtfulness.* Portland, OR: APRICOT, Inc.

Attwood, T. (1998). *Asperger's Syndrome: A guide for parents and professionals.* Philadelphia: Jessica Kingsley Publishers.

Aylward, E. H., Minshew, N. J., Goldstein, G., Honeycutt, N. A., Augustine, A. M., Yates, K. O., Barta, P. E., et al. (1999). MRI volumes of amygdale and hippocampus in non-mentally retarded autistic adolescents and adults. *Neurology, 53,* 2145-2150.

Ayres, J. A. (1979). *Sensory integration and the child.* Los Angeles: Western Psychological Services.

Baron-Cohen, S., Ring, H. A., Wheelwright, S., Bullmore, E. T., Brammer, M. J., Simmons, A., & Williams, S. C. (1999). Social intelligence in the normal and autistic brain: An MRI study. *European Journal of Neuroscience, 11,* 1891-1898.

Berard, G. (1993). *Hearing equals behavior.* New Canaan, CT: Keating Publishing, Inc.

Bookheimer, S. (2004). Overview on learning and memory: Insights from functional brain imaging. In *Learning Brain Expo Conference Proceedings – Functional brain imaging in children: Applications in typical and atypical language development.* San Diego, CA: Brain Store.

Bragdon, A. D., & Gamon, D. (2000). *Brains that work a little bit differently.* San Francisco: Brainwaves Pub.

Baylor College of Medicine. (2002, October 11). *Brain anticipates events to learn routines.* Houston, TX: Author.

Buron, K. D. (2003). *When my worries get too big!: A relaxation book for children who live with anxiety.* Shawnee Mission, KS: Autism Asperger Publishing Company.

Buron, K. D., & Curtis, M. (2003). *The incredible 5-point scale.* Shawnee Mission, KS: Autism Asperger Publishing Company.

Caine, G., & Caine, R. N. (1994). *Making connections: Teaching and the human brain.* Alexandria, VA: Association for Supervision and Curriculum Development.

Calvin, W. H. (1996). *How brains think: Evolving intelligence then and now.* New York: Basic Books.

Carruthers, P. (1996). *Language, thought, and consciousness: An essay in philosophical psychology.* Cambridge, MA: Cambridge University Press.

Chiat, S. (2001). Mapping theories of developmental language impairment: Premises, predictions and evidence. *Language and Cognitive Processes, 16*(2/3), 113-142.

Coch, D. (2002). Word and picture processing in children: An event-related potential study. *Developmental Neuropsychology, 22*(1), 373-406.

Cooper, J. D. (2003). *Literacy: Helping children construct meaning.* Columbus, OH: Houghlin-Mifflin.

Corso, R. M., Santos, R. M., & Roof, V. (2002). Honoring diversity in early childhood materials. *Teaching Exceptional Children, 39*(3), 30-36.

Countryman, J. (1992). *Writing to learn mathematics: Strategies that work.* Portsmouth, NH: Heinemann.

Courchesne, E., Karns, C. M., Davis, H. R., Ziccardi, R., Carpu, R. A., Tigue, Z. D., Chisum, H. J., et al. (2001). Unusual brain growth patterns in early life in patients with autistic disorder: An MRI study. *Neurology, 57,* 245-254.

Damasio, A. (1986, November). *Learning and language.* A presentation for the Science and Technology Series, Portland, OR.

Damasio, A. (2003). *Looking for Spinoza: Joy, sorrow, and the feeling brain.* New York: Harcourt Brace.

Dethlefs, E. (1989). Making math meaningful. *News from: Apricot, Inc., Volume II, No. 2.* Portland, OR: APRICOT, Inc.

Diamond, M., & Hopson, J. (1998). *Magic trees of the mind.* New York: A Plume Book, Penguin Putnam, Inc.

Eimas, P. D., Siqueland, E. R., Jusczyk, P. W., & Vigorito, J. (1971). Speech perception in infants. *Science, 171,* 303-306.

Fields, D. R. (2005, February). Making memories stick. *Scientific American, 292*(2), 74-81.

Fombonne, E. (2003). Epidemiological surveys of autism and other pervasive developmental disorders: An update. *Journal of Autism and Developmental Disorders, 33*(4), 365-382.

Friend, M. (2006). *Special education.* Boston: Pearson-Allyn & Bacon.

Gagnon, E. (2001). *Power cards: Using special interests to motivate children and youth with Asperger Syndrome and autism.* Shawnee Mission, KS: Autism Asperger Publishing Company.

Gil, D. (2004). *Babel's children.* Retrieved January 8, 2004, from www.economist.com/science

Goldberg, E. (2001). *The executive brain: Frontal lobes and the civilized mind.* New York: Oxford University Press.

Goldblum, N. (2001). *The brain-shaped mind: What the brain can tell us about the mind.* Cambridge, MA: Cambridge University Press.

Grandin, T., & Scariano, M. M. (1986). *Emergence: Labeled autistic.* Novato, CA: Arena Press.

Grandin, T. (1995). *Thinking in pictures.* New York: Doubleday.

Grandin, T. (2005). *Animals in translation.* Orlando, FL: Harvest Book-Harcourt, Inc.

Grandin, T., & Barron-Cohen, S. (2005). *Unwritten rules of social relationships.* Arlington, TX: Future Horizons.

Gray, C. (2000a). *Comic strip conversations.* Arlington, TX: Future Horizons.

Gray, C. (2000b). *The new social story book, illustrated edition.* Arlington, TX: Future Horizons.

Greenfield, S. A. (1997). *The human brain: A guided tour.* New York: Basic Books (Harper Collins).

Greenough, W. T., Black, J. E., & Wallace, C. S. (1987). Experience and brain development. *Child Development, 58,* 539-559.

Hagiwara, T., & Myles, B. S. (1999). A multimedia social story intervention: Teaching social skills to children with autism. *Focus on Autism and Other Developmental Disabilities, 14,* 82-95.

Hannaford, C. (1995). *Smart moves: Why learning is not all in your head.* Arlington, VA: Great Oceans Publishing.

Hannaford C. (1997). *The dominance factor: How knowing your dominant eye, ear, brain, hand, and foot can improve your learning.* Arlington, VA: Great Oceans Publishing.

Halliday, M.A.K. (1994). *An introduction to functional grammar* (2nd ed.). London: Arnold.

Hampson, R. E., Pons, T. P., Stanford, T. R., & Deadwyler, S. A. (2004). Categorization in the monkey hippocampus: A possible mechanism for encoding information into memory. *Proceedings of the National Academy of Sciences (USA), 101*(9), 3184-3189.

Hart, L. A. (1983). *Human brain and human learning.* New Rochelle, NY: Brain Age Publishers.

Hart, M. (1992). Making math meaningful. *News from: Apricot, Inc., Volume V,* No. 4. Portland, OR: APRICOT, Inc.

Heilman, A. W. (2002). *Phonics in proper perspective.* Columbus, OH: Merrill-Prentice Hall.

Holmes, V. M., & Davis, C. W. (2002). Orthographic representation and spelling knowledge. *Language and Cognitive Processes, 17*(4), 345-370.

Individuals with Disabilities Education Act (IDEA, 1997). Public Law 105-17. U.S. Department of Education, (1999). *Federal Register, 34,* CFR Parts 300 and 303.

Jensen, E. (1998). *Teaching with the brain in mind.* Alexandria, VA: Association for Supervision and Curriculum.

Joanisee, M. F., & Seidenberg, M. S. (1998). Specific language impairment: A deficit in grammar or processing? *Trends in Cognitive Science, 2,* 240-247.

Kotulak, R. (1997). *Inside the brain.* Kansas City, MO: Andrews McMeel Publishing.

Kovalik, S. (1994). *Integrated thematic instruction: The model* (3rd ed.). Kent, WA: Susan Kovalik and Associates; distributed by Books for Educators.

Lovaas, O. I. (1987). *Teaching developmentally disabled children: The ME book.* Austin, TX: Pro-Ed.

Lucas E. (1976). *An alternate approach to oral communication for an autistic child.* A videotape theater presentation at the ASHA Convention, Houston, TX.

Lucas, E. (1977). The feasibility of speech acts as a language approach for emotionally disturbed children (Doctoral dissertation, University of Georgia). *Dissertation Abstracts International,* 1978, *38,* 3479B-3967B.

Lucas, E. (1980). *Semantic and pragmatic language disorders.* Rockville, MD: Aspen Systems Corporation.

Lucas, E., & Hoag, L. (1976). *Speech acts: A language therapy strategy for emotionally disturbed children.* A paper presented at the Interdisciplinary Linguistic Conference: Language Perspectives, Louisville, KY.

McAfee, J. (2002). *Navigating the social world.* Arlington, TX: Future Horizons, Inc.

McGuinness, D. (2005). *Language development and learning to read.* Cambridge, MA: MIT Press.

McKay, D. G., & James, L. E. (2001). The binding problem for syntax, semantics, and prosody: H. M.'s selective sentence-reading deficits under the theoretical-syndrome approach. *Language and Cognitive Processes, 16*(4), 419-460.

McQueen, J. M., & Cutler, A. (2001). Spoken word access processes: An introduction. *Language and Cognitive Processes, 16*(5/6), 469-490.

Mehler, J., Jusczyk, P. W., Lambertz, G., Halsted, N., Bertoncini, J., & Amiel-Tison, C. (1988). A precursor of language acquisition in young infants. *Cognition, 29,* 144-178.

Merzenich, M. M., Schreiner, C., Jenkins, W., & Wang, X. (1993) Neural mechanisms underlying temporal integration, segmentation, and input sequence representation: Some implications for the origin of learning disabilities. In P. Tallal, A. M. Galaburda, R. R. Linas, & C. vonEuler (Eds.), *Annals of the New York Academy of Sciences* (682, pp. 1-23). New York: Academy of Sciences.

Met, M. (2001). Why language learning matters. *Educational Leadership, 59*(2), 36-40.

Myles, B. S., Cook, K. T., Miller, N. E., Rinner, L., & Robbins, L. A. (2001) *Asperger Syndrome and sensory issues: Practical solutions for making sense of the world.* Shawnee Mission, KS: Autism Asperger Publishing Company.

Myles, B. S., Trautman, M. L., & Schelvan, R. L. (2001). *The hidden curriculum: Practical solutions for understanding unstated rules in social situations.* Shawnee Mission, KS: Autism Asperger Publishing Company.

Naugle, R., Cullum, C. M., & Bigler, E. D. (1998). *Introduction to neuropsychology: A case book.* Austin, TX: Pro-Ed.

Obler, L. K., & Gjerlow, K. (2000). *Language and the brain.* Cambridge, MA: Cambridge University Press.

Osterhout, L., & Holcomb, P. (1995). Event-related potentials and language comprehension. In M. D. Rugg & M.G.H. Coles, *Electrophysiology of mind. Event-related brain potentials and cognition.* Oxford, UK: Oxford University Press.

Owens, R. E., Metz, D. E., & Haas, A. (2007). *Introduction to communication disorders: A lifespan perspective* (3rd ed.). Boston: Pearson Education-Allyn and Bacon.

Piaget, J. (1971). *The language and thought of the child.* New York: World Publishing Company.

Pierce, J. C. (1992). *Evolution's end – Claiming the potential of our intelligence.* San Francisco: Harper and Row.

Piven, J., Arndt, S., Bailey, J., & Andersen, N. (1996). Regional brain enlargement in autism: Magnetic resonance imaging study. *Journal of the American Academy of Child and Adolescent Psychiatry, 35,* 530-536.

Piven, J., Saliva, K., Bailey, J., & Arndt, S. (1997). An MRI study of autism: The cerebellum revisited. *Neurology, 49,* 546-551.

Portes, A. (2002). English-only triumphs, but the costs are high. *Contexts, 1*(1), 10-15.

Restak, R. (1984). *The brain.* New York: Bantam Publishing Co.

Ruhlen, M. (1994). *The origin of language.* New York: John Wiley & Sons, Inc.

Sadato, N. (1996, July). Breakthroughs. *Discover,* 27-28.

Santrock, J. W. (1997). *Psychology* (5th ed.). Madison, WI: Brown and Benchmark Publishers.

Savner, J. L., & Myles, B. S. (2000). *Making visual supports work in the home and community: Strategies for individuals with autism and Asperger Syndrome.* Shawnee Mission, KS: Autism Asperger Publishing Company.

Searle, J. (1969). *Speech acts: An essay in the philosophy of language.* Cambridge, UK: Cambridge University Press.

Selsor, K. (2004, February). Stories persuade and motivate. *Brain Store Newsletter, 6*(2).

Shlain, L. (1998). *The alphabet versus the goddess: The conflict between word and image.* New York: Penguin Group.

Simmons, A. (2002). *The story factor: Inspiration, influence, and persuasion through the art of storytelling.* Cambridge, MA: Perseus.

Singh, H., & O'Boyle, M. (2004). Interhemispheric interaction during global-local processing in mathematically gifted adolescents, average ability youth, and college students. *Neuropsychology, 18*(2), 371-377.

Sobotka, H. (2000). *Bird watching and bird habitats.* Portland, OR: APRICOT, Inc.

Sobotka, H. (2000). *Pond and stream habitats.* Portland, OR: APRICOT, Inc.

Sousa, D. A. (1995). *How the brain learns: A classroom teachers' guide.* Reston, VA: National Association of Secondary School Principals.

Sprenger, M. (1999). *Learning and memory: The brain in action.* Alexandria, VA: Association for Supervision and Curriculum Development.

Sturmey, P., & Sevin, J.A. (1994) Defining and assessing autism. In J. L. Matson (Ed.), *Autism in children and adults: Etiology, assessment, and intervention* (pp. 13-36) Pacific Grove, CA: Brooks-Cole.

Sylwester, R. (2003). *A biological brain in a cultural classroom: Enhancing cognitive and social development through collaborative classroom management.* Thousand Oaks, CA: Corwin Press.

Tortora, G. J., & Anagnostakos, N. P. (1990). *Principles of anatomy and physiology* (6th ed.). New York: Harper.

Trott, M. C. (1993). *SenseAbilities: Understanding sensory integration.* Tuscon, AZ: Therapy Skill Builders.

U.S. Department of Education and Office of Civil Rights. (1999). *Free appropriate public education for students with disabilities: Requirements under Section 504 of the Rehabilitation Act of 1973.* www.ed.gov/offices

U.S. Department of Health and Human Services. (1999). Children and mental health. In *Mental health: A report of the Surgeon General* (p. 17). Rockville, MD: Author.

Vygotsky, L. S. (1962). *Thought and language.* Cambridge, MA: MIT Press. (originally published in 1934).

Walker, H., Ramsey, E., & Gresham, F. (2004). *Anti-social behavior: Evidence-based practice* (2nd ed.). Belmont, CA: Wadsworth-Thompson Learning, Inc.

Wallace, M. T., Ramachandran, R., & Stein, B. E. (2004). A revised view of sensory cortical parcellation. *Proceedings of the National Academy of Sciences (USA), 101*(7), 2167-2172.

Webster, D. B. (1999). *Neuroscience of communication.* San Diego, CA: Singular Publishing Group, Inc.

West, T. C. (1997). *In the mind's eye.* Amherst, NY: Prometheus Books.

Wiley, L. H. (1999). *Pretending to be normal: Living with Asperger's Syndrome.* London: Jessica Kingsley Publishers.

Winner, M. G. (2000). *Inside out: What makes a person with social cognitive deficits tick?* San Jose, CA: Michelle Garcia Winner, SLP. London: Jessica Kingsley Publishers.

Wesson, K. (2004). Looking at learning through the lens of the latest brain research. *Learning Brain Expo Conference Proceedings,* San Diego, CA: Brain Store.

Yeargin-Allsopp, M., Rice, C., Kanapurkar, T., Doernberg, N., Boyle, C., & Murphy, C. (2003). Prevalence of autism in a U.S. metropolitan area. *Journal of the American Medical Association, 289*(1), 49-55.

GLOSSARY

Acoustic features – pitch, loudness, and duration/time, which the ear receives as sensory input.

Agent – someone who does something with someone or something; part of a basic semantic relationship.

Asperger Syndrome – a neurological disability named after Hans Asperger. Persons with Asperger Syndrome are generally thought to have normal intelligence but have difficulty with reciprocal social interactions and show a repetitive repertoire of interests and activities.

Auditory language – thinking expressed in spoken words.

Auditory learning system – acoustic patterns integrated with visual and tactile patterns to form language-based auditory concepts.

Auditory memory – the ability to retain and recall information presented through the auditory channel.

Authoritarian – a parenting style that is restrictive, punitive, and controlling. It is a style of raising children without allowing for open discussion or differences of opinion.

Authoritative – a parenting style that encourages children to be independent while placing consistent limits and controls on their actions in a nurturing, supportive way.

Autism spectrum disorders (ASD) – a term that encompasses autism and similar disorders as listed in the DSM-IV. ASD includes autism, Asperger Syndrome, PDD-NOS, childhood disintegrative disorder, and Rett's Syndrome.

Behaviorism – a philosophy supporting the scientific study of observing behavior in order to understand how individuals act in a variety of environments through the principles of operant conditioning.

Behavior – series of acts.

Behavior analysis – originated with the famous behavioral scientist B. F. Skinner, who believed that in order to experimentally analyze human and animal behavior, each behavioral act must be broken down into three key parts: discriminative stimulus, operant response, and reinforcer/punisher.

Cerebrum – the part of the brain responsible for body sensation, muscle movement, and thinking; divided into the right and left hemispheres.

Cognition – the physiological organization of sensation into the basic thought patterns; or how we think.

Cognitive dissonance – basic thought patterns that are in discord (i.e., replacing one set of expectations with another set of expectations to help people feel better about what their child does, not necessarily understanding who the child is).

Communication – the conveyance of an intended message through language and speech that acts to alter a listener's or receiver's attitudes, beliefs, or behaviors.

Concept – the idea or thought that comes from developing an overlap of sensory perceptual patterns (e.g., a person, place, or thing are basic concepts whereas government and respect are more complex concepts).

Context – the immediate environment of the speaker and listener, including past interrelated experiences that each brings to the situation. Context refers to people, their actions, and their locations.

Contextual story – an event-based story using words and ideas in real time to help create mental pictures that overlap in meaning, developing the concepts for better social development.

Continuum – a range that accounts for both high-end and low-end skills and severity of need.

Conventions/conventional – the mutually used tools of sign representation between a speaker and a listener. An example would be writing, which is a motor process that can be communicated and shared with others.

Developmental domains – typical areas of development, which include social/emotional, language, motor, physical, and cognitive areas.

Discrete trials – an instructional method that uses a discrete pairing of stimuli with reinforcers that act as rewards/punishers.

Discriminative response – the pairing of a reward with a specific behavior to elicit a very specific response. For example, teaching the concept of tree by always using the same specific card, allowing for only one specific response or reward.

Displacement – a linguistic principle that refers to how far away from a physical location or a physical object communication occurs; using language to communicate information about another place and time.

Dyadic – two individuals who maintain a sociologically significant relationship.

Echolalia – a language disorder resulting from an inability to attach meaning to perceptually organized features; the repetition of acoustic patterns without attaching meaning.

Ecological perspective – the importance of assigning meaning to different contexts. An ecological approach would examine how a behavior changes within a context or according to environmental stimuli (e.g., every time the environment changes, the information the child receives through his/her learning system also changes).

Etiology – a branch of knowledge that is concerned with causes and origins of diseases.

Extension – adding semantic features or layers of meaning to ideas such as all four-legged striped animals are no longer tigers but cats, zebras, etc.

Frontal lobe – the anterior division of each cerebral hemisphere responsible for executive functioning, problem solving, and long-range planning.

G-signs – gestural sign language connecting two relationships of meaning (e.g., pointing).

Generalization – to bring into general use or knowledge across environments.

Grounding – point of reference in relationship to the ground (e.g., when a child puts his/her body against any of the people or objects within that space to become part of the space, thereby gaining a feeling of comfort).

High context – lots of information provided about a certain situation to avoid the listener having to guess, infer, and/or assume.

Hypersensitivity – supersensitivity to all sensory input that does not become organized.

Hyposensitivity – undersensitivity to sensory input.

Iconic – a sign (as a word or graphic symbol) whose form suggests its meaning.

Inhibition – information that has already been recognized by the brain and, therefore, is no longer new and no longer attended to.

Integration – neurological term that refers to connecting sensory system information together to create patterns, therefore allowing for learning and developing of language.

Jargon – patterns of speech that do not have conventional meaning.

Language – a set of arbitrary symbols that communicate conventional and shared meaning among two or more people.

Learning – the way new concepts are acquired; specifically, the neurobiological process of cells creating meaning from sensory to perceptual sets that overlap with past information to form systems of concepts that language represents or shows a change in behavior.

Learning styles – preferences for learning that may be a result of specific training or education and may not be the same as the neurobiological learning system's way of learning new concepts.

Linguistics – the science of languages, including the study of human speech and semantic development.

Low context – insufficient information about a given situation that requires guessing, inferring, and assuming to increase understanding of ideas.

Marking – the attachment of meaning to an object, action, and/or event represented or labeled by an idea or word (e.g., the written word *tree* is attached to represent the concept of the picture of a tree).

Metacognition – the language used to think about thinking.

Metalinguistic – the language used to talk about language.

Natural consequence – occurs when there is a physical internal change as a result of an act, leading to permanent learning (e.g., a child's clothes get wet when he/she goes outside to play without an umbrella or jacket on a rainy day).

Neurobiological – the knowledge of how cells interact based on their biological nature.

Negative reinforcer – the absence of or removal of a reward that causes the likelihood of a behavior reoccurring. A negative reinforcer can be pleasant or unpleasant depending on the situation or person.

Occipital lobe – the posterior lobe of each cerebral hemisphere, which contains the visual areas.

Ontogeny – the development or course of development of an individual organism or the history of the beginning as well as course of development of a language or any other human artifact.

Operant conditioning – includes a set of methods that stem from the philosophy of behaviorism; pairing a desired need with a desired behavior; that is, a behavior occurs and something either positive or negative happens. For example, a child throws food from a high chair and the parent says "no."

Parietal lobe – a part of the brain that deals with the reception of sensory information from opposite sides of the body. It has a role in calculation, reading, writing, and language.

Patterns – sets of sensory input that form recognizable input (e.g., seeing the squiggles of "John" on a page but not knowing what the squiggles say).

Perceptual patterns – the organization of sensory-received stimuli into usable features; that is, sounds, tastes, touch, smells, and sights all integrate as sets of perceptual patterns that overlap into concepts.

Phonation – the vibration or production of speech sounds.

Phonemes – acoustic patterns in a language that correspond to a set of similar speech sounds; one of the smallest units of speech that distinguish one word or utterance from another.

Phonemics – branch of linguistic analysis that consists of the study of phonemes.

Phonics – a method of teaching beginners to read and pronounce words by learning the sound patterns of letters, letter groups, and especially syllables.

Pictographs – the representative symbols belonging to a pictorial graphic system.

Pragmaticism – term coined in the 1800s by Charles S. Pierce; means that the "whole is greater than the parts."

Pragmaticism methodology – a termed coined by Dr. Ellyn Arwood; based on the principles established by Charles S. Pierce. Refers to working with the whole learning process, not just the child's products.

Primary reinforcers – include drink, food, and sleep.

Proprioceptive system – the system that connects the muscles, tendons, and joints from inside the body to the movements of the body.

Prosody – the rhythm of speech and intonational aspects of language.

Reading fluency – an educational method of assessing reading speed by calling out the individual words in a paragraph or story.

Reinforcer – a reward or a punisher that precedes or follows a behavior.

Semantics – the study of meaning – verbal, nonverbal, and contextual – as interpreted by the listener.

Semantic relationship – the connection between basic concepts such as agents or people and their actions or objects that may be expressed verbally or nonverbally. For example, a child looks at Mom and then points to the toys indicating a semantic or meaningful relationship between Mom and the toys, and Mom says, "I will pick up the toys."

Semiotics – the study of signs and symbols, especially as elements of language which also includes the value of the signs and symbols.

Sensory input – information from the skin, eyes, ears, and motor system.

Social contract theory – a philosophy that postulates that all members wish to follow the parameters of societal rules (e.g., a child with ASD needs to know what the social rules are for friendship in order to comply with expectations).

Social competence – the ability to initiate and maintain healthy relationships.

Social skills – communication, problem solving, decision making, self-management, and peer relations skills that can be taught.

Socialization – the process of learning how to fit into a group, such as society, through interpersonal and intrapersonal relationships.

Social narratives – stories that are written to provide information in a social context.

Spatial orientation – where a person is in relationship to an object or the ground.

Spatial planes – points of reference for a person in relationship to his or her orientation to the ground; that is, a child's brain must incorporate all three of the dimensions of input known as planes in order to recognize and actually see an object such as a ball.

Speech – consists of acoustic-motor patterns that will represent language (e.g., oral language expression such as spoken English).

Speech act – an action performed by means of language, such as describing something, asking a question, making a request, ordering, or making a promise. Other common examples of speech acts include greeting, apologizing, or insulting.

Stereotypical movements – movements such as rocking, flapping, and/or spinning that persons with ASD may display when searching for information to process for meaning.

Stimulus – an action or condition that causes or provokes a response.

Synergism – the interaction of two or more agents or forces so that their combined effect is greater than the sum of their individual parts.

Temporal lobe – a part of the brain that deals with hearing, listening, language, and some memory storage.

Vestibular system – the system of the body located in the inner ear that controls the sense of movement and balance even with the eyes shut.

Visual features – light and movement as perceived through the visual sensory system.

Visual language – thinking in visual ideas; iconic or graphic.

Visual perception – the way a learner organizes sensory input from the eyes in the brain.

Glossary Resources

Arwood, E. L. (1983). *Pragmaticism: Theory and application.* Gaithersburg, MD: Aspen Systems Corporation.

Arwood, E. L. (1991). *Semantic and pragmatic language disorders, second edition.* Gaithersburg, MD: Aspen Systems Corporation.

Jensen, E. (1998). *Teaching with the brain in mind.* Alexandria, VA: Association for Supervision and Curriculum Development.

The Merriam-Webster online dictionary. (2005). Print version of Merriam-Webster's collegiate dictionary, tenth edition. New York: Merriam-Webster.

Santrock, J. W. (1997). *Psychology.* Brown and Benchmark Publishers.

www.autism-resources.com/autism-glos.html

Index

A

Abilities, 13–14
Acoustic, meaning of term, 308
Acoustic features
    competing, 42
    definition, 315
    processing, 44
    sorting, 42
Acoustic patterns
    blocking out, 94–95
    imitation, 31, 45–47, 61
    integration with visual patterns, 47–49, 50
    production, 44, 45
    recognition, 61
    teaching, 54
    without conceptual meaning, 47, 48, 49
    See also Speech
Activities of daily living (ADL), 126–128, 147–148
Agency
    development, 104, 105–107, 209–210, 274–276, 278
    difficulty in acquiring, 106–107
    levels, 106
    social contract approach, 208
    types, 106
Agents, 60, 315
American Sign Language (ASL)
    symbols, 61
    use of, 149, 166, 183
    as visual language, 71, 79, 81
American Speech and Hearing Association, 149
APRICOT II pictures, 280
Arithmetic. *See* Calculating
Articulators, 162, 163
Arwood, E., 48, 72, 149, 190–192, 231, 280, 301
Arwood's Language Learning Theory, 61, 77, 165, 209, 308–309
AS. *See* Asperger Syndrome
ASL. *See* American Sign Language
Asperger Syndrome (AS)
    conceptual development, 56
    definition, 11, 315
    developmental differences, 14
    responses to tastes, 16
    See also Autism spectrum disorders
Assigning meaning
    to behavior, 157, 180–187, 236
    changing, 188
    to children with ASD, 181–187
    consistency, 187
    to gain security, 98–101
    guidelines, 183–187
    importance, 181

    levels, 180, 193
    modalities, 184
    to nonverbals, 273
    opportunities, 188
    with oral language, 190–192
    to patterns, 34–35
    sabotaging environment, 188–190, 238–239
    to sensory input, 98–101
    social, 276
Auditory, meaning of term, 308
Auditory concepts
    formation, 68–69
    of time, 79, 82, 257–258, 260
Auditory cultures, 50, 53, 79, 81–82, 156, 257–258, 260
Auditory languages
    concept formation, 68–69, 71–72
    definition, 315
    properties, 78, 79, 82
    use of context, 81
Auditory learning system, 50, 315
Auditory memory, 85–86, 308, 315
Auditory pathway, 68, 308
Auditory patterns
    conceptual development from, 47–49
    difficulty in forming, 69
    integration of acoustic and visual patterns, 47, 50
    spelling, 48
    in teaching English, 68
Auditory semantic memory, 85–86
Auditory teaching methods, 137–138
Authoritarian parenting style, 293, 315
Authoritative parenting style, 315
Autism, definitions, 11–12, 15
Autism spectrum disorders (ASD)
    abilities, 13–14
    definition, 315
    developmental differences, 12
    diagnosis, 11–15, 217, 293
    incidence, 15
    See also Asperger Syndrome

B

Balance, 19
"Because" language, 283
Behavior
    aggressive, 114, 157
    assigning meaning to, 157, 180–187, 236
    auditory ways of teaching, 118
    communication through, 217
    computer signs for, 240–241
    conceptual development of, 124–132
    definition, 315
    development, 111–113

Stimuli, 198, 199, 201–202, 319
Stories
    contextual, 248, 280–281, 316
    event-based, 280–281
    social narratives, 319
Swaddling, 182
Swallowing therapy, 168
Symbolic drawings, 237
Symbols
    in language, 60, 61
    use in language-based therapy, 244–246
    See also Signs
Synergism, 216, 319

T

Tactile defensiveness, 143–144
Tactile system. *See* Touch system
Taste system, 16–17
Teaching modalities, 77
Technology. *See* Computers
Temporal lobe, 319
Therapy. *See* Language-based therapy; Speech
  therapy
Time
    auditory concept, 79, 82, 257–258, 260
    clock, 257–262
    development of concept, 258–262
    external and internal, 260
    measurement words, 285
    visual concept, 82–84
Touch system
    pressure, 17, 143–144
    sensory input, 17–19
    See also Hand-over-hand methods
Transitions, difficulty with, 148
Typewriters, 148, 273
Typical learning systems, 31, 32, 52–53, 61–62,
  97–98, 210

V

Vestibular system, 19, 319
Viewing, 156
Visual cues, 280
Visual cultures, 80–81
Visual features, 31, 43, 44, 55, 319
    See also Light; Movements
Visual languages
    concept formation, 68, 69–71
    definition, 319
    properties, 78, 82–83
    relational, 236
    use of context, 81
Visual learning system, 51, 72–73
    See also Visual thinking
Visual-motor system, learning behavior through,
  119–124

Visual patterns
    conceptual development from, 49–51
    integration with acoustic patterns, 47–49
    for language, 69–71
    of light, 28, 55, 78, 104, 141, 254
    linking to movements, 73
    use in language development, 64–65
Visual perception
    definition, 319
    development, 17, 28
    of letter shapes, 138–140
    of light, 28, 55, 78, 104, 141, 254
    of patterns, 28, 42
    sensory input, 20, 42
Visual thinking
    concepts as shapes, 141–142
    by majority of U.S. population, 72–73, 79, 158
    by persons with ASD, 69–71, 78
    semantic memory, 85, 86–87
    stages, 116
    time concept, 82–84
    use of grounding, 107
Vocal system, 162–163
Voice therapy, 167
Vygotsky, L. S., 61

W

Watching. *See* Viewing
Words
    measurement, 285–286
    as patterns, 119, 149–150
    shapes, 142, 149, 152, 254
    spatial, 285
    typed, 119
    See also Spelling
Writing
    language development through, 144–145
    learning, 152
    learning before drawing, 145–146
    learning behavior through, 131
    relationship to reading, 150–151, 152
    speech development through, 146–147, 164,
      165–167
    variations in development, 145–147
    See also Hand-over-hand methods

APRICOT, INC.

PO Box 230138
Tigard, OR 97281-0138
www.apricotclinic.com

CPSIA information can be obtained
at www.ICGtesting.com
Printed in the USA
FSHW02n0059090618
48948FS